W9-CGQ-687

JEWISH ETHICS FOR THE 21ST CENTURY

BY STEPHEN RITTNER

Copyright © Stephen Rittner, July 1977.
345 Marlborough St., Boston, Ma. 02115

All rights reserved. No part of this book may be reproduced in any form or by any means, electronic or mechanical including photocopying, recording, or by any information storage and retrieval system, without permission in writing from the author.

All the characters, places, situations etc. in this book are fictitious (unless otherwise noted) and any resemblance to actual persons living or dead, true life places, situations etc. is purely coincidental.

i

Library of Congress Catalogue Card No. 77-82273

ISBN: 0-930444-51-5

Cover:

. . . And they will beat their swords into plowshares, and their spears into pruning hooks. Nation will not lift up sword against nation, neither will they learn war anymore. And each person will will sit under his fig tree and vine, and none will make them afraid . . .
Micah 4:3, 4

Printed in U.S.A.

acknowledgements

A number of people contributed in many ways to the formation of this book:

I would like first of all to acknowledge the fact that Rabbi Roland B. Gittelsohn has had a profound impact upon my theological development and understanding of Judaism.

I would like to thank Bill Finn whose terrific drawings add so much to this book. Bill's sensitivity, expert artistic ability and enthusiasm were crucial for this undertaking.

I would also like to thank Debra Rittner. Debby worked very closely with me in smoothing off the rough edges in this text. Her suggestions, additions and modifications were very important and are greatly appreciated.

The photographs, Unit 12 by Tom Rickles
The photograph p. 212 by Alan Schwartz
My thanks to them both. (All other photos are by the author).

The Hunter p. 252, by Johnny Meeko.
The Chase p. 89, by Johnassie and **Family** p. 87, by A. Temela.

Geometric design p. 22, from Treasury of Design for Artist and Craftsman, by Gregory Mirow, Dover Publications.

Additional thanks to:

Mrs. Lillian Beauvais, my principal at Temple Israel, Boston; Edward Butler, for his technical advice and helpful aid; Ismail Resul; my cool Grandmother Gussie Rittner who's really where it's at; Phyllis Rittner, Len Rittner, Paul and Elvira Showstark — Directors, School of Bio-medical Photography Mount Sinai Medical Center, Miami Beach; Ms. Ann Travis; Prof. C.B. Wellington of Tufts University and Ms. Elaine Wilton.

My students at Temple Israel, Boston.

And of course, my parents.

To Samuel Nemzoff
a pioneer in
Religious Education
whose vision of excellence
has inspired
all of us.

contents

vi

unit one

Defining Our Terms

ETHICAL AND MORAL QUESTIONS vs. QUESTIONS CONCERNING FACTS

"Jewish Ethics for the 21st Century" . . . "Yeah right" you say. "So what's that all about and what does it have to do with me?" Well it's always smart when starting something, to first define our terms and make sure we are all talking about the same thing. Let's begin with the basic word:

ETHICS

What exactly does the word "ethics" mean? Well, one possible definition is that "Ethics is the study of **moral problems**." "Oh no," you groan. "Here I asked for a definition of Ethics and he gives me another strange word":

MORAL

Perhaps we could clarify the situation a little by giving a few examples!!
When we are dealing with questions concerning **facts**, it is pretty obvious what we are talking about:

1.   *What is the name of Boston's baseball team?*
                                Answer: The Boston Red Sox.

2.   *In what year did Christopher Columbus "discover" America?*
                                Answer: 1492.

3.   *Why would the ancient Hebrews want to leave Egypt with Moses?*
                                Answer: They were slaves.

4.   *During what season is Rosh Hashanah and what do the words mean?*
                    Answer: Fall — Head of the year — The Jewish New Year.

5.   *Name the organ in the body that pumps blood.*
                                Answer: The heart.

These are pretty clear cut. They are questions asking about things which have occurred to which there are straightforward factual answers.
While different people may disagree about facts — it still remains that a **fact** is a **fact!**

On the other hand, here are examples of the kind of questions that are raised when discussing moral problems:

1.   *Is it right to be competitive?*

1

2. *Were the big powers of the world such as Spain, France and England justified in laying claim to areas in the "New World"?*

3. *Was Moses being disrespectful in his dealings with Pharoah? Why? Why not?*

4. *Is a person who attends religious services only on Rosh Hashanah and Yom Kippur really a "good Jew"? Why? Why not?*

5. *Given a large sum of money for medical research, and a number of possibilities as to its use, how do we decide which projects should receive greater funding?*

I think you can readily see the difference between the concerns of the first set of questions, as opposed to those of the second set!

Both sets of questions deal with the same five general areas of concern: Sports, The New World, Moses-Hebrews-Pharoah, Rosh Hashanah, and Medicine, but the focus is far different! In the first set of questions we are dealing with **facts** — things that definitely are, or things that certainly have occurred: reality as we know it! The second set of questions deals with **moral** problems. In these items we are concerned with the issue of whether or not something is right or wrong, whether it is justified or not, or whether something could or should be done in a different manner.

While the factual questions presented above were quite easy to answer, that is not always going to be the case. Indeed some factual questions can be very sophisticated and difficult. If you were asked to solve a problem in math (or any other subject, for that matter) requiring the use of knowledge which you haven't yet learned, it would be difficult if not impossible. Thus it is quite common to confront obstacles in solving factual problems because one is unaware of other facts which are indeed both available and necessary. Sometimes facts that are known are lost to us forever (e.g. What was Moses' favorite color?). Then again, sometimes something that is a fact isn't yet discovered. For example we know that a sure way of finding the square of the hypotenuse of a right triangle is to take the square of each of the other two sides and add them.

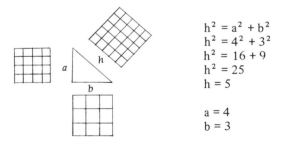

$$h^2 = a^2 + b^2$$
$$h^2 = 4^2 + 3^2$$
$$h^2 = 16 + 9$$
$$h^2 = 25$$
$$h = 5$$

$$a = 4$$
$$b = 3$$

This relationship may be fairly obvious to us now. Before Pythagoras figured it out around 2500 years ago, it was still true, but no one (except possibly the Babylonians who also figured it out at an even earlier time) was really aware of this fact. There is a great deal about the universe that we still don't know. That's why scientists "do their thing". They are trying to find out facts that are not yet known or understood.

Anyhow if you think that questions of fact can be a challenge to answer, just wait until you deal with moral problems or questions! They have many of the difficulties of factual problems. They also include an added dimension. Common questions that are asked when confronting moral issues are:

Is it "right" or "wrong"?

What is "good" or "bad"?

When is something "good" or "bad"?

Why be "good"?

Am I dealing fairly with someone else?

Who is more important — the individual or the group?

Let's give you a few more examples of moral problems:

1. *The Hero on the late, late, late show arrives at the lumberyard. The heroine, in the clutches of the dastardly villain, is in a nasty predicament. The villain has her tied down and is about to saw her in half! Fortunately the hero arrives! He fights with the villain and utterly defeats him. The heroine is saved. They ride off into the sunset with the implication of a long and happy life together. Now what if the heroine was a homely, old spinster? What would you do if you were the hero?*
   Is the above situation in any way sexist? Why? Why not? Is that a moral problem? Why? Why not?

3

2. *There is a prediction of a massive earthquake in South America. If you could delay it for twenty-four hours by repeating every word that anyone says to you back to them, for an entire week, would you? Why? Why not?*

3. *What if you were offered $500,000 to simply make a telephone call and say "yes"? You have no idea whom you are calling and to what you are saying yes. The other party on the phone will not say anything to you. Would you agree to make the call? Why? Why not?*

4. *There is ill will between your country and country "X". The situation has deteriorated to the extent that an outbreak of war will most likely occur. However, diplomatic relations have not yet been severed. You are a florist and have received an order for 23 red and 2 yellow roses to be delivered to the embassy of country "X". You suspect that it is a code or message of some kind. What would you do? Why?*

You may say, "Well these situations could never happen to me." Well, wait a second. Let's look at a few more situations:

5. *Mr. Green has just interviewed two women who have applied for the job of being his secretary. Both seem to be equally qualified and quite capable. One is young and in her twenties. The other is middle-aged. Green is thinking to himself that he always has much more "fun" with younger women!*

6. *John's brother Charlie does not type. John, however, refuses to type Charlie's term paper for him. John justifies his actions by saying that he has read the term paper, and that it is so bad that Charlie will probably flunk anyway!*

7. *If Mrs. Wingrat gives the advertising account to the Stone Advertising Company, McCleary Advertising Agency, which has previously done all of her firm's work, will be hard hit and possibly go out of business. Both agencies do work of equal quality. Both are charging the same rate. Mrs. Wingrat, however, is thinking back. The Stone Advertising Company ran a nice dinner party last May. . . . What would you do if you were Mrs. Wingrat? Why?*

You may wish to compare these latter three cases with the first four!

You probably have heard the terms "moral" and "ethics" being tossed around with various shades of meaning in conversation. It should be clear by now, that moral questions are concerned with whether something is "right" or "wrong". You may hear someone say "Oh, his morals are shady"; shady meaning the speaker believes that the person (being talked about) behaves in a less than upright manner. This person's standard of what is right and wrong are apparently not the same as (or possibly not up to par with) the speaker's.

Similarly Ethics is the study of what is good and what is bad, of moral problems. Yet sometimes you may hear someone say, "She was very ethical in that situation" or "She has no Ethics". Again this implies that the person who is being discussed either behaved (or didn't behave) according to some standard that the speaker had in mind.

4

VALUES

A study of Ethics inevitably involves one's **values**. A value is something that someone believes to be very, very important to him/her. If, for example, you are a very sociable kind of person, then you value (put a great deal of emphasis upon, believe it to be very important) friendship. If you can't stand people who lie, then honesty is an important value for you. Whenever we deal with ethical problems we are forced to decide what our values are and which ones we choose to follow. "Which ones we choose to follow?" Sure. Some of the most difficult ethical problems are ones where two or more of our values are in conflict! For example, let's examine the following situation:

Joe was a slob! Whenever he did his homework the books and papers were all over his room. Actually by spreading these things out he had developed a system which helped him organize his work and finish his lessons much faster. His mother, however, objects to his mess. Joe himself can't stand the mess either.

Here we have a number of values in conflict. Joe values other activities far more than doing homework. This is indicated by the fact that he is trying to figure out a system in order to finish his work quickly. The fact that he can't stand the mess indicates that he also values cleanliness and neatness. Here we have a conflict:

Messy — but		
fast system enabling	*vs.*	*Cleanliness, neatness*
more valued activities		*and standard slow way.*

Then there is the problem of whether he puts value upon continued good relations with his mother and to what extent those relations will be impaired by his system. Moreover, he probably doesn't value at all any punishment that could result from impaired relations with his mother over this issue. What will the result be? That depends on which values he feels are more important! My guess is that should his mother force the issue, his system will be doomed. (Most students value getting along with parents pretty highly). If his mother does not actively pursue the matter, the conflict of the remaining values (more valued activities vs. neatness) could go either way depending on Joe! This, of course, is a very simple example of a value conflict.

There are two main points to remember:

1. *One's values are very important in determining how ethical problems will be solved.*

2. *It is quite common to encounter conflicts in a given situation, between two or more values. What values are more important to a person can also influence how the problem will be dealt with.*

WHY THIS COURSE?

So **why** bother with a study of Ethics? (After all if you are going to spend time studying something, you should at least have an idea as to why!) The primary reason is that ethical problems are extremely common. They affect each and every one of us. No . . . you may never be offered a half a million dollars to simply say "yes" on the phone, but it is almost 99.9% certain that you have already experienced situations where you have had to make a decision as to what was the "right" thing to do. These problems of an ethical nature never cease. You will encounter them all the days of your life. Moreover, these problems aren't trivial! (Face it, the problem of whether you should buy a candy bar or gum is unimportant). The problem of whether to cheat (be it on a test or

These are (and have been) highly valued in American Society:

1. Rational thinking —
   (Scientific Approach).
2. Democracy.
3. Equal Opportunity.
4. Material Comforts.
5. A sense of moral purpose.
6. Work.
7. Conformity.
8. Achievement (success).
9. Freedom.
10. Superiority.
11. Efficiency.
12. Individuality.
13. Humanism and charity.
14. Nationalism.

5

on a job) can have serious consequences. Ethical dilemmas can not only affect you, but indeed have a strong impact upon the welfare and well-being of many others as well.

Everybody has a way of dealing with ethical or moral problems that occur in everyday living. However, few people encountering an ethical dilemma stop and say to themselves "O.K. myself, this is a moral problem. Where do we go from here?" Most don't **consciously** consider the value conflicts that may be involved. In general most people just act automatically. Sometimes they wander from crisis to crisis, that they themselves may be causing, without realizing the actual implications of their own behavior. Thus it is not unusual to find people whose values and ethical behavior are quite **inconsistent** and **contradictory**. Here's an example.

I am sure that you have seen "cops and robbers" movies where the crooks murder people, steal etc., yet are shown being nice to their families, pet canary etc. . . But it's more widespread than that! In fact here are some views which are fairly common in our society:

> *It's good to give to charity — as long as one is not inconvenienced to the extent of being deprived of the second T.V. or car.*

> *If one is a good thief, steals a lot — and doesn't get caught — one is cool. If one is caught — she/he is a bum.*

> *Social progress in housing, education and jobs is great — as long as my personal lifestyle is unaffected. Let it happen elsewhere.*

Thus another reason you are studying Ethics is to give you a chance to examine moral issues as such and to get your own thoughts together about a lot of different areas.

"O.K." you say. "But the title of this book is **Jewish Ethics for the 21st Century** . . . What's so Jewish about ethics?" The answer: Judaism doesn't believe that one can be called "religious" if his/her ethics are lousy. If you consider it for a second, there are two major areas with which religions deal:

1. Concern with God, prayer, important questions (e.g. How did we get here? What's the purpose of life? — HEAVY STUFF!), ritual, etc. . .

2. Righteous conduct, interpersonal relationships, ethics.

Thus it should come as no surprise that there are comments in the Traditional Sources indicating that prayer and ritual without proper conduct is empty. We therefore find that Judaism did not develop as something to be applied only on special occasions (like a band-aid), but rather should be conceived of as a way of life. Indeed, Jewish teachings are so broad in their scope and application that they extend to virtually every aspect of daily living. At this stage you are probably saying "So?" Look at it this way. For many, many years now during your career as a religious school student you've probably been hearing this bit about "Judaism being related to all of life . . . being relevant etc. . ." Well here's where we put it on the line. In a course based on this book you are going to see how Judaism can be relevant and can be practical — and not just on Hanukkah when you, perhaps, receive a gift. — but in your everyday life!

THEORY AND ACTION

There are four types of people who attend the Bet Hamidrash, the house of study:

One who goes and does not act — has the reward for attending	One who both goes and acts — a sainty person
One who acts but does not go — has the reward for action	One who neither goes, nor acts — a wicked person

from Pirke Avot

He whose wisdom is greater than his deeds — what is he like? He is like a tree whose branches are many but whose roots are few — and the wind comes and uproots it and overturns it —

But he whose deeds are greater than his wisdom — what is he like? He is like a tree whose roots are many so that even if all the winds in the world blow against it — it cannot be moved.

From Pirke Avot

Now a little about this book and what it covers. **Jewish Ethics For The Twenty-first Century** is divided into fifteen sections. The topics in it vary greatly. Having defined ethics in this section, the book goes on to discuss various problem solving techniques. If you think about it, ethical dilemmas are just problems, waiting to be solved. Generally people find it much easier to solve a math problem than an ethical one, because it's easy to stay cool and detached when dealing with numbers. When one is dealing with people all kinds of emotions get involved! At any rate, all kinds of techniques to help cope with ethical situations are set forth. When we consider ethics we are thinking in terms of standards of what is right and what is wrong. Generally these standards are translated into forms made usable by society through the use of rules, customs and laws. Just about every group, whether large or small, simple or complex, has some set of guidelines which its members try to follow. Thus in unit four we get involved in the basic issue of "Why bother with laws?" In unit five we check out some sources of Jewish ethical guidance. These include the Bible, the Mishnah and Talmud. Units six through fifteen are intended to give a sampling of a wide range of ethical problems. Such issues as ethics of communication, war, and monetary dealings are presented. The last few units "Some Bio-medical Ethics", "Ecology", and "Ethics of Technology" center around ethical problems involving humankind's technological abilities.

Throughout this book Jewish approaches to some of these ethical dilemmas will be presented. **This isn't meant to preach to you.** Where we have five thousand years of accumulated experience in our tradition — we'd be plain stupid to simply ignore it. Moreover, when you have class discussions based on this text you will be expected to do some hard thinking of your own! Your **own** opinions and reactions to ethical situations will be an important contribution to the course. The amount of enthusiasm and discussion that you put into this ethics course will actually determine how interesting and valuable it will be for you. A study of Ethics can and should be one of the most dynamic and fascinating courses around, for it deals with everyday life!

Oh yes, one more thing — the title of the book is **Jewish Ethics for the 21st Century**. So far we've discussed the "Ethics", and the "Jewish" parts of the title but what about this "for the 21st Century" business?

The reason for "The 21st Century" is that by then — you will be the establishment! You will be the teachers, doctors, lawyers, and bosses of tomorrow. The kinds of moral decisions you make will affect the type of world you live in. You will even be sending your kids to synagogue to take a course in Jewish Ethics!

SUMMARY

In this chapter we defined our terms as a basis for our study of ethics. A distinction was made between questions dealing with facts, and questions dealing with moral problems. We found that moral concerns deal with the "right" or "wrong" of a subject. A number of examples of moral problems were presented. Ethics, the study of moral dilemmas, is concerned with values. One's personal set of values will play an important role in determining how an ethical problem will be solved. We also examined the rationale for undertaking a study of Ethics. Ethical issues are extremely common in our everyday lives. You have already been faced with situations where you have had to decide whether it was right or wrong to do something. You will undoubtedly face them again. Ethical problems are important for they can have serious consequences for you as well as others.

Religions in general, and Judaism in particular, have been concerned, not only with beliefs about God, prayer, ritual, etc., but indeed with one's relationships with his/her fellow human beings. Judaism has been concerned with virtually all aspects of life and has much to offer us in terms of ethical wisdom and guidance. Nonetheless, this is not meant to be an ethics course in which you will be preached to and expected to give back the teacher's opinions. Your involvement and discussion is a must, as you analyze and give your **own** reactions to a number of ethical issues!

CONSIDER THIS:

1. a. List ten factual questions.
   b. List ten questions that raise moral problems.

2. This will give you an idea of just how much our lives are filled with ethical situations. In a twenty minute period I heard the following stories on the local news:

> *A local politician was put into jail.*
> *A discussion of unemployment vs. inflation.*
> *Discussion of honesty in organized charities.*
> *An increase in the cost of coffee.*
> *Shoe imports affect the domestic industry: Should protective tariffs be imposed?*
> *Warning concerning sale of a bad stock.*
> *Local public official's wife contesting a divorce – charges she's been publically humiliated.*
> *Will an ex-politician return to acting? – "No" he states, "I'm too old to take my clothes off."*
> *Public Editorial: on nursing homes.*
> *Weather: Cold air coming in has implications for home energy use.*
> *Sports: Salaries of 6 baseball players total nine million dollars.*
> *Commercial: Eve tries to get Adam to eat an apple. Adam refuses because it's Wednesday, which is _____ spaghetti day.*

9

Thus an ability to evaluate ethical problems is of basic necessity to get along in our society.

Watch the news on T.V. for a half hour. List different ethical problems that are featured. Discuss them in detail.

3. The following game has thirty–two personality characteristics that are highly valued, (e.g. fair) and eight characteristics that are often not valued at all (e.g. hostile).

   a. Find and circle them.
   b. List them on a separate sheet of paper.
   c. Find 10 (of the 32) that you value most highly and list them in order of how much you value them (e.g. most valued first, least valued last).

```
T S E N O H I P L E A S L R Q S N V B E A T L E S P
O N S U T E X N F C G M T A R E P N E U I R T L S O
Q N A E R S U F T E G R A V R F I L L E A R S E U L
A L I R O C R H M L R I Q E P L A C I T C A R P A S
I N O P E U L F A J E L C T O E E H R E A L T I Y A
O V D T X L X Y T X S N I F T X L D A E R H C I T Y
U T O R A H O A U E I F T N S I M O E S A O B E R I
S T E V E L I T N S V S A L E B I D U D S T A T I U
T H O P E F U L B U E E V I S L U P M I N J I U A N
N I R D O T F H E H Y I L N D E L I T S O H R V S S
D N D D U D I F I D F A I R R O Y N U F P I N G E E
I Q E F F I C I E N T A A A Y T A I F O E R I N E L
L U R H A R D E L O V S T O S T P I T L A N E R I F
L I L E C A R I N G I M R E P S H O S I C A N E R I
S S Y S I G M F I I L U N E U E M P E R E W H A T S
A I C U G B I U L N A R I O L F A I T H F U L I U H
L T R L A R Z N Y D A I R P O I T I N I U F I R R P
A I U A C A O H E E A E F P I N A B I O L I C H F E
M V N N I V E B I P N U F O N L E B D U P E F D E N
I E M O D E S T A E L S P O C K R E L Z I T S E C S
R C T I T H R V G N L G O U T K E E R E U N O C N O
Y A I T E L I J A D T N H T S U J E R A I E N A E L
E N N A E M E R Y E I I B O S T O N H I D L E F R O
E R D R C E L T S N T V G N I Z I L A I C O S O O M
M O S E S T O N I T E O S H O W I D U O O I T W O O
O O R E S P O N S I B L E T V N O I U F R V T T O N
T A N A C H N E I O N O T S U B F R I O E N G L E T
I A S E N I Y H T R O W T S U R T S O N E T A R Y U
O N R I V U B R O T H E R L O E P E A Z O R A C E N
N E A R O I A N A E N A B P O P I L F E E L A R S I
A B A R M I T Z V A H E I U P A T I E N T R I G G N
L O R D S T B L I S H I S U R E I N P T E O U S N G
```

10

4. Toys can (believe it or not) be a reflection of values held by society in general. Go to a store and take a look at the toys that are being sold. Based on your observations answer the following questions:

  a. What particular items did you see? (list them!)
  b. Were there any individual objects that occurred in great frequency (e.g. many of the same type of object but made by many different manufacturers etc.)?
  c. From the toys that were for sale, what can you deduce about the values of our society? (If possible find specific values in specific toys, games etc . . .)
  d. Were there any differences in toys intended for girls as opposed to boys? What (if any) were they?

5. **Pretend**: You are told that in two hours your house will blow up! There is no possible way for you to stop this event. You are allowed to remove fifteen things (alive or inanimate) from your house before the zero hour! What fifteen items would you take? Why? What do these things tell you about your own values?

6. Finish the following statements:

   The one thing that really annoys me is —
   If I had one wish that I know would come true, I'd pick —
   That boy has green hair. He is —
   I can't stand —

What do these tell you about your own values?

7. These statements are from Pirke Avot — a collection of ethical sayings in the Mishnah (books of Jewish law which we'll talk about later!) Evaluate the following as they relate to this chapter:

> *He whose deeds exceed his wisdom — his wisdom endures; but he whose wisdom exceeds his deeds — his wisdom doesn't endure.*

> *Shammai said — "Make your study of the law a fixed duty — say little and do much — and receive all people with a cheerful face!"*

> *. . . It isn't so much the study of the law . . . but the practice of it — that's crucial!*

And how about this old Hasidic saying —

> *A man who studies the law but doesn't actually follow it with actions is like a bookcase filled with books. They both just sit there. What is really needed is a reader!*

8. In this chapter two important areas that religion deals with are mentioned.

   a. What are they?
   b. Evaluate the following two examples. According to the comments made earlier would these individuals be considered religious? Do you feel they are religious? Why? Why not?

   Mr. Holmes is a member of the Temple Board of Directors. He feels it is very important to be involved in religion. He goes to Synagogue weekly. He contributed a great deal of money to the Temple building fund. Mr. Holmes earns his money by selling second hand cars. He realizes that many of the cars he sells are fixed up in such a way that they will "die" when his protective warranty is up. But he feels that that's O.K. — After all, business is business.

   Mrs. Zwitterhorn hasn't been in a Church or Temple for the past thirty years. She states "Religious services leave me cold. I don't believe in God, and certainly not in prayer." Mrs. Zwitterhorn spends her free time on weekends working with retarded children. She is a very active member of the community and has contributed a great deal of both time and money to many charitable organizations. In addition she is widely respected for the hospitality she shows to anyone who comes to her door.

9. Look up the following Biblical passages. Discuss them as they relate to this unit:
   a. Isaiah 5:16,20
   b. Amos 5:14-15, 21-24
   c. Micah 6: 6-8
   d. Zechariah 4:6
   e. Malachi 2:10

12

Decision Making I - General Problem-Solving Techniques

One question that comes up from time to time in Ethics classes involves the "how" of Ethics. "**How** do we go about evaluating ethical situations?" . . . "What's the best way to solve the problem?" These are questions involving problem solving techniques. Now, we don't expect to teach you all of the methods of decision making in two chapters. There are, believe it or not, entire courses devoted to different methods which you can use when evaluating problems! But, read this chapter and the next one. Try to keep some of the basic principles and ideas in the back of your mind. You will find that they will make ethical problem solving (and problem solving in general) much easier.

Also please keep in mind that we aren't telling you that **you must** use principles 1, 2, 3 etc. when confronted by a problem. These are but a listing of techniques that have been found to be very useful. It is my hope that by considering these points, you may find something in them of value to yourself.

13

Here then, are some basic principles to keep in mind when solving problems:

1. Don't fool around — be serious!
2. Decide as to just what the problem is.
3. Don't ignore the obvious.
4. Get as much information as you can.
5. Try to look at stuff different ways.
6. Break problems into pieces, or work backwards.
7. Don't get trapped by preconceived ideas.
8. Get a little help from a friend.
9. Sleep on it.
10. See if you can find similar examples or guidelines from the past.
11. Always evaluate the possible consequences of any proposed course of action.

1. DON'T FOOL AROUND

This means you! Listen, problem solving and decision making is serious business! You just can't get stuff accomplished if you are fooling around or keep changing your focus of attention. If you've ever gone to the library with a friend to do homework (ugh! — nasty word) and then started to talk about the "big game on Saturday" or "the party at Joe's house", you know how much work got done! So when working on a problem — stick to it (you can always discuss the party later!) As our ancestors commented in Ecclesiastes 3:18. —

To everything there is a season and a time for every purpose under heaven:
A time to be born and a time to die
A time to plant and a time to uproot
A time to kill and a time to heal
A time to pull down and a time to build up
A time to weep and a time to laugh
A time to mourn and a time to dance
A time to scatter stones and a time to gather them
A time to embrace and a time not to
A time to seek and a time to lose
A time to keep and a time to cast away
A time to tear and a time to mend
A time for silence and a time for speech
A time to love and a time to hate
A time for war and a time for peace

2. JUST WHAT IS THE PROBLEM?

If you are going to make a decision about something, you've got to decide just what the actual problem is. "But of course I know what the problem is," you say. Well sometimes it's not that clear! Perhaps several examples would be useful. Here is a problem:

$$3^2 + 25 - 13 = ?$$

"Obviously the problem here is to find the answer," you say. Yes that's true. But before you can find the answer to the entire problem you have three **smaller** problems that must be considered:

    a. What is 3^2?
    b. How do I add 25 to 3^2?
    c. How do I subtract 13 from $25 + 3^2$?

Naturally when you solve something as easy as this example you don't consciously think in terms of each step being a separate problem. You just automatically think of the entire item as one big problem. Nonetheless if you had not been able to deal with each of the separate parts you would never have been able to find a solution.

Here is another example. This one is non-mathematical.

It is twenty degrees below zero, the coldest day of the year. As you sit reading, you suddenly begin to feel a chill in the air. After a while you conclude that the heat in the house is off.

It may seem obvious at first glance that the general problem is the fact that the heat is off. There are however, a number of items inherent in this situation which could be considered problems:

    a. How do I keep warm?
    b. Has the heat been off so long that the pipes have frozen?
    c. Why is the heat off?

What course of action you follow will depend on which problem you decide to

focus upon! Of course, like the math example above, this is a relatively simple problem. You might very well ponder b and c simultaneously while you run to get a sweater (to solve a)!

At this point you may very well be tempted to ask "Hey, aren't you really taking something that is actually quite clear cut and easy, and making it far more complicated than it really is?" In the simple cases given above that may very well be true. Not all problems that you will encounter will, however, be that simple! Let's say you are contemplating an issue such as "crime". Crime is certainly a problem. But even the so-called "experts" are tearing their hair in frustration trying to deal with it. Part of their difficulties stem from trying to work out **what** the basic underlying problems are, and then deciding how to best cope with them.

"Maintaining the quality of our environment" is another problem. But again, in order to effectively cope with it one really has to first decide what the basic problem is, that must be dealt with. Is it overpopulation? Is it pollution? What exactly is it? Then there are problems involved **with each** of the problems! If the basic problem is overpopulation, then don't the real issues of concern become "Should we control population growth, and if so what methods should be used?" At that stage there are many problems involved with the various methods. (see chart). The major point here is **not** to give an in-depth analysis of the problem of "maintaining the quality of our environment" (The chart could easily be expanded!). The important thing is that you realize **that when trying to solve more complex dilemmas it is important to look carefully at the situation and decide exactly which problem is to be focused upon.** Perhaps it is the fact that people are often unclear in their own minds as to this procedure, that makes problem solving much more difficult than it need be. Now before you go on to the next "principle" for problem solving — take a quick look (about ten seconds) at the picture on this page. Then **without** looking back at the picture list the things you saw in it!

16

EXAMPLE OF THE DIFFICULTIES INVOLVED IN DEFINING JUST WHAT THE PROBLEM IS!

Sample Problem:

Maintaining the quality of the environment

BUT IS THAT THE ACTUAL PROBLEM?
WHAT DO WE FOCUS UPON TO SOLVE?

POLLUTION?

Problem: Is pollution a major threat to the environment?
Problem: If so, what are all of the major causes of pollution?
Problem: How much pollution can the earth's ecosystems tolerate?
Problem: How do we control pollution? What are some general approaches and specific guidelines?

More Specialized problems:

1. What kinds of legislation must be passed?
2. How should special interest groups be handled?
3. How to coordinate international cooperation on specific issues?
4. How can decisions be enforced?
5. What specific technological improvements or solutions may be found?

More **problems** are involved with the specifics of any of the above:

A. **Technological problems** – Is it feasible?
B. **Ethical problems** – Is it feasible?
C. **Economic problems** – Is it practical?
D. **Administrative problems** – Is it practical?
E. **Political problems** – Is it practical?
F. **Choice problems** – What should overall program be?

OVERPOPULATION?

Problem: Is population growth a major threat to the quality of the environment?
Problem: How much population growth can be tolerated by the earth's ecosystems? Is it desirable to allow it to reach that limit?
Problem: How do we go about controlling population growth? Should we?
Problem: If it is necessary to control population what general methods and specific approaches should be used?

More Specialized problems:

1. Voluntary methods (what are they?).
2. Involuntary methods (what are they?).
3. Educational approaches (what are they?).
4. Changes in societal institutions. (what are they?)
5. Economic benefits or penalties.

More **problems** are involved with the specifics of any of the above:

A. **Technological problems** – Is it feasible?
B. **Ethical problems** – Is it feasible?
C. **Economic problems** – Is it practical?
D. **Administrative problems** – Is it practical?
E. **Political problems** – Is it practical?
F. **Choice problems** – What should overall program be?

There are numerous problems involved with each one of A–F. To give some examples, here are some **ethical problems** in population control:

- How can a specific proposal be fair?
- How can it be set up so as not to penalize any one group (e.g. disadvantaged?)
- How can it avoid becoming an end in itself?
- How can maximum freedom of choice be maintained?

This leads us to our next principle:

3. DON'T IGNORE THE OBVIOUS

The reason you were asked to look at the picture and then list the items from memory was to emphasize a point. **Very often we will look at something, but not really remember what we saw!** How many of the items were you able to remember? How many did you miss? If you were able to remember everything in the picture then you are quite unusual! In this particular instance you were given advance notice! You were told to look at the picture for a short time and then to try to remember what was in it. There are, however, many things that you have looked at, as part of everyday life. If you were suddenly asked for details about them, (without advance warning that you were going to be asked) you might find the task even more difficult. For example consider the following:

1. *The man on a U.S. nickel is — — — —.*
2. *There are — — — — doors painted blue on your block.*
3. *(Don't look!) I am wearing — — — — — colored socks today.*
4. *Close your eyes. Pretend you are in your living room! Orient yourself in one place and then mentally "wander" around the room. Can you remember* **exactly** *where everything is? How about the details? Is it easy?*
5. *How many keys are there on the family typewriter? . . . or buttons (dials) on the stove?*
6. *How many doors (windows) are there in your cousin's house?*

I hope that by now you are convinced that there may be many things that we **look at** but never **really** pay attention to! Incidently this same kind of thing occurs with music and listening.

Very often you will **listen** to a song and get the general melody down; but can you remember **all** of the harmonizing notes, the little trills and doo-dads worked in? Not always. (Try it!) Again — we pick up a lot of stuff with our various senses that we ignore! Normally the fact we do this isn't that bad. After all we are bombarded with so much information all the time that naturally we "filter" it. But when trying to solve a problem it's important not to ignore **any information** — especially the obvious! Oh yes, there is some neat stuff from our tradition that relates to this! First an old tale:

> *There was once a Hasidic Rabbi who lived in style. Another Rabbi came to visit and asked him, "What is going on?" The first Rabbi responded — "I have three funds: The first is of donations from the very pious. That pays for my basic needs. The second is from people who are not too pious, but not bad. — That goes to charity. The third fund is of donations made by sinners. That I use for my indulgences. How can I help it if that is the largest fund?"*

That Rabbi **made sure** he saw the obvious! And how about this comment which was an old Rabbi's way of telling us to be aware of the obvious:

> *If one man calls you a jackass — just ignore it; but if two or more call you a jackass — consider getting a saddle!*

When confronting any problem, take a careful look at all the information that

is available and don't ignore any details. What sometimes may at first glance appear trivial or even obvious, could in the final analysis, be important for the solution of your problem.

4. GET AS MUCH INFORMATION AS YOU CAN – IF POSSIBLE

This is somewhat of an extension of our last principle. Aside from being careful not to overlook any given information one is always smart to seek any additional information about the problem at hand. Extra information can often make the difference between solving a problem and not solving it. It can affect the quality of your decision making. A solution which might be barely adequate can be modified with extra data, into a solution that is tops. Sometimes it is just not possible to get anymore information than what is given. In that case you simply have to work as well as you can with what you have. But in many real-life problems involving moral issues it is possible to get extra details. For example:

> *Mr. Extell has a problem. His head foreman, Bertrand has been acting strangely lately. Bertrand has been moody, sullen and has even come to work drunk. Extell has tried to talk to Bertrand about it, but can't seem to break through to him. Bertrand has been a loyal employee for the company for twenty years and has always done more than his share of the work. Extell finds the thought of firing Bertrand distasteful but if this behavior, which has been going on for several months should continue, he may be forced to let him go.*

Extell has a moral problem on his hands. He could sit back, see if Bertrand's behavior continues to be strange and eventually make the decision as to whether to fire him or not. He could, however, seek further information from Bertrand's friends, family etc. What if he found the following?:

Bertrand's marriage is in trouble. His wife is an alcoholic. To add to the stress, Bertrand's only daughter (age 14) was hit by an automobile, several months ago. She was hurt very badly and is still in the hospital. Bertrand has been doing his best to pay the bills, but his insurance simply won't cover all of the expenses. Consequently he is in debt and even stands in danger of losing his home.

Doesn't this extra information add greatly to our knowledge of the situation? If you were Extell and became aware of this extra data wouldn't it affect the quality of your decision? How? The point is clear. Seek as much information as you possibly can about any problem before making any decisions!

5. TRY TO LOOK AT STUFF DIFFERENT WAYS

This sounds strange, but it is actually one of the most important principles of problem solving. Sometimes when people look at a problem they may not view it as an opportunity to experiment with new approaches and to be creative. It is, however, the willingness to look at things in different ways that will often hold the key to the best solutions to problems. You're not convinced? Look at the following:

A. What do you see? . . . The container or the faces?

20

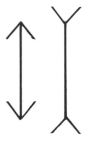

B. Which of the two lines are larger? Measure them and compare!

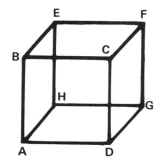

C. What is the nearest surface of the cube?
Is it A, B, C, D?
or
Is it E, F, G, H?

I think you can get the point. Very often our senses can fool us. The real value of these illusions is that they demonstrate quite vividly how it is often **possible to see the same thing in various ways**. Here are some more:

D. Divide this square into four equal parts in as many ways as you can.

E. Describe this picture in as many ways as you can.

F. Which is the top and which is the bottom of these stairs?

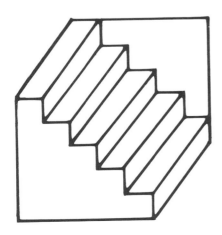

And how about these pictures —

G—J Describe what is happening in each as many ways as you can.

Of course it can be argued that the examples given here are visual situations which really aren't the same as moral problems. True, we are making a comparison. However, the ability and the desire to consider something various ways is by no means limited to any one area. It can be applied to viewing anything. A comedian takes the ordinary and by approaching it from a slightly weird perspective makes it funny and unique. A scientist who is having difficulty solving a problem may intuitively try something new or different, hoping that she/he will have better results. Art can give us great examples of this kind of thing. Tell an artist to paint a picture of the same thing at four or five different times in his/her life, and you will be amazed at how different the pictures can sometimes be. So it should come as no surprise that "trying to look at things different ways" can be quite useful when confronting ethical issues as well!

One hundred and fifty years ago when I was a student I was told an old Jewish tale which demonstrates how you can look at something from varying perspectives:

> There was once a man who after winning his case in court called the judge brilliant. Sometime later he lost a case in the same judge's court. Then he called the judge an idiot. After word got around, whenever people saw this man they said "Brilliant one day — an idiot the next!"

There are several methods by which one may try to view a problem in different ways:

1. One involves putting aside your preconceived notions and trying to think of as many ways of dealing with an issue as possible. This can involve brain storming techniques as well as principle six etc.

2. A second approach to viewing problems in different ways is inspired by Pirke Avot (a book in the Mishnah dealing with ethics — See p. 94):

Don't judge your fellow man until you are in his place.

An extremely useful approach in handling ethical problems is to pretend that you are each of the different people involved and to try to consider the problem from their perspectives. You'll be surprised at how much insight this can provide. You will become more aware of why other people are behaving as they are and how they might continue to act under the circumstances.

BRAINSTORM!

When one tries to solve a problem by approaching it from many different angles an excellent procedure to use is brainstorming. Here are some rules to follow:

PHASE ONE:

1. List as many ideas as you can concerning a problem. — the more the better.
2. This can be done alone but even more ideas turn up when you Brainstorm in a group!
3. As the ideas are suggested no **immediate** criticism or evaluation should be made. Wild ideas are just as good as conservative ones. Remember we are interested in **quantity**.
4. Sometimes one wild idea suggested can lead to another. Try to build on ideas suggested.

PHASE TWO:

5. After your paper/board is full of ideas or you've run out of ideas — **then** start evaluating.
6. Don't just junk weird or unusual approaches. There just might be something sound or usable in even the strangest ideas. An old saying from Jewish mystics (people looking for ultimate reality) was "There's a Kernel of wheat in the mass of chaff." Look for the Kernel!

6. BREAK PROBLEMS INTO PIECES OR WORK BACKWARDS

A guy named Ben Bag Bag (cool name, huh?) made the comment in the Mishnah "Turn it this way and that (it - being the Torah) for everything is in it." He was suggesting a practical method for the study of Jewish law.

The same method can be useful when trying to solve problems. You take a problem and consider it from one end, and then the other. You take it apart, analyze it and then put it together again. Rather than starting at one spot in the problem, you start at another. You may even work backwards. "Strange" you say? No, not at all. Just think of all the times you weren't sure how to solve a math problem. You might have looked at the answer given at the end of the book, and then tried to work your problem so as to arrive at that answer. In a sense that's working backwards. Whenever you try to solve a mathematical word problem you start with what you know, work what sections of the problem you can, and then go to the final solutions.

I hope the difference between this principle and the last one is clear. Here we are concerned with solving a problem by cutting it into pieces and concentrating on the various sections, working backwards, etc. The last principle suggested that you look at problems in different ways. That **includes** concentrating on various sections, etc, but it is far more general, involving coming up with unusual solutions, looking at the problem from the perspectives of all of the individuals involved, etc.

Perhaps it is best to summarize these two principles with a cool midrash:

> *A Roman philosopher spent many years of scientific research and finally discovered certain facts about the reproduction of serpents. When a few Jewish wise men visited Rome, he asked them questions to see if they knew his facts. Well, at first they went into shock but after consulting a few Jewish sources they figured out an answer. When the philosopher heard it he got pretty uptight. In fact he got so uptight that he started to mess up a wall as he beat his head against it. "Here I wasted seven years in research," he cried, "and these characters come up with the answer in a short time!"*

Thus to find the answer to a problem, there are many avenues of analysis!

Now look at the picture on the opposite page. **Write down what you think** each person is like. If you were a multimillionaire and were to give one million dollars away, to which of these people would you give it? (Yes, you **have** to give it away to one of these people – Don't be greedy!) STOP HERE! **Look immediately at the picture before proceeding further.**

Now that was a sneaky exercise to show that we all do have preset or preconceived notions or ideas about people and/or things. (After all how do you **really** know whether the people in the picture **are** what they appear to be. The "sweet little old lady" could be the toughest character there!) Preconceived notions can sometimes affect the way we make decisions. This leads us to our next principle.

7. DON'T GET TRAPPED BY PRECONCEIVED NOTIONS

It can limit the possibilities when you try to solve problems. Here is one of my favorite stories, an old Hasidic legend about having preconceived notions. (It also shows us a Jewish view of over-indulgence!):

> There was once a hunter who liked to indulge in alcohol to excess. One day he heard that a big bear was seen in the vicinity. Although he had no money he headed to the local inn where he could get a drink. When asked about payment, he told the innkeeper about the bear. "I'll pay you after I get a lot of money from the bear's hide!" Well, the hunter had one drink after another and after a while he was "sozzled!" He then went out to seek the bear. Suddenly the bear charged out of the woods! The hunter shot at him but was so drunk that he missed! The bear continued to charge at him! The hunter fell to the ground and played dead. The bear came over, sniffed at his head and finally left. The innkeeper ran out of the Inn. "Are you all right?" he asked the hunter. "Yeah I'm fine," was the answer. "What did the bear say to you when he came so close?" asked the innkeeper. "He said," responded the hunter, "not to promise payment for drinks with money from his hide, before I know for sure that I'll be able to get it!"

Moral of the tale — No preconceived notions please!

STEREOTYPES

When discussing preconceived notions one can't help but touch upon the subject of Stereotypes.

Stereotypes are preconceived notions, generally over simplified, and formulated without adequate knowledge about a person or group of people.

You have possibly heard comments like: "Such and such group is noisy or lazy" etc. These are examples of stereotypes. Stereotypes are quite dangerous preconceived notions. They can lead to acting towards others, based on labels rather than on the basis of personal knowledge. Stereotypes can cloud our perceptions and prevent us from responding to other human beings uniqueness and individuality.

Jews should be particularly concerned about false preconceived notions, for our ancestors have been victimized by them. For example:

I. The Blood Libel — This a particularly nasty one. It is the charge that Jews murder non-Jewish people in order to obtain their blood to use in a wide variety of things ranging from medicines, and aphrodisiacs, to ritual use at Passover. It's thought that this was early propaganda spread by Antiochus (the bad guy of the Hanukkah story). While this charge is totally false and contrary to Jewish customs and procedures, enough people blindly accepted it, to cause our ancestors great misery. The blood libel has been raised in such a variety of places as Syria, England, Italy, Spain, Russia, Greece, France and Poland. Even during modern times the Nazis tried to revive this in their propaganda. It has led to the torture and murder of Jews in hundreds of communities throughout the ages.

II. The Black Death — During the mid 1300's an epidemic of plague (caused by the organism bacillus pestis) swept through Europe. Plague is not a very pleasant disease. The three forms, pneumonic (attacks the lungs), bubonic (produces swellings of the lymph glands) and septicemic (poisons the blood) are fatal. It is characterized by high fever, great pain and death in five or six days.

The epidemic from 1348 — 1350, killed somewhere between one quarter and one half of the population of Europe. No one at that time had any idea as to how to prevent or cure the disease. People reacted in various ways. Some believed that the plague was God's punishment for their sins, and turned to prayer. Others saw the plague as an opportunity for crime and violence. As some individuals prayed, others kept busy mugging and robbing. Terrified, the people tried to find someone to blame for their problems. Among others (including witches, and physicians) the Jews were blamed for the Black Death. The charge was that Jews had been poisoning the water and food supply. In hundreds of cities Jews, dying of plague were attacked by non-Jews, dying of plague. In spite of Pope Clement VI's efforts to protect the Jews, thousands lost their lives and property.

The point should be clear. Preconceived ideas are quite common. We all have opinions, some of them very strong, about various situations and/or people. To a degree, these conceptions and ideas are necessary for us to be able to get along in the world. For example, if you did not have the preset idea, based on years of experience, that misbehaving in class could lead to punishment, then you would continually be having hassles with your teacher. So there is a good side to preconceived notions. However, if we do not recognize our preconceived notions to be just that, and blindly follow them all of the time, then we can run into difficulties. These opinions can and do influence our judgement when we deal with ethical issues. If we are not on guard they can slow us down and prevent us from finding new, different or possibly better solutions to problems. It is not always easy to totally ignore preconceived ideas. Nonetheless, if you have preset ideas about something and make an effort to **at least recognize them as such**, then it is less likely that you will be trapped or unconsciously led by them.

8. A LITTLE HELP FROM A FRIEND

Very often when faced with a problem, comparing notes with a friend(s) can be very useful. There are times when another person can think of an approach that you possibly ignored. A saying in Pirke Avot "Who is wise? — he who learns from all men.", kind of highlights this point. Perhaps you've heard the Talmudic story of two dogs who were guarding sheep. They found that it was a lot smarter to work together against the wolf, than for each to go off on his own. Similarly when you solve a problem, it might be in your best interest to adopt a similar approach.

With a little help from some friends.

9. SLEEP ON IT

Sometimes it is possible to have a problem, a bad one, and nothing, simply nothing, seems to help you solve it. You have tried everything:

- *You have seriously and carefully defined just what the problem is with which you are concerned.*

- *You have examined everything, sought information, and have not missed any obvious points.*

- *You have tried to think of new and different ways of approaching the problem, including breaking the problem into pieces and/or working backwards — (but have only a headache for your efforts!)*

- *You have checked possible guidelines from tradition but are still unsatisfied.*

- *You have even asked friends for suggestions — and only received an earache listening to them.*

In short you have gone through everything and are still BLANK!!!

Sometimes the best way to deal with a situation such as this is to simply "push the problem to the back of your mind" and get a good night's sleep. You may find yourself waking up in the middle of the night with the answer. Preposterous? No, not at all. There are numerous cases recorded throughout history of this kind of thing occurring. One that always impressed me was the experience of a guy named Kekule. He knew that the chemical compound Benzene was made of 6 carbon and 6 hydrogen atoms — but he was having a terrible time figuring out **how** it was put together. He dozed off and dreamed of a snake grabbing its own tail. This led him to discover the actual arrangement:

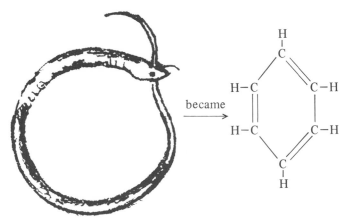

became

This was an important chemical discovery, and to this day the ringed arrangement is known as "The Kekule structure of benzene." So you see it can happen! Incidently three further comments are necessary:

1. *If you wake up in the middle of the night with an answer write it down so you won't forget it.*

28

2. *This approach is a last resort method. It's not guaranteed. It only works sometimes. Moreover, it should **never** be used to avoid dealing with problems in a conscious straightforward manner. Trying to wait and let problems "solve themselves" usually only makes them worse.*

3. *A variation upon this theme, is that if you are trying to solve a problem and seem to be running into difficulties simply go away from it for awhile and come back to it later. (e.g. in an hour) It often helps . . . Again as mentioned above, never use this approach as an excuse to avoid dealing with problems.*

10. SEE IF YOU CAN FIND SIMILAR EXAMPLES OR GUIDELINES FROM THE PAST

This principle is extremely important. If you were told by a teacher that you had to write a report on a given topic, you would most likely first check out what had already been written about that subject by others, before starting to write your own paper. If you were a scientist developing a new invention or theory, you would first make certain that you were aware of similar projects that had been done in the same field. After all, it would be plain stupidity to disregard other research and to end up repeating by trial and error work that had already been done by someone else. It is the same kind of thinking that would suggest this principle! Why not take advantage of the vast amount of materials offering ethical insight and/or guidance? Well, while this might sound neat, it isn't that simple. There is no book entitled "Ethical Guidance," with straightforward recipes for ethical dilemmas. It is possible, however, to find insights concerning ethical issues from all kinds of sources; in novels and general literature and even in specialized law books. A major source of materials offering moral guidance is to be found in the Jewish Tradition. Later in this book an entire unit will be devoted to Jewish sources that offer ethical guidance. In the next unit we will be discussing some general Jewish Guidelines.

29

11. ALWAYS EVALUATE THE POSSIBLE CONSEQUENCES OF ANY PROPOSED COURSE OF ACTION

I'm sure you've heard of Newton's third law at one time or another — A simplified wording would be "To every action there's a reaction." Well similarly whenever you do something in an ethical situation, there is a reaction. This reaction may be good or bad, depending on what you've done! One should therefore always consider the possible **consequences** of a proposed course of action to see if that is the way one **really wants** to proceed. Some of you might be saying "Yeah but that's common sense. I do that anyhow." That's true, it is common sense. But you'd be amazed at how often people don't think through the possible results of their actions. One of the biggest problems with our Science and Technology today is that often new things are invented or developed, but comparatively little thought has been given to the impact of these things on society. This is a clear case of ignoring consequences by so-called "smart" people. By now you are probably waiting for a midrash illustrating this point, and of course I'm not going to disappoint you! Here is an example of someone not considering the consequences of his actions:

One day a Rabbi was traveling and was feeling pretty happy with himself. He came across a man who was really ugly. When the man greeted him the Rabbi answered. "Wow are you ugly!" The man answered "If you have any complaints . . . take them up with God who created all of us." Later this man made the incident public knowledge when the Rabbi arrived at his destination.

So here's a case where being proud and ignoring possible consequences didn't do a person any good! Then of course there is an old saying in the Zohar (book Jewish mystics used) which definitely shows awareness of the possible consequences of an action:

One who wishes to sing praises to God in a loud voice should have a good voice. If he doesn't have a good voice he shouldn't pray aloud!

One final comment about this principle. No person is a mind reader or can possibly predict the future with one hundred percent certainty. When the suggestion is made to evaluate possible consequences the stress is on the **possible** While you may not know for sure, whether or not something will happen as a result of a proposed course of action, you can often make an **educated guess** based on your knowledge of the situation.

SUMMARY:

In this section we examined eleven hints to help solve ethical problems.

Let's put the whole process together in diagram form:

30

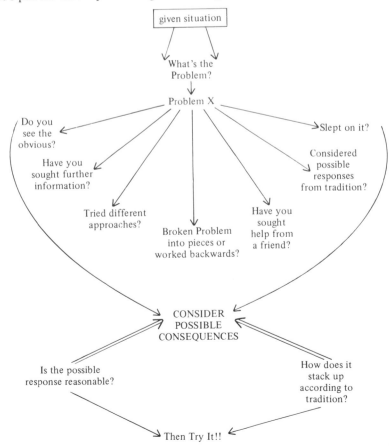

given situation

What's the Problem?

Problem X

Do you see the obvious?

Slept on it?

Have you sought further information?

Considered possible responses from tradition?

Tried different approaches?

Broken Problem into pieces or worked backwards?

Have you sought help from a friend?

CONSIDER POSSIBLE CONSEQUENCES

Is the possible response reasonable?

How does it stack up according to tradition?

Then Try It!!

Just as A Chess Player is careful of his moves so too should we be careful of our moves in the game of life.

Rabbi Bunam

1. Write out three problems (ethical if possible). Analyze each one in terms of at least eight of the problem solving principles discussed in the chapter. (Note: In order to get anything out of this, or any of the other questions you must be prepared to spend some time and do some very careful thinking).

2. Close your eyes (Not now; only after you read this problem!). Visualize every step of your coming from (or going to) school. Write it down. Can you describe your surroundings perfectly?

3. This is a common problem that teachers like to give their classes when discussing problem solving. Connect the twelve spots without lifting your pencil from the page. How **many** ways can you solve this problem?

32

4. As you recall in the chapter, we often overlook or ignore the obvious. Here are a few more exercises that deal with that principle. After you try them — compare your answers with the actual answer. Write both sets of answers down on paper.

      a. Is your front door knob on the right or left side of the door?
      b. What is the color of your best friend's glasses?
      c. Does your father part his hair on the left or the right side?
      d. What color is a $25 bill?
      e. When you get up in the morning do you put on your left shoe or right shoe first?
      f. When you eat an ice cream cone, do you
          I. Lick it in a circular fashion?
         II. Push the ice cream down with your lips and tongue, then bite at the cone?
        III. Use another method?
      (Wasn't that a nice exercise?)
      g. How much change do you have in your pocket?
      h. Where is the fire station nearest to your house?
      i. How many poles (streetlights, telephone poles etc.) are there on your block?
      j. How many houses are there on your block?

5. Hopefully by now you are becoming more aware of the obvious. We tend to ignore data from senses other than our vision. This exercise (and others like it that you can make up yourself) will help you sharpen up your other senses. When solving problems you must use all of your capabilities. Imagine the following:

a. The smell of burning eggs
b. The sound of a fire engine
c. The taste of a soft drink
d. The smell of a rose
e. The feeling of being dizzy
f. The feel of velvet
g. The smell of chocolate
h. The feel of bark of a tree
i. The taste of peppermint

j. The feel of sandpaper
k. The smell of coffee brewing
l. The sight of a sunset
m. The sound of a horse galloping
n. The taste of a hamburger
o. The sound of glass breaking
p. What you are actually hearing right now
q. The pain of scratching or scraping yourself

Take your time going through these. After you imagine each one write down (for each) a description of what you experienced in your mind. (It isn't easy!)

6. Find as many connections among the following things as you can. Even if there doesn't seem to be much of a relationship between them, try to think of some. List them.

   a. ice cream, pen, bowl, apple
   b. desk, sugar, automobile, pen
   c. chair, fan, steak, spoon
   d. cat, window, light bulb, cash register
   e. penny, dog, stork, grass
   f. tape, cord, sofa, baby

7. Write a paragraph using all the words in number six. (It must be clear and coherent!) Underline the words.

8. Write a paragraph (a clear and coherent one) using all the following words (underline them, please):
   run, kettle, danced, feeble, ethics,
   lemon, swirl, chicken wire, tasty, cat,
   annoyed, healthy, porch, nervous, paint,
   stink, dull, smell

This paragraph must present some kind of **ethical problem** (slave drivers aren't we?).

9. Look at the following picture:

Which is longer — S or R? Are you certain?

10. A nice tasty hamburger is on a tray suspended fifteen feet above the floor. How many ways can you get at the hamburger? Describe.
   You have the following equipment:

   — a large rubber band
   — a 3 ft. cord
   — an apple
   — a wire coat hanger

   — three pieces of paper
   — a box of dog biscuits
   — a saw
   — paper clips

33

TEMPLE ISRAEL LIBRARY

11. Look at the following picture.

    a. List everything that could be going on here.
    b. Write two different stories about the picture.

12. Given the following:

Situation One: The J.C.E. Corporation recently fired a large number of their employees.

Situation Two: The exact same as above but add to it the following facts:

    a. J.C.E. is doing extremely well financially.
    b. The people who have been laid off were those who had seniority (were with the company for 15–25 years).
    c. These individuals were replaced by young people willing to work for cheap wages.
    d. The president of J.C.E. recently bought an expensive yacht.

  I. What is your evaluation of the J.C.E. Corporation given only:
    Situation one?
    Situation one plus two a?
    Situation one plus two a and b?
    Situation one plus two a, b and c?

II. How does the addition of each particular bit of information affect your evaluation?

13. List the numbers 9—16 in the boxes in such a way that no consecutive numbers are next to each other (e.g. 9, 10, 11 can't be in boxes next to each other).

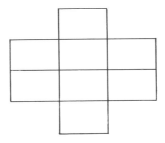

14. Take the numbers 6—14. Arrange them in the grid so that the sum of the numbers in each column, row or diagonal adds to thirty.

15. Now evaluate the following situation:

John was playing hockey with his friends. The game got hot and heavy and he accidently got hit in the head with a stick. His father who was coaching tried to revive him, but to no avail. He rushed his son to the hospital. In the emergency room the physician on duty gasped, "I can't treat the boy . . . he is my son!"

How would you explain this?

Were you trapped by preconceived notions?

BEN SIRA ON BEHAVIOR AT
THE DINNER TABLE

Ben Sira wrote this in Hebrew over two thousand years ago!

If you're sitting at a big table don't lick your lips and say "Hey, what a spread!" . . . Don't reach for everything you see and bump into other guests . . . Eat what's put in front of you like a gentleman, and don't chomp and make yourself obnoxious . . . If you're eating out with a large group, don't reach before others . . . A moderate eater sleeps well . . . but a pig suffers from insomnia and indigestion . . . If you can't avoid overeating at a party leave the table and get relief by vomiting! . . . If you are giving a party don't be cheap; it's bad public relations! If someone knows when to drink and when to stop, wine can be enjoyable . . . but in excess it can result in bad feelings and expose one to injury . . . Don't try to prove your manhood by boozing! . . . At a feast don't reprimand or belittle another guest while he's having a good time . . . that just isn't the time to argue with him or bug him to pay his debts! If you are master of ceremonies, don't be high and mighty . . . Take care of others before you sit down! Speak if you're old, it's you're right . . . but come to the point and don't interrupt the entertainment! Speak if you're young . . . but be brief. Don't be the last to leave . . . Oh yes . . . and make sure you thank your maker who has blessed you!

unit three

Decision Making II-
The Jewish Approach

In the last chapter I indicated that one approach to problem solving can involve checking out similar examples or seeking guidance from the past. This is a key area where Judaism can help us in the study of Ethics — where it is very relevant and useful. We can explore the tradition for suggestions as to what to do, and we can evaluate our own actions by traditional guidelines. There are two ways we can apply Judaism to ethical problem solving:

1. The Specific Situation Approach.
2. The General Guideline Approach.

When I talk in terms of the **specific situation approach** I mean that given a certain problem, what detailed hints, suggestions etc. does Judaism give that may be specifically applied to that or to similar situations. For example — what information can we get about good table manners, (see p. 36), ransom of captives (p. 127) etc. Here and there, in this book we will give specific insights of Judaism about various topics.

The **general guideline approach** is what it's name implies — general guidelines. Does Judaism have any comprehensive or all-embracing teachings which would be useful for us to keep in mind as we analyze any ethical issue? I would answer yes! A consideration of these general Jewish approaches forms the basis for this unit.

Well then, what are these general Jewish approaches to ethics? I would list them as follows:

1. Survival and self-fulfillment plus societal enrichment.
2. Treating another as if you're in his/her place.
3. The middle course.
4. The "world is sustained" approach.
5. The "wise person" approach.

A number of problem solving techniques were presented in the last unit as basic tools to use when dealing with ethical issues. So too, can these basic Jewish guidelines be helpful to you! O.K. so here goes:

1. SURVIVAL AND SELF-FULFILLMENT PLUS SOCIETAL ENRICHMENT

This is an extremely important guideline to consider whenever confronting moral problems. Before explaining its meaning, I'd like to tell a story about an individual who said some very important stuff about this approach! The person is Hillel. Have you ever heard of him? He was quite an interesting character. Hillel lived about two thousand years ago. There is an interesting story about what happened to him when he was young. He wanted to learn Jewish stuff very much, but there was a problem. He was poor, very poor. Normally he was able to scrape a little cash together to pay for his entrance to the school. (They charged admission, like private schools today.) One day he was **broke**. I mean zonko — no cash! Well that didn't stop him. If he couldn't get in the academy through the front door he could always find a different route! So up went Hillel onto the roof. He made his way over to a skylight, sat down and started to listen. Well, Hillel became so involved listening to the lesson going on inside that he didn't notice that it began to snow! In fact it snowed and snowed and Hillel began to freeze — and almost turned into a Jewish popsicle! Inside the building these other characters who were studying noticed that it was getting dark in the room! They weren't exactly too thrilled about that ... After all, how can you study anything if it's too dark to see? (Remember lighting techniques then were rather primitive compared to today). They said to themselves "Ourselves — what's messing up our skylight?" They noticed a big blob covering the skylight. Further investigation revealed that the blob was Hillel! Well after considering the situation they figured that it just wouldn't be right to leave him out there! He was messing up the architecture in addition to spoiling the lighting. So they brought him in and thawed him out!

This story gives us some idea of Hillel's determination to gain an education. It also shows the great stress that Judaism puts on learning. Even poverty didn't stop Hillel! It was fortunate for Judaism that Hillel wasn't left up on that roof, for he eventually became a big shot scholar and religious leader. He said some pretty cool things (no pun intended)! One of them was:

If I am not for myself
Who will be for me?
And if I am only for myself
What am I?
And if not now — then when?

To me, this short saying is one of the most profound in our tradition and nicely summarizes much of Jewish Ethical thinking.

IF I AM NOT FOR MYSELF, WHO WILL BE FOR ME?

This certainly displays a high regard for the individual's own situation. Hillel seems to be indicating to us that if a person isn't interested in furthering his/her own welfare, then certainly she/he shouldn't expect someone else to look out for his/her concerns. If you think about it, this statement makes a great deal of sense.

— *If an individual on a job is really trying to learn all about the work she/he is doing and wants to better him/herself, many companies will make an effort to help by providing further training, etc. Whereas another person who doesn't really care about self-improvement on the job, is less likely to have the company concerned with his/her taking that kind of training.*

— *A person gets change after buying something and fails to make certain that she/he received the correct amount. If that person isn't concerned enough to check —who will be?*

— If there are possibilities to make specific improvements in a town, the people living there will decide what exactly has to be done, and then seek state and federal help. If the town **itself** *doesn't at least take the first vital steps to decide what needs doing and to try to get the project moving, the probability of accomplishing its goals might be drastically reduced. (While help can be initiated by outside sources, the chance that that particular town, among many, would get exactly what its population wants would be much less, if the town didn't actively get involved on its own behalf!)*

Thus I think you can see that this first part of Hillel's statement, uttered many hundreds of years ago, is as true and as applicable now, as when it was first formulated. **A person should look after him/herself and be concerned with his/her own interests.** To do otherwise is plain stupid. We have an interesting story from our tradition that relates to this:

Time: Just after the children of Israel fled from Egypt.
Place: The shores of the Red Sea.
Remember when Moses and the children of Israel (the good guys) were being chased by Pharoah's Army (the bad guys)? Well they all came to The Red Sea and Moses began praying to God. God said to Moses — "Look, here you are with the sea in front of you. Your enemy is close behind, and you just sit there praying. Prayer is a good thing but sometimes it's better to be brief. You do your thing and I'll do mine and we can discuss it later!" And of course the sea opened up and our ancestors crossed.

40

Here is a clear cut example from our tradition. It would have been suicidal for Moses to stop and worry about the well-being of Pharoah and his troops. If Moses and the children of Israel didn't start taking care of themselves — and fast, then the outlook for them would have been grim indeed. They had to be concerned with their own survival!

IF I AM ONLY FOR MYSELF — WHAT AM I?

If Hillel's saying was merely, "If I am not for myself, who is for me?" and nothing more, then one could say "Well, that's good and fine. I agree that one has to look out for him/herself but isn't that statement a bit selfish?" Indeed if you consider the first statement alone and without additional clarification it does sound like some kind of conceited person on an ego trip looking out only for him or herself and not really that interested in the welfare of others. Hillel's second comment provides a correction to the first statement. While he acknowledges the importance of an individual's (or group's) concern for self-interests, he asks the basic question, "If one is **only** interested in him/herself, what kind of human being would that person be?" Well, even though Hillel phrased this as a question, you can pretty much guess what he would intend as an answer. Thus, after acknowledging the individual's obligation to him/herself he goes right on to indicate that we must also pay attention to the needs of others. Perhaps a midrash is in order here to illustrate this point:

This is the story of an old man who was working hard planting trees. A Roman Emperor happened to wander by. He asked, "How old are you, old man?" The answer came back "One hundred." "Well, then," said the

Emperor, "why are you working so hard planting trees? . . . Do you really expect to eat the fruit that they will produce?" "I don't know." responded the old man. "If I eat them, fine. If I don't — well, just as my father worked for my benefit . . . so too am I working for my kids' benefit."

This is so typical of the strong interest that Judaism has in the welfare of others. The individual does not live in a vacuum, in isolation from other human beings. Thus we find that Judaism shows great concern for "the other guy." The general approach so neatly outlined by Hillel, representative of much of Jewish thinking, would be "No don't neglect yourself by any means, but also keep other people in mind too."

IF NOT NOW . . . WHEN?

What about this "If not now . . . when?" bit? Well, the first two parts of Hillel's statement were primarily concerned with an individual's attitude towards himself and others. This third statement is more concerned with another aspect of ethics— the "when?" aspect. As was indicated in unit one, Judaism views ethics as an important part of everyday life. You just don't live according to high moral standards on special occasions. A concern with doing the "right" thing should be with the individual all of the time. This small concluding comment that Hillel makes puts the responsibility for ethical behavior right back upon the individual. It tells us that one shouldn't just sit back and say "Well I suppose that one of these days I'll start living ethically!" — It suggests that each person take **immediate** responsibility to live in an upright manner.

41

If I am not for myself *Who is for me?* *If I am only for myself* *What am I?* *And if not now, when?*	*Personal* *Survival and Self-* *fulfillment* *+* *Societal Enrichment*

This very short statement displaying a concern not only with oneself, but with others as well, forms an extremely important guideline to keep in mind when dealing with ethical issues.

2. TREATING ANOTHER AS IF YOU ARE IN HIS/HER PLACE

In the last chapter we mentioned that one part of approaching things from different perspectives involves trying to look at stuff like the different people involved would (p. 23, now remember?) It isn't far from that comment to this very Jewish approach.

Another general guideline would be — **treat the other guy the way you yourself would want to be treated in a given situation.** Interestingly enough, Hillel (among others) had his hands in this one too. As was indicated above, Hillel managed to survive his education (as most of us do!). Later when he became a renowned teacher (establishment type) he attracted a number of followers. At about the same time another fellow named Shammai also attracted many students. A strong rivalry grew between Hillel and Shammai and their students. They ended up having all kinds of arguments on all kinds of issues . . . (You know, if Hillel and his followers said that it was raining outside, then Shammai and his group would say it was snowing!). Incidentally in the Talmud, we find over three hundred different things that these two groups disagreed about. Anyhow, getting back to the point about treating another as if you are in his/her place, we have the following story:

> *One day a guy came along and said to Shammai — "Teach me the entire Torah while I stand on one foot and I'll convert to Judaism." Well Shammai was notorious for his quick temper and, sure enough he lost his cool. He chased the guy out swinging a stick at him! Baiting Shammai was fun so the guy now went off to see Hillel. He made the same suggestion to him. "Teach me the entire Torah while I stand on one foot and I'll convert to Judaism." Hillel calmly said, "What you don't like to be done to you, don't do to your fellow man. That's the whole Torah . . . The rest is commentary. Now go learn it."*

Generally when teachers tell this story, they do it with a touch of awe in their voices . . . What control Hillel had! . . . How wise he was! . . . I somehow suspect that for all of his cool, calm, appearance, Hillel was getting as fresh with the wise guy, as he was with Hillel! At any rate the moral is there. When challenged to teach the Torah in such a way that a person could learn it while standing on one foot, (obviously not a very long period of time), Hillel did set forth an extremely important guideline. The idea of not doing to another what you would not like to have done to yourself, while simple in its statement, can readily be applied to just about any ethical dilemma. It's rather ironic that we get such a positive result from a situation in which someone was "wise mouthing" a great teacher (not a recommended procedure: another moral of the tale!).

42

Incidentally the idea that Hillel expressed is also stated in our tradition in other varying ways. In Pirke Avot we read:

> *Let the honor of your fellow man be as precious to you as your own.*

Doesn't this really state the same idea but in a different manner? Here the emphasis is on someone's honor. The statement suggests that one shouldn't put anyone else into an embarrassing position or hurt another's reputation. After all no one would like that done to him/herself. Here's another comment:

> *Let the property of your fellow man be as important to you as your own.*

No, don't get the wrong idea here. This doesn't mean that you should go and steal someone else's stuff! It does, however, suggest a pretty good guide as to how to treat anything you may have borrowed! And here are several more:

> *Don't rejoice when your enemy falls or be happy when he has a setback.*

> *Despise not any man!*

Sometimes both are tempting but would you like them done to you? Thus another guideline to keep in mind when dealing with ethical situations might be "How would I want to be treated if I were in that person's place?"

3. FOLLOW THE MIDDLE COURSE

Here is a neat story:

> *Once a great Rabbi who was asked "how to be a good human being" told the story of two convicts. These two convicts were originally going to be killed but their sentence was reduced. They were brought to a very dangerous river. A rope bridge was extended from one side to the other. Their new sentence was to cross the river using that bridge. The first managed to make his way across safely. The second hollered over to the first, "Hey, do you have any suggestions as to how I can get across without killing myself?" The first one responded, "Yeah; If you find yourself leaning too far in one direction try leaning in the other direction for balance." "So," the Rabbi concluded, "If you really want to be a fine human being, try not to lean too far in any direction and should you find a shortcoming in your personality try to lean in the other direction to balance it."*

A balance, a middle way between two extremes — this is the approach advocated. I always like to use diagrams when explaining things, so here goes:

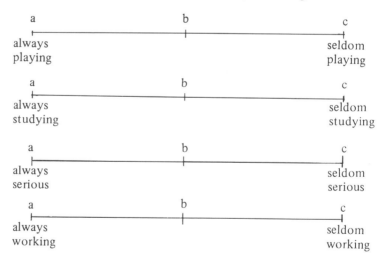

I am sure that you know people who are **always** (or almost always) studying, or who are **always** serious etc. It is also likely that you have known (or will meet) people who are never really serious about anything, or who generally do the minimal amount of work etc. Generally speaking, going to extremes in any regard can often cause problems. Thus positions a and c on the chart aren't the recommended route. Position b, where someone is sometimes serious, sometimes not; makes a habit out of doing a certain amount of work, but doesn't overdo it and has fun too etc., the middle position, is the approach suggested here.

We find comments within our tradition against both extremes. In the Talmud, for example, there's the comment that if a person who refrains from drinking wine is called a sinner — how much greater a sinner is one who refrains from all enjoyments. This certainly would seem to be against abstaining from pleasures. It tells us that one **should** enjoy the pleasures of life on earth!

45

On the other hand, we also have within our traditions a neat story about Noah. (Noah, as you will recall, was the best meteorologist of his day — he had inside information. He also ran a dating service — bringing together two of each kind of animal):

> One day Noah was busy planting a vineyard. Satan happened to come along. "Hey, Noah what's doing?" "Oh, not too much Sate. I'm planting a vineyard." "Well, what's in it for you Noah?" "The fruit is good, and from the fruit I can even make wine!" "Hey groovy," responded the Devil. "Can I be your partner?" "Sure," said Noah. Satan then killed a lamb, lion, pig and monkey and spilled their blood under the vine. (Yich!) That was his way of saying:
> 1. Before wo/man drinks wine s/he is as innocent as a lamb.
> 2. When one drinks moderately s/he feels as strong as a lion.
> 3. When one drinks too much s/he resembles a pig!
> 4. If one really gets sozzled s/he is like a monkey chattering around, singing etc. oblivious to the world.

Here is the opposite kind of statement to the one we read earlier. This story certainly does not seem to recommend overindulgence in any way!

The key to the Jewish approach is **moderation**, not to go too far in either direction. "So what," you say? "That is only common sense." Of course it is! The "Middle Way" approach is an extremely (pardon the pun!) reasonable, and common sense one.

So why make a big thing of it? When you eventually take a few courses in comparative religion (and it is my hope that you eventually do — they can be quite interesting) you will find that there have been some other approaches to life which don't follow the "Middle Way" at all. There have been, for example, many pagan religions where **unrestricted pleasure** was very important! On the opposite side there have been, in other religions, the view that **bodily pleasures are evil**. Perhaps you have read books or seen movies where there was a big noise made about playing cards, or dancing or showy clothes. Strict self-denial as a way of being religious (often called Asceticism) is frowned upon by mainstream Judaism, as is total self-indulgence. The "Middle of The Road" approach is a common sense and very Jewish way of looking at many ethical problems.

4. THE WORLD IS SUSTAINED APPROACH

To me this is a rather fun kind of approach to ethics. It also follows from statements found in our tradition. There is a midrash, for example that tells us that **there is no generation in history where there aren't at least thirty righteous people. The existence of these people prevent the destruction of the world.** Isn't that an interesting thought? (Well I think it is, whether or not you do!) First of all it points out just how hard it is to be ethical! Do you have any idea as to how many people are alive on our planet? The number around 1975 was approximately four billion! Even in 8000 B.C.E. it's estimated that there were as many as five million people. Can you imagine what a small number thirty is when compared to numbers such as these? This midrash not only indicates the difficulty of always being ethical, but it also implies the huge number of ways that one can harm another. Moreover, it leaves us with an interesting question. "Could you or I ever be among those thirty?"

Here is a comment from Pirke Avot which carries this theme a step further:

The world stands on three things; On Torah (law), on divine service and on acts of loving kindness (charity).

And here is another comment, also from Pirke Avot:

The world stands on three things; on justice, truth and peace.

One of the things that has always fascinated me, has been how some of the ancient sages were able to take some very sophisticated ideas, and to express them in short sayings that simply burst with meaning! While I shouldn't be surprised, (for the Talmud does tell us that teachers shouldn't talk too much — Yay!), I always do find that these little sayings are really neat! When one first looks at them s/he might be tempted to merely shrug them off and say "Big deal . . . nice phrases . . . So what?" But stop and take a very careful look at them. Consider them for a while. Such things as law, charity, justice etc. are fairly important. If there were absolutely no kind deeds, peace etc. anywhere, societies might well fall apart.

Here is one example. You know how sometimes something might happen, that just doesn't seem **fair** I'm sure you remember just how outraged you probably were. Can you imagine how annoyed people might get, on a societal level, if they feel they're not being dealt with in a just manner? I'm sure you can readily understand the kind of turmoil that could result. Here is an interesting example from our own Jewish History. You remember King Solomon? ("Oh yes, good personal friend," you answer). Well, Solomon was quite a character! Face it, he believed in living like a king! He had forty thousand stalls of horses, and fourteen hundred chariots. He had a fancy ivory and gold throne. Solomon had so much gold that he even had hundreds of shields made of the stuff. He directed the building of the Temple. Solomon also had seven hundred wives and three hundred concubines (Remember, there was no T.V. in those days!) Solomon also had a huge and lavish palace complex set up. (With that large crowd to house, you'd need to build a palace too if you were Solomon). Naturally all of this required money and labor! The construction of the Temple alone required over 180,000 laborers. Moreover can you imagine what it must have cost to feed all of Solomon's household (just in terms of sheer amounts of food)? When Solomon died, his son Rehoboam became king. Rehoboam was asked by the people to reduce the heavy taxes and forced labor (In order to get enough laborers to work on his various building projects Solomon had to draft people!). When Rehoboam was unsympathetic ten of the twelve tribes rebelled and established their own separate kingdom. What had once been a great unified nation split into two second-rate powers. Isn't it ironic that a taxpayer revolt and unhappiness with a draft could have contributed to the unified kingdom's demise? The point here should be clear. The people were unhappy. They didn't feel that they were being treated in a **just** manner. The story illustrates and underscores the quotation from Pirke Avot. A perceived lack of **justice** on behalf of the people cost Rehoboam half of his kingdom.

Well, this is but one example using one of the things that the quotations indicate are necessary to maintain the world. The other items are also quite important.

"The world is sustained approach" — short, seemingly "simple" statements that contain a great deal of insight into the maintenance of society, forms another guideline in living ethically.

Incidentally in 1751 The royal household in France spent about 25% of the French government's revenue. It is believed by historians that the high living of the French royalty also contributed to the revolution in that country — Apparently the French royal family didn't read the Bible very carefully, or neglected it's lesson: history does repeat itself!

THE WISE PERSON APPROACH

Curiously enough there seems to be a lot of concern in our Jewish literature about the characteristics of a wise person. You ask me "Why?" I will tell you. "I don't know." Maybe there were a lot of wise guys wandering around in those days (or a lot of fools?). So at any rate our ancestors had a great deal to say about the distinctions between the two! For example in Pirke Avot there is a discussion of seven characteristics that distinguish the wise person from the uncultured pig:

1. A wise person doesn't talk before one who's smarter than him/her.

2. S/he doesn't break in, in the middle of a discussion.

3. A wise person isn't hasty to answer — S/he considers the situation.

4. S/he asks questions that relate to the subject at hand, and answers questions to the point.

5. S/he is analytical discussing the first thing first, and the last thing last.

6. If s/he doesn't understand something, s/he admits it.

7. S/he admits the truth, and if proven to be wrong, is flexible.

The foolish boor, we are told, displays the opposite characteristics to those listed above. Again, in spite of the fact that these comments were written centuries ago, one can't help but feel that they are quite contemporary and relevant to us today! Such points as considering a situation carefully, asking relevant questions etc. are quite useful when tackling ethical dilemmas.

An accompanying chart gives some other observations concerning the differences between a wise person and a fool!

THE WISE PERSON VS. THE FOOL

A wise son brings joy to his father; a foolish son is his mother's grief.
(Proverbs 10:1)
A wise son gathers in summer; but one that sleeps at harvest time is shameful.
(Proverbs 10:5)
A wise person will take on commandments; but a babbling fool will fall.
(Proverbs 10:8)
Wise men lay up knowledge; but when a fool speaks disaster is near.
(Proverbs 10:14)
He that utters slander is a fool.
(Proverbs 10:18)
A fool thinks he's always right; a wise man listens to advice.
(Proverbs 12:15)
A fool's anger is shown immediately; a wise man conceals his feelings.
(Proverbs 12:16)
A wise man doesn't brag about his knowledge, but a fool soon reveals his stupidity.
(Proverbs 12:23)
Walk with wise men and be wise; walk with fools and you'll be destroyed.
(Proverbs 13:20)
A wise man is careful and stays clear of evil; a fool is over-confident.
(Proverbs 14:16)
A fool enjoys folly; but a wise man walks uprightly.
(Proverbs 15:21)
Even a fool, if he keeps quiet, is thought wise.
(Proverbs 17:28)
To answer a question before you listen to it is dumb.
(Proverbs 18:13)
Even if you pound a fool in a mortar with a pestle, his foolishness won't depart from him.
(Proverbs 27:22)

SUMMARY

Just as we analyzed some general problem solving techniques in unit two, we turned in this unit to some Jewish guidelines for approaching ethical situations. Judaism can shed insight on moral problems in terms of specific detailed hints for dealing with particular problems. It can also give us general guidelines that may be useful. In this unit we touched briefly upon five of these general guidelines:

1. *A concern with oneself coupled with societal considerations under-scores —* **Survival And Self-Fulfillment** plus **Societal Enrichment**.

2. *Often, when in doubt concerning specific ways of handling a situation* **treating another as if you were in his/her place**, *is a good rule of thumb to keep in mind.*

3. *One reason why people sometimes mess up their lives is because they tend to excesses. By avoiding extremes and* **sticking to the middle way**, *one can eliminate problems before they even occur.*

4. *The* **World is Sustained Approach** *is a fun approach to Jewish Ethics, based on some very short statements, which are very full of meaning!*

5. *The* **Wise Person Approach**, *seeks insights from our traditions as to what makes a wise person different from a fool (The obvious useful-ness of this approach is to help us be wise rather than foolish!)*

50

CONSIDER THIS:

1. Write an essay discussing the "wise person" vs. "the fool."

2. A friend once made the comment:

    Do unto others before they do unto you.

    Does that seem like a realistic approach to life? Why? Why not? Is it an ethical approach? Why? Why not?

3. Discuss any relationship between Hillel's statement:

    If I am not for myself
    Who will be for me?
    And If I am only for myself
    What am I?
    And If not now — then when?

    and general guideline number two in the text. Give examples.

4. Discuss any relationship between Hillel's statement (above) and general guide-line number three in the text. Give examples.

5. One of the general guidelines is to stick to the middle of the road. Give three examples where going to an extreme could cause problems.

6. Another comment in Pirke Avot was made by Judah ha Nasi:

> *Which is the right path that a man should choose for himself? Any that is an honor to those that pursue it and brings him honor from mankind.*

Why do you suppose the author did not include this as a general guideline? What are the ethical problems raised by this statement?

7. Sandy Ideal has a problem. She has just graduated from medical school and has completed her internship. She must now decide where to set up her practice. She knows that should she work in the affluent suburbs, she will be able to collect high fees and make a fine living. On the other hand she also knows that there is a strong need for physicians in the inner cities, in rural areas and on Indian reservations. However, she is aware that the second option could result in substantially lower wages and/or reduced standard of living.

How should she solve this ethical dilemma? Using ethical guideline one? Using ethical guidelines two? three?

8. The Smith Family has just moved into the upper middle class neighborhood of Moneysville. The fact that a family has moved into that neighborhood wouldn't normally cause a furor. The Smith Family, however, is black. Mr. Smith is a janitor. He originally came from the South but moved North seeking opportunity. Mrs. Smith works as a waitress. Both have worked very hard and have saved their money in order to put their children through college. Neither child however wanted to go. Thus, the Smiths were able to afford buying a new house. The neighbors are in an uproar. They feel that the fact that the Smiths have moved into Moneysville could hurt the property values there. Already two families have put up their homes for sale. Mrs. Albright would like to go over and welcome the Smiths but is afraid that she will be ostracized by her neighbors if she does.

51

    a. Discuss the ethics of the situation.
    b. Relate this situation to the general guidelines of the unit.
    c. What would you suggest that Mrs. Albright do?

WHAT IS THE RIGHT WAY FOR A PERSON TO GO?

R. Eliezer — A Good Eye (generous, kind etc.)

R. Joshua — A Good Companion.

R. Jose — A Good Neighbor.

R. Simon — One who sees the Consequences.

R. Elazar — A Good Heart.

Pirke Avot

WHAT IS AN EVIL WAY THAT A PERSON SHOULD AVOID?

R. Eliezer — An Evil Eye (jealous, stingy etc.).

R. Joshua — An Evil Companion.

R. Jose — An Evil Neighbor.

R. Simon — One who borrows and doesn't repay.

R. Elazar — An Evil Heart.

Pirke Avot

When asked these two questions, these five Rabbis gave the above answers:

— What do you think each meant? Discuss in detail.
— Which do you agree with most? Why?
— Which do you agree with least? Why?
— Add some more to their lists!
— When another Rabbi looked at the responses he preferred the comments of one Rabbi to the others for he felt that all of the others' statements were contained in that one person's comments. Whose statements do you think he preferred? Why?

SPACE ODYSSEY
SIMULATION

This exercise is to be conducted in class (before the "Why Laws" unit). Your class is to divide up into groups, with no more than five people per group.

> It is the year 2086. You are on a scheduled airliner on a routine trip to Israel. The trip took up to ten hours during the mid-twentieth century. Due to modern xenor propulsion, an extremely high altitude, and utilization of the earth's rotation, the travel time has been considerably shortened — to one half hour.
>
> You have taken off and are now in orbit. Suddenly a cosmic storm generated by a solar flare-up causes a malfunction in the robot control. The ship is thrown off course!! You are hurtled out of the Solar System and crash land on a planet in another part of the universe.
>
> Before crashing the sensors indicated that the planet has earthlike characteristics although there is no sign of intelligent life.

Your problem — What do you do now?
Consider carefully and discuss at length.
After a period of time specified by your teacher, each group will report its results to the rest of the class.

Why Laws?

In earlier units we've considered such problems as "What is ethics?", "What are values ?" and "What are various problem-solving techniques?" Now I am sure that sooner or later such questions as:

"Why do we even bother with ethics — **what's in it for me?**"
"What are the functions of laws concerning human behavior?"

are going to enter your mind. These are extremely important questions. As a rule people aren't going to do anything (including living ethically) unless they feel that there are **pretty valid reasons** for doing so.

LAWS AND ETHICS

You will note that one of the above questions, (as well as the title of this unit) raises the fundamental issue of "why even have laws in the first place?" Before dealing directly with that problem a few words should be said about the relationship between **laws** and **ethics**. After all why should we even waste time talking about the why and wherefore of laws, if we are really supposed to be discussing ethics. There must be some connection between the two to even justify this unit! Well, in a sense there is. Take a look at the following chart on p. 56.

55

We are all influenced to a large degree by leaders of society in many fields. Politicians, scientists, military, business, labor and religious leaders all have an impact. So too, do educators, artists and the mass media. All of these sources make a strong impression upon us and affect our values. What values are held in society as a whole will affect what a society wants to accomplish, or in other words, its goals. Our officials on all levels of government (local, state and national) help try to bring about our desired goals. They decide on various policies and pass laws to get the resources needed to bring about these policies, thus (hopefully) accomplishing our goals.

Perhaps a few examples would further clarify the situation. A common American value is equal opportunity — the idea that each person, regardless of background, should have an equal chance to realize his/her ambitions and to attain happiness. This value has been encouraged among our people by various leaders (e.g. mass media, religious etc.). As it has been adopted as an important value in the American conscience, it has affected our goals. Our elected officials have been, through all kinds of legislation, trying to bring about the goal of making equal opportunity a reality. Another example: a few years back, various leaders in society began to oppose the war in Vietnam. When enough people valued removing American troops from combat, the U.S. national goals were affected, and change was brought about.

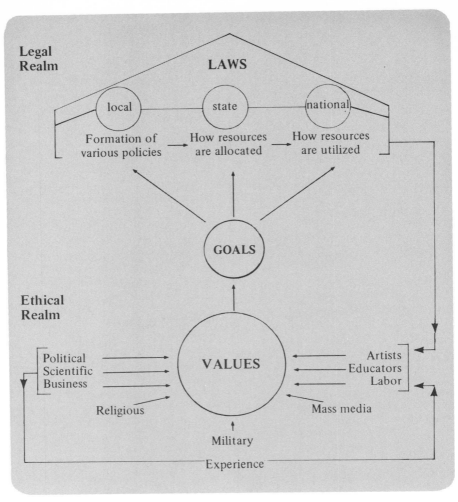

Now this is, of course, **greatly simplified**. For example you can have a people in country "X" with very nice ideals, and even laws on the books that would reflect their values, and a **dictatorship** running that country, in total disregard of the people's inherent desires. Even in a nation such as ours, many factors often complicate the translation of values into reality:

> There are often variations of law from place to place and details in them that seem contrary to majority values.

> Law makers are often unsuccessful in totally realizing their goals due to a wide variety of reasons (e.g. interest groups, etc.)

> Sometimes loopholes are available in laws etc.

So you can readily see that in practice the translation of values into reality by laws **doesn't always follow as easily** as in the chart.

Still a major point is to be made here. Values are an important area in the field of ethics. They affect our ethics. **Values do have an impact on laws**. While there may indeed be a number of problems involved, you cannot escape the fact that in general there is an **important relationship between the values people hold and a nation's legal structure.** For example our ancestors held a number of important values about human beings, God, and ethics. These values were translated into practice through the various rules and regulations that they had. In the United States today such things as freedom of the press and the right to privacy are highly prized, and we constantly hear of various legal decisions made to try to uphold these values. In a dictatorship you may find that while laws reflecting the people's values may be ignored, new laws contemptuous of human rights, and reflecting the rulers' values may come into play. One area, (the ethical realm) does affect the other (the legal realm). There is indeed a relationship between the two, although to be sure, it doesn't always work perfectly!

WHY LAWS?

O.K., so we've established that there is a relationship between values and laws. "Why then," you may ask, "do we bother following laws in the first place?"

Let's go on to try to get some perspective as to why we even are concerned with rules and regulations concerning human behavior:

Reason One: WE FOLLOW LAWS BECAUSE OUR PARENTS SAY WE HAVE TO:
Well I admit that seems to be a pretty strong reason. "I don't steal because Dad and Mom would . . . . .

a. Disapprove of it.
b. Punish me severely."

But it still doesn't really solve the basic problem. While we may follow certain rules because of family pressures, it doesn't explain why our parents believe **they** should follow the rules. (You could say because of **their** parents, and so forth — but in continuing the chain backwards you still aren't really answering the question).

Reason Two: WE FOLLOW LAWS BECAUSE SOCIETY SAYS WE MUST — IT'S THE LAW OF THE LAND.

Again at first glance, that seems reasonable. One follows the law because one has to. After all, if we break laws we run the risk of being caught and punished. The fear of being punished for breaking a law of the land is enough to motivate most people to obey the law. But it still doesn't really answer the very basic problem of why laws are set up in the first place, and why they are worthy of being followed!

Reason Three: THE RELIGIOUS APPROACH

Another reason given for obeying laws, and now I am referring in particular to laws in a religion such as Judaism, is that they are God's laws. If you recall your Jewish history, the various rules and ordinances given to our ancestors by Moses were considered to be straight from God.

Moreover, just as you would think twice about breaking a city, state or national law today (for fear of punishment), so too were our ancestors also concerned about the possible bad consequences of their actions, should they disregard laws given by God. Time and time again throughout the Bible we are presented with the view that when the people lived proper lives in an upright manner in accordance with the laws they would prosper. When the people strayed from the laws and "did wrong in the sight of the Lord" they would be punished. (e.g. Why did God create a flood to destroy all life on earth? Because God was fed up with the amount of sin and corruption on earth). The idea of punishment, not just by human institutions, but by God is pretty strong stuff, huh?

Reason Four: LAWS, A NECESSITY TO REALIZE OUR VALUES. THEY PROMOTE ORDER AND MINIMIZE CONFLICT.

Let's look at the following situations:

Situation one: *You are in Boston's downtown subway station at Park Street. The door of the train opens. About fifty people try to leave the train. Another fifty are trying to board – simultaneously. What happens?*

Situation two: *The map shown on p. 59 is Kenmore Square. Kenmore Square as you can see poses interesting problems in traffic flow. It also is strategically placed near Boston's Fenway Park, home of The Red Sox.*
Your problem, The Red Sox have just played a game. The Police Officers normally on duty, went off to get some coffee. The lights are broken. What happens?

Situation three: *The next day you happen to be at point X on the map. The officers are still off sipping their coffee, but the lights have been repaired. Unfortunately you are faced with a red light. Suddenly you hear a siren behind you. It's an ambulance. What happens?*

58

I think, that at this stage of the game, you can begin to appreciate just why laws are so important. It is quite likely that during the space trip simulation, you came up with an orderly progression of doing a, b, c, or d to accomplish your goals. It is even possible that your group hypothetically set up committees or groups to handle certain tasks. The point here is that laws and rules of conduct are set up for some pretty specific purposes:

I. To Promote Order

Face it, Kenmore Square without the policeman or lights was a mess. We'd all like to do our own thing, but if we each did our own thing without regard for each other — boy, what a mess it would be.

IMAGINE A WORLD: *Where every person would steal all the time from each other.*

IMAGINE A WORLD: *Where a person could kill anytime, anyone who gets him/her angry.*

Would you be safe?

KENMORE SQUARE: A MONUMENT
TO THE GENIUS OF URBAN PLANNING

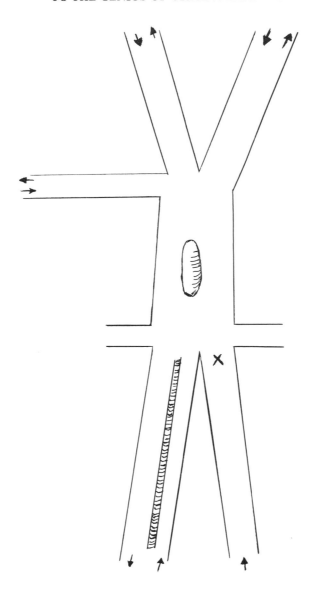

Isn't that strange? It would seem that having laws and rules seem to be "built into" the world, in order for it to function.

II. To Try to Minimize Conflict

It follows that if there were no laws or rules, and everyone did exactly as s/he wanted, then people would most likely be doing things that would get other people really up-tight. There would be many more arguments and fights over who really should be doing what than there are now. Think of what it would be like if every time two cars met at an intersection, the drivers had to discuss who should go first. Think of all of the fights that would occur if there were no set procedures for selling property. How often would people get into quarrels if there were no laws protecting both consumers and sellers of all kinds of things?

III. To Realize Our Values

It seems ironic that rules and laws actually end up helping us accomplish our goals (and therefore are actually less restrictive than they would, on first examination, seem to be). Because they promote order and minimize conflict, rules, regulations and laws allow us to be more efficient. As was indicated earlier, laws can provide a means for the realization of our values and goals.

MORE ON PUNISHMENT — ANCIENT AND MODERN CONCEPTS

"O.K" you say, "Let's assume I agree with you. There is a very practical reason as to why we have laws and rules; to maintain order in society, minimize conflict, and attain societal goals. This is a strong clue as to why our parents say we should obey laws. It would also explain why society insists that we have them. But a few pages back you talked about people being "punished" by God if they didn't live according to ethical rules and regulations. Well that's all good and fine for those Biblical folks, but does it have any practical meaning for us today?"

In a sense our ancestors viewed God as a kind of "superdaddy." God kind of kept watch over man, and from time to time got involved in human affairs. God was, in a sense, like a person who approved, disapproved etc. God sometimes even suspended (stopped) the laws of nature and performed miracles. God punished people who didn't live in a proper manner.

Today we know more about science than our ancestors did. Just as styles of clothing have changed over the past few thousand years, so too have some of our ideas of what God is like.

First of all modern Jews still believe that there is something which we call God. Let's face it when you see something like a chair you know that it didn't just happen. Someone designed it and manufactured it. That is true of just about every article you have around you. With living things it's a bit more complex. Sure, living things now come from other living things — but how and why did it all begin? Even the simplest organisms are incredibly complicated. Thus we feel that there must be something behind it all, something that created and sustains the laws of nature. We call that something God.

61

Nowadays many Jewish theologians (people who sit around and worry about what God is like) don't think of God as a "superdaddy." Some put greater stress on God being more like a "superpower" or "superforce." **God is the force behind the laws of science** . We know that the universe is constructed in such a way that given a certain set of conditions you will get a certain result. For example, if I add hydrogen and oxygen together under the proper experimental conditions, I will get water. Given those exact same conditions, I will **always** get the same results. This is what we mean when we talk about God being behind the laws of science.

Well you might say, "What if there is a hurricane and a major city almost gets blown off the map . . . Is God responsible?" In a sense yes, and in a sense no! God is responsible in the sense that scientific laws say that given certain environmental conditions there is a strong chance that there will be a hurricane. God is the power behind those laws. God is not responsible in that it is highly unlikely that there was any Divine plan to zap that city. God wasn't considering whether to zap the city or not. The city just happened to be there.Similarly, say you go on a picnic and it rains. God is the power that insures that given the proper meteorological conditions rain will fall. God however didn't decide to purposefully mess up your picnic. A force doesn't actively "decide" to do things the way people do. You just happened to pick a cruddy day!

Well, let's say that somebody does something. S/he should expect that given the laws of science there will be a predictable reaction. For example, say Stanley Scatterbrain is wandering around on the ledge of a fifty story building. (Don't ask me why; maybe his pet cat wandered out and he is trying to rescue it!) At any rate, should he accidently happen to wander off of the edge . . . You know what will happen! SPLAT!!! Stanley will really mess up the sidewalk below! Yuch! In a sense you could say that Stanley is being "punished." He isn't being punished by a God who is consciously trying to zap him. But by ignoring gravity (a scientific principle — God is behind the laws of science) Stanley could court disaster. In that sense he would certainly be "punished."

Similarly let's say you do the following. What will happen?

You put your hand in a fire.

You never brush your teeth a day in your life — or go to the dentist.

You walk on a pond that has very thin ice.

In a very real sense you are "punished" for your actions, not that God is consciously or deliberately giving you a hard time — but in the sense that you didn't cooperate with the scientific principles that are a basic part of our reality.

As you can see this is a rather interesting, and common sense approach to the concept of being "punished" by God. If a person eats a lot and then goes swimming, s/he may be "punished" by getting cramps. Not that God is actively and consciously trying to zap that person. Rather, the distressed person ignored basic laws of physiology that would point to that result. Because we acknowledge God as the power behind the laws of nature, we can still say that the person was "punished by God," though in a different sense than what our ancestors may have intended.

"So far so good" you say. "But as you said earlier, these examples are instances of going against scientific principles. Naturally I'm in for trouble if I ignore them. But if I'm **bad** that doesn't necessarily mean I'll get zapped. After all it's not the same thing, is it?" Well it's true that our knowledge of the laws governing behavior is **very** primitive when we compare it to our ability to predict results in Chemistry or Physics. Nonetheless, note the following:

> If you're high on drugs and then drive, it's **more** likely that you will get into an automobile accident — (Our knowledge of the human body and how it works confirms this).

> If you beat a dog everyday when s/he is young, there's a strong probability that the dog will turn vicious (and maybe bite you or someone else).

> If a country doesn't allow its people to follow the religion of their choice, human behavior indicates a possible strong reaction (e.g. warfare that led to the holiday of Hanukkah).

> Say a wo/man deals ruthlessly and viciously with people in business. There is a strong chance that somebody will eventually give him/her the same treatment in return.

> If a shopkeeper is unethical and cheats or deceives his/her customers, human nature being what it is — those customers would be unlikely to return.

> Indeed they may even spread the word about that shopkeeper. (It's ironic that often the small amount that individual may have made dishonestly is probably much less then s/he might have eventually made, had s/he been honest).

> What about the person who cheats right and left in his/her business dealings, yet seems to be "getting away" with it. Well, s/he could be "punished" by guilt. Moreover, the personality traits, which this person displays in business could also be ruining his/her personal life. There are many instances we know of where people who are outwardly "successful" in spite of "bad" behavior, have frustrated and extremely unhappy private lives.

> Then of course, as we mentioned earlier, rules and laws seem to be built into the system. All societies seem to need laws to function. If one breaks laws there is always the danger that s/he will get caught and be punished by society. The frequency of people getting caught, sooner or later, is fairly high — evidenced by a common fascination people have concerning the so-called "perfect crime." If everyone always got away with unlawful behavior, there would be no discussion of such an "ideal."

Now all of the above examples dealt with moral situations. In each case there was a strong probability of "punishment" of one kind or another. Conscious punishment by God? Possibly not. But just as there are laws (sustained by God) governing such things as gravity etc., so too are there scientific principles governing human behavior. No, to be sure, we don't know nearly as much about the scientific principles governing human behavior as we do about those behind other sciences. Nonetheless it seems likely that lousy behavior can often result in "punishment" of one kind or another. From our limited knowledge today we can't say that it always works with the same certainty as gravity does, etc. It would certainly be interesting to come back in two hundred years and find out what future scientific knowledge can add to our understanding of these principles!

FOCUS ON: WHY DO THE GOOD SOMETIMES SUFFER?

Four men sat in silence. One of the four had formerly been a fortunate and happy man. He had had great wealth and a nice family. He was a good man and had always lived ethically. (For now, we shall call him "J"). Then came bad times. All of J's children were tragically killed — all ten of them. If that weren't enough, a weird series of mishaps destroyed all of his wealth. Harassed and dejected, J came down with a skin disease. Depressed in spirit, itching all over, J sat in the dust scratching, feeling like a born loser!

A sadness was over him . . . so sad . . . Finally after seven days and nights he could be silent no longer. J cursed the day he was born! He couldn't understand why a person destined to suffer had to live. After all, he had nothing now . . . nothing! He looked forward to dying. He was itchy and it all just didn't seem fair!

His friends were in shock! They had come to be properly sympathetic, but J was getting out of line! Starting off lightly, but gradually becoming more bold and outspoken his "friends" began the cross examination. "Come on J . . . come clean," said one. "Yeah right J . . . spill the beans." . . . added another. "You know one always gets what he deserves." . . . "You must have been a real crumb to get this kind of punishment." "Sure, God wouldn't come down on you this hard if you weren't a sinner!"

"No! No! No! No!" J went through every possible thing he could have done wrong. He was positive that he had lived ethically! While he wasn't totally renouncing God, J wasn't entirely sold on his current situation!

Finally God decided to get involved. "Who are you J to question my justice? . . . Where were you when I laid the earth's foundation? . . . Tell me if you know . . . Have you descended to the depths of the seas or do you understand death?" Well God went on for some time. J finally admitted that a mere human being can't really understand everything!

> Who is J and where can we read about him? (If you don't know, ask your teacher).

> The problem of why a good individual who has never hurt anyone should suffer, has haunted our theologians for many thousands of years.

> a. What does the above story suggest as a possible reason.
> b. What do you think about the subject? Why?

FOCUS ON: SHOULD WE OBEY ALL LAWS?

Evaluate the following:

In 1846 War broke out between the United States and Mexico. The Mexicans were still smarting from the loss of Texas. (Texas belonged to Mexico; the Americans who settled there declared and won their independence, and eventually joined the U.S.) Mexico viewed the U.S. as a land-hungry monster. The U.S. on the other hand, remembered the massacre at Goliad where Texan forces who had surrendered were brutally murdered. The U.S. also felt that the constant internal instability in Mexico was a threat to the lives and properties of people of other nations. While it takes two to make a conflict, many people felt that war was unnecessary. Henry David Thoreau at that time refused to pay his taxes, lest his money contribute to what he perceived to be an unjust war.

In the play **Antigone** two brothers Polynices and Eteocles led armies against each other outside of Thebes. In the course of combat both die. Creon the ruler orders that Polynices who had attacked the city should be left unburied. (Eteocles is, however, to be given a decent funeral). Creon furthermore orders that anyone who tries to bury Polynices is to be put to death. Polynices and Eteocles have two sisters Ismene and Antigone. Ismene feels that it's too risky to disobey the order. Antigone however, defies the order and buries her brother. She is, incidentally, caught . . . (For grimy details check this play out!)

Time: The middle to late 1940s. Place: Palestine under British law. World War II has ended. Many thousands of Jews, refugees from Europe, want to settle in Palestine. British law, however, limits Jewish immigration to the holy land. In spite of this large numbers of Jews are being smuggled in. Moreover, Jewish settlers are importing and hiding weapons. Attempts to stop the breaking of laws have involved mass arrests and even hanging some individuals. Radical elements of the Jewish underground have replied by terrorism and killing of British officers.

We hold these truths to be self evident: that all men are created equal; that they are endowed by their creator with certain unalienable rights; that among these are life, liberty, and the pursuit of happiness; that to secure these rights governments are instituted among men, deriving their just powers from the consent of the governed; that whenever any form of government becomes destructive of these ends it is the right of the people to alter or abolish it and to institute new government, laying its foundation on such principles and organizing its powers in such form as to them shall seem most likely to affect their safety and happiness.

The U.S. Declaration of Independence,
Jefferson, 1776

THE EVILS OF KINGSHIP

After the ancient Israelites managed to settle in the land of Canaan (Israel), after returning from Egypt (remember the Passover story?) each tribe more or less did its own thing. The problem was that without a strong central government the tribes were not a cohesive unit. There was also that "small" matter of the Philistines who had superior military weapons, worked together effectively in battle, and caused our ancestors much difficulty. The Israelites occasionally worked together under popular leaders — The Judges, but finally the people came to the prophet Samuel and asked for a full-time King. Samuel warns the people that with a strong king there would be problems (I Samuel Ch. 8: 11-18).

- He will take your sons and make them serve in his chariots and with his cavalry (a draft!)

- Others will make weapons of war and equipment for mounted troops (military industrial complex?)

- He will take the best of your fields, vineyards and olive yards and give them to his servants (patronage, honesty in government)

- He will take a tenth of your vineyards . . . and your sheep . . . (taxes)

It seems that in those days, as today, strong government had not only advantages but disadvantages as well!!

67

"Isn't that strange? Here he gives us a chapter stressing how laws and rules are important, and then he follows it with those last four examples! What's going on here?" I think that this section will serve as an interesting postscript to a discussion of "why laws?"

First of all, it should be stated that traditional Jewish sources put a high regard on following laws. In Pirke Avot we read the following:

> *Pray for the welfare of the ruling power, for without fear of it people would swallow each other alive.*

In Judaism following the laws of the Torah is also considered extremely important. Again in Pirke Avot:

> *Love peace, pursue peace, love your fellow beings and bring them to the Torah.*

After a while, a rather interesting problem arose. In the course of Jewish history, Jews were living in many different countries. It's all good and fine to talk about obeying the law, but the problem came up as to "Just what laws should be followed?".

In Jeremiah (29:7) the following advice is given:

> Seek the peace of the city where I have caused you to be carried away captives and pray to the Lord for it; for in the peace thereof will you have peace.

The Talmud goes on to make it pretty clear that with regard to all civil matters **one should follow the law of the land s/he lives in.** Interestingly enough this has led to some strange situations.

For example: during the American Civil War, Jews fought on both sides. During World War I, just as Jews served on the Allied side, so too were about twenty percent of Germany's Jews in that country's army. About eleven thousand five hundred were even given the Iron Cross (a decoration).

Nonetheless, there is also within our tradition a recognition that just as men aren't perfect, so too can governments have corruption, or laws be unjust. Another comment in Pirke Avot:

> Love labor, hate domineering, and don't be intimate with the ruling power.

And also:

> Be on your guard in your dealings with the ruling power for they bring a person near for their own interests. While they are friendly when it's to their advantage, they don't stand by a person in his hour of need.

The father of the man responsible for that rather cynical comment was a friend of the Emperor of Rome.

O.K., let's assume one should follow the laws of the land. **What if there is a conflict between the laws of society and one's own conscience? What if a law(s) is an evil or unjust one? What should one's response be?** Maybe we can get some insight from the Biblical story of Jephthah. First of all a little background information is necessary before I tell the story. **FLASHBACK!**

After the children of Israel returned to Canaan under Joshua, they took over and divided up the land. There was then a period of time before Saul became king. During this period each of the various tribes of Israel "did its own thing." Occasionally, when there was danger, they might work together. From time to time popular leaders arose. These were known as "Judges." Samson, who like the author of this book didn't like getting haircuts, was one of those "Judges." Another of those "Judges" was Jephthah. O.K., now Jephthah was originally from Gilead. As he was the black sheep of his family he was kicked out of Gilead with the approval of the village elders. He went off roaming with a gang of drifters to the land of Tob.

Gilead was then attacked by the Ammonites. No one in Gilead had the intestinal fortitude to take them on, so they sent for Jephthah. He wasn't too sympathetic until they told him that if he'd help, he'd be made the boss of Gilead (If this sounds like the plot of the late movie — it is; now you know where they got it from!) Jephthah vowed to God that if his army won, he would make a sacrifice of the first creature that came out of his house to meet him upon his return. Well the big battle came. The Ammonites were defeated. The first person, however, that Jephthah saw come out of his house was his only child, his daughter — his pride and joy! (Boy, this is getting even better than the late show!) Well, Jephthah broken-hearted, fulfilled his vow! (Judges 11, 12) Now at this stage you're probably thinking "Interesting plot, but what does it have to do with the problem of confronting a law that seems unjust?" Well there is a legend based on this story: — there was a high priest Phinehas who had knowledge of the law that could have saved Jephthah's daughter from that unjust fate. But Phinehas was proud and said to himself "Myself — I'm not going to help that fool . . . let him stew in his own juices!" Jephthah was also too proud to consult Phinehas. The legend goes on and tells us that **because Phinehas refused to get involved, even though he could have, he lost his inspiration from God.** (rather disastrous for a religious leader!).

I think you can see the moral. In Judaism each person is held accountable for his/her own actions. Respect for law is necessary, vital and stressed. Nonetheless in situations where a law is unjust, if a person refuses to get involved, (as Phinehas) s/he is in a sense responsible for the possible consequences of that law.

SUMMARY

This unit started off by discussing the general connection between laws and ethics. An important component of ethics, the study of moral problems, are the values one holds. Our values are influenced by a number of societal leaders (such as political, artistic leaders etc.). These values affect what societal goals we would like to accomplish. Government and laws are the means by which we try to translate our values and goals into reality. As was discussed, there are sometimes problems involved in this process. Nonetheless an important connection between the legal and ethical areas was noted.

Why specifically do we have laws or rules? A number of reasons were set forth:

1. **We follow laws because our parents say we must.** *While this reason seems logical, it really didn't answer the question fully.*

2. **We follow laws because society says we must. It's the law of the land.** *Again, as in reason one, this really doesn't answer the very basic problem as to why laws are set up in the first place!*

3. **The religious approach.** *The idea that some laws are given by God, with the possibility of divine punishment, should those laws be ignored.*

4. **Laws are necessary to promote order, to minimize conflict and to help realize our values.**

We returned to the problem of being punished for ignoring God's laws. The view was presented, that perhaps we aren't punished by a God who is consciously showing displeasure at our sins. Rather, the universe is set up in such a way that there are certain scientific principles that will always hold true. These principles are maintained by what we call God. When we ignore them, we run the risk of facing the consequences. In a sense that is still "punishment" for breaking God's laws, but possibly in a different sense than what our ancestors intended. While it is easy to see this in action for such things as chemical and physical relationships, it is much harder to see this in behavioral situations (e.g. a person behaving in an unethical manner). Nonetheless we noted some examples where living unethically could also result in disaster. **Actually when considered from this perspective, living according to a standard of ethics becomes a very practical and realistic goal.**

Finally we considered two very difficult problems. One concerns the person who is always good, yet suffers. The other issue raised, was the problem of whether we should always obey all laws.

CONSIDER THIS:

1. What is the connection between laws and ethics? Discuss.

2. Does the fact that values affect laws mean that laws will be ethical? Why? Why not?

3. What are the various reasons given for why we have laws? What are the strengths and weaknesses for each reason? Discuss in detail. List any addional reasons for laws not mentioned in this unit.

4. If you could form an ideal state — what laws would you pass? List and discuss at least ten.

5. Look up Judges 21:25. Discuss the statement in relation to this chapter.

6. Mr. Bertrand was having a serious conversation with Ms. Essenson. Bertrand commented that he believed that the only valid law is one's own conscience. Essenson, on the other hand, pointed out that the consequences of that statement would be anarchy and chaos. How would you react to those two views? Why?

7. Is one ever justified in breaking a law? What would justify breaking one law as opposed to another?

8. Is there a difference between dissent and civil disobedience? If so what is it? Why?

9. What are some Jewish insights concerning following laws?

10. In this unit we discussed God a little bit. Different people have different views of God. For example, the suggestion was made that God is like a "superforce" that sustains the laws of nature. Many people however feel very uncomfortable with a concept of God that isn't a "personal" God, (e.g. one whom you can relate to, like Tevye did in "Fiddler On The Roof").

    a. *What do you think of the concept of God as a "force" behind the laws of nature?*

    b. *What is your concept of God?*

11. In the Bible we read of the Prophet Elijah. Elijah could not find God in the wind, an earthquake or fire. He finally experienced God as "a still, small voice" What do you think he meant? (I Kings 19:11-12)

12. A friend of mine from Israel once wrote me the following in a letter:

> *No, I don't believe there is such a thing as a God. If there were a God how could he permit the murder of six million Jews in World War II? The fact that the holocaust occurred leads me to believe that there is no such divine being.*

   a. How would you react to this person's comments?
   b. From what you read in this unit, how do suppose the author would respond?

13. A child is born grossly deformed. The mother believes she's being punished by God. Analyze and evaluate in detail.

14. In the Bible we are given numerous examples of God "speaking" to human-kind. Do you believe that God could actually speak to people? How can we interpret such events?

15. If God is the force behind laws governing our behavior (governing so-called "Moral Laws") how can we go about discovering what laws we humans should make?

16. Here is a tough ethical dilemma. It's all good and fine to talk about following customs and laws, but sometimes standards vary from one society to another. For example:

   a. *As Jews we are not allowed to eat pork according to Jewish law, yet for the Maring of New Guinea pig eating plays an important part in adjusting the size etc. not only of the animal population – but of the human population as well. When the pig population increases to a certain extent, all of the human population holds a big pig eating festival which lasts about a year, and is followed by clan warfare, which then stops until the pig population is high again. The cycle then repeats itself. In this situation not only is pig eating considered "good" but even warfare and killing seem to take on a "positive" quality.*

   b. *Will Durant points out that at one time giving a coffin to an older relative, particularly a sick one, was considered good taste in China. (Would we feel the same way today?)*

   c. *Depending on where you live in the world covering your head may or may not be seen as a sign of respect.*

   d. *At one time some Eskimos, tribes in Brazil and other places would kill or abandon their elderly.*

   e. *A traveller in Tibet in the early 20th century noted that sticking out one's tongue at someone was considered a show of respect.*

   f. *In some societies kissing has been looked down upon!*

While these are but a few examples, I'm sure you can see the problem. Granted it's important to follow rules, laws etc. If there is variation in standards depending on where you are, does ethics simply become a matter of "doing what others

71

around you are doing"? Does that mean that such things as killing or stealing would be justified in a society that condones it? Are there any absolute standards of ethics? If so, what would they be? Why?

17. In Pirke Avot we read — "Rabbi Jannai said, It is not in our power to explain either the prosperity of the wicked, or the tribulations of the righteous." Analyze in detail in accordance with what you have read in this unit.

18. In Leviticus 19:16 we read "Thou shalt not stand idly by the blood of your neighbor." Analyze in accordance with this unit.

A DIFFICULT SON

David had a terrible time with his son Absalom. Absalom decided that it was about time for his father to have an **early** retirement from his job as King! Moreover, Absalom wanted to take over and run the Kingdom! To accomplish his aims Absalom worked hard at gaining popularity with the people. Eventually when he had a large enough following, he had himself proclaimed ruler. David found it necessary to leave Jerusalem in a hurry! Eventually in a battle between David's troops and the rebel forces, Absalom was killed. His ending was rather gross. While riding on a mule, Absalom passed under an oak. His head got caught in a fork of the trees, and as he was hanging there, he was slain! David was quite upset as he had given orders not to harm Absalom, and grieved for his son (II Samuel 13-19).

1. Was David morally responsible for his son's death? Why? Why not?

2. Should a government or society take **any** necessary measures to protect itself? Why? Why not?

3. Is the leader of a government above his/her society's laws? Why? Why not?

THE DUNSMORE DILEMMA

Mrs. Dunsmore entered the smoke filled room. "John, must you persist in that crazy habit of yours?" "Now look honey," responded Mr. Dunsmore, "the fact that you managed to give up smoking six months ago doesn't mean that I must! Does the smoke really bother you?" He asked. "No," she responded, "but you know that statistics indicate that smoking can ruin your health!" "Possibly," replied Mr. Dunsmore "but I happen to enjoy smoking . . . More importantly . . . I'm not really hurting anyone else . . ."

a. Is Mr. Dunsmore's reasoning valid? Why? Why not?

b. Mr. Dunsmore feels that his actions aren't really harming anyone else. Let us take his comments at face value and simply assume for a second that that is so. Is the fact that one person is not harming another (even though s/he may be doing damage to him/herself) valid justification for a course of action? Why? Why not?

c. Does society have the right to pass laws on every aspect of individual behavior? Are there areas of private concern where behavior should not be regulated? If so what are they? Why?

d. Let's assume that one took the attitude that every aspect of behavior should be governed by laws; how would those laws be enforced?

unit five

Sources

When you were a small kid, chances are that your first visit to a library was quite an experience. You were confronted with a whole messload of stuff that possibly seemed rather confusing until you got used to it. Similarly one's first experiences with Jewish sources can also seem rather bewildering. In this chapter we will be discussing some of these sources of Jewish ethical material (and hopefully remove the "bewilderment"). No, you won't receive a detailed in-depth analysis of all of the Jewish sources that can give us ethical guidance. What I hope is accomplished, is that you get an idea of **some** of the materials that are available. I like to view these sources as very practical tools — tools which we can consult as we seek guidance in solving ethical problems. It is my hope that just as in units two and three, you may find information here that will be useful to you in the years ahead.

O.K. then, just what are some of these sources of Jewish ethics?

THE BIBLE

Probably the most obvious source of ethical teaching in Judaism is the Bible. Now don't start groaning. The Bible is actually one of the most interesting collections of writings that has ever been created. All too often students tend to read "condensed" and "watered down" versions that lose a great deal of the impact of the actual text. I always marvelled at the fact that the Bible is so popular in religious schools. Oh, of course it would be, for it contains the religious beliefs, history and ethical teachings of our people. But in its unedited versions it also contains an incredible amount of violence, "blood and guts," and gore! Some of the stories in the Bible are extremely dramatic. No glorification is made of our ancestors. They are shown as **real** human beings with **real** faults. We find that one of our greatest leaders, Moses, had a speech defect. Samson was a great hero and judge. His claim to fame was fooling around with Philistine women and fighting Philistine men! Do these revelations detract from the Bible and its "cast"? No, not at all. The fact that there is this touch of humanity adds to its credibility and to its impact. I'll bet you didn't know that there's a book in the Bible made up of love poems (sexy, x-rated in spots, but very beautiful literature). It's called Song of Songs, and we read in the Talmud that the Rabbis even had a debate as to whether it was divinely inspired or not. Here's an excerpt:

Behold you are fair my love; behold you are fair. You have the eyes of doves within your locks: Your hair is like a flock of goats that appear from Mount Gilead . . .

S.S. 4:1

(It gets even better). The Rabbis decided that it was divinely inspired. They interpreted the book's lovers as being symbolic of the special relationship between the Jewish People and God. Incidently tradition tells us that Solomon wrote this. (Solomon as you'll recall had about 1000 wives and concubines — so he was considered to be pretty knowledgeable about the subject).

THE BIBLE — TANACH

THE FIVE BOOKS OF MOSES — TORAH

>   Genesis, Exodus, Leviticus, Numbers and Deuteronomy.

THE PROPHETS — NEVIIM

>   Joshua, Judges, 1st and 2nd Samuel, 1st and 2nd Kings, Isaiah, Jeremiah, Ezekiel, Hosea, Joel, Amos, Obadiah, Jonah, Micah, Nahum, Habakkuk, Zephaniah, Haggai, Zechariah and Malachi.

THE WRITINGS — KETUVIM

>   Psalms, Proverbs, Job, Song of Songs, Ruth, Lamentations, Ecclesiastes, Esther, Daniel, Ezra-Nehemiah, 1st and 2nd Chronicles.

Anyhow, this is but one of the books of the Bible. One of the books? Yes. The Bible isn't really one book, but can be considered to be a whole library of books all wrapped up under one cover! In Hebrew the Bible is called Tanach. Tanach is really an abbreviation of three words: **Torah, Neviim** and **Ketuvim**. The **Torah** is the scroll that we read in the Temple. These are the so-called Five Books of Moses, or the Pentateuch. Neviim are the Prophets. (A Haftarah part that you may have read at your Bar/Bat Mitzvah was taken from Neviim). The third section **Ketuvim**, are the writings. The writings include such things as Psalms, Proverbs and Job. How many books are there altogether in the Bible? Well that depends on how you count them. Very often the Minor Prophets (Hosea through Malachi) are considered as one book and Ezra-Nehemiah, Samuel I and II, Kings I and II and Chronicles I and II are considered one book each. In that case there would be twenty-four books in the Bible. If you count each Minor Prophet as one book and each of the two part books as two books, then you end up with thirty-nine books in the Bible. At any rate you end up with a lot of books forming the Bible!

You have, I am certain, heard the phrases "Old Testament" and "New Testament". Believe it or not, the word Bible means different things to Christians and Jews:

To a Jew, Bible = Torah, Neviim, and Ketuvim — Tanach — This is sometimes called the "Old Testament" by the Christian World.

To a Christian, Bible = Tanach **PLUS** the "New Testament."

Jews believe that Tanach alone is sufficient as the Bible. Many Jews are unhappy with the terminology "Old" vs "New" Testament, feeling that calling one part Old as opposed to calling the other New is a "put down" of the Jewish Bible.

"Well," you say, "It's all good and fine that you are telling us about the Bible — but how does it constitute a source for ethics?" Actually it constitutes a source in a few very important ways:

1. The various stories and the morals they suggest.
2. Sections of advice.
3. Legislation — laws and commandments.

The Various Stories and the Morals They Suggest

Much of the Bible is made up of literary and historical material. Can this stuff be a source for ethical guidance? Yes, of course it can. Let me give you an example. You are probably acquainted with the story of Noah's Ark and the flood. Well, flood stories are a "dime a dozen". Archaeologists and scholars have found them in other Near Eastern cultures and even in India. So what's so special about the Biblical version? When you check out the Biblical story you find a moral.

God wipes out all but the Ark's inhabitants **because the earth has become so full of sin!** Later at the end of the story God promises never again to wipe out life that way. "While the earth remains seedtime and harvest, cold and heat, summer and winter shall not cease." — Genesis 8:22. Thus, the story also becomes an affirmation of the regularity of the laws of nature. (If that seems unimportant think of what it would be like if things like gravity turned on and off unpredictably). The main thing here, however, is that our ancestors tied this quite common flood story in with humankind's ethical behavior. Because ethical behavior was not practiced, life was destroyed.

77

Another example would be the story of the "sacrifice of Isaac". As you'll recall Abraham's loyalty was being tested by God. He was told to offer his son Isaac as a sacrifice. Of course just in the nick of time, Isaac was saved. In actuality, this story displays a Hebrew reaction to the offering of human sacrifices, practiced at that early time. The story, in a sense reaffirms the importance of life. Now it would be very easy for our ancestors to say "O.K. life is important". You would yawn and probably forget the message. But the Bible builds up a very dramatic sequence of events in which Abraham is first told to sacrifice his son, the apple of his strudel. The tension rises as we watch the two go on their journey, make preparations for the sacrifice etc. Face it, that story (whether you are tired of it or not by now) has a great deal of impact, and quite effectively portrays its message far more than a mere statement.

Another example of a moral can be found in the life of Jacob. As you'll recall (or if you don't I'll tell you now) Jacob was a pretty sneaky fellow. When Esau came in dying of hunger, Jacob was glad to give him some food — in exchange for Esau's birthright. Later Jacob even cheated Esau of his proper blessing. (See Genesis Ch. 25, 27). Of course Jacob gets his just reward. Just as he cheated his brother earlier, so too, does he get the same treatment. He falls in love with Laban's daughter Rachel, a very pretty young lady. Well Laban is very happy to have Jacob as a son-in-law ("Sure Jake, work for me for seven years; I'll teach you the business!"). Well Jacob got the business all right. At the end of seven years when he's all ready to marry Rachel, Laban wishes Leah on him. Leah as you'll recall, was apparently nothing special to look at — Yuch! — and for seven years work too! Laban let Jacob marry Rachel also. But in return Jacob had to work for another seven years! Later Jacob is deceived again this time by his sons, when they report to him that Joseph was killed (when he really wasn't). Is it not ironic that the plot insures that the trickster gets two good doses of his own medicine?

Well, I could go on and on, but I think you can get the point. Many of the stories in the Bible present ethical insights. By becoming familiar with these stories, not just reading them at face value, but rather, analyzing them carefully, we can find a great deal of ethical commentary and guidance.

Sections of Advice

There are within the Bible several sections which concentrate on giving advice quite directly. One of these is the **Book of Proverbs**. A proverb is a popular saying. The Book of Proverbs in the Bible contains many hundreds of these sayings. They were meant to be quite practical and useful. Perhaps you've heard the sayings:

> *"Hope deferred makes the heart sick."*
> *"Pride goes before destruction and a haughty spirit before a fall."*

These are but several of the many proverbs that are found in this section of the Bible. While scholars still argue one way or another, the Book of Proverbs is traditionally supposed to have been written by King Solomon, renowned for his wisdom! (a wise guy!)

HAVE ANYTHING YOU WANT!

Have you ever wondered what you would pick if you were given the opportunity to have any one wish fulfilled? Well our traditions tells us that King Solomon was given that opportunity! One day he fell asleep . . . ZZZZZZZZZZ . . . ZZZ . . . (That's him snoring!) and dreamed that God was offering him anything he wanted. Solomon asked himself . . . "Myself . . . what do you want?" Well he considered all kinds of goodies. "Let's see, how about money? . . . No that's no good. I could lose it as quickly as I receive it . . . How about power? . . . No, that doesn't last forever." . . . On and on; Solomon considered one thing after another. Finally he chose wisdom. We are told by the sages that his choice was a good one, for because of his wisdom all of the other things which he had considered, wealth, power, and even a long life were brought about.

Another section consisting of advice is **Kohelet** or **Ecclesiastes**. Kohelet is a very strange book. It is a rather pessimistic book. It's written by some old person who has been looking for the meaning of life, and doesn't seem to be finding it! It starts off:

> *Foolishness! All is foolish . . .*
> *What does a man gain for all of his labor under the sun?*
> *One generation passes away, and another generation comes, but the earth goes on forever . . .*
>
> *Ecclesiastes 1:2-4*

The author of Ecclesiastes has tried to find happiness in various ways, through hard work, wealth, sensuous pleasures and wisdom! One almost gets the idea that his approach to life is "Eat, drink and be merry for who knows what to-morrow may bring!" Yet he can't seem to find any lasting satisfaction. He con-cludes, however:

> *Let's hear the conclusion of the*
> *matter: Fear God and keep his*
> *commandments, for this is man's duty.*

Ecclesiastes 12:13

A strange book of advice, yet one with some passages and sayings of unparalleled beauty.

Another book of advice that I'd like to mention here never even made it into the Bible! It's called **Ecclesiasticus** or **The Wisdom of Ben Sira**. Ben Sira lived around 180 B.C.E. The book is similar to the Book of Proverbs and contains advice on almost all aspects of life. It is found in a volume known as the Apocrypha. (The Apocrypha is a bunch of books that weren't included in the Hebrew Bible . . . In spite of that fact I feel that Ecclesiasticus is extremely interesting and worthy of being mentioned here!)

Legislation — Laws and Commandments

Naturally an important source of ethical guidance in the Bible is contained in the various laws and commandments found there. The most famous of these, is the **Decalogue** — or **Ten Commandments.** In Hebrew the Ten Commandments aren't even called the Ten Commandments! They are known as **Aseret Hadibrot** or the ten words!

A very traditional Jew would tell you that the Decalogue (and possibly even the whole Torah) was given to Moses by God. Other Jews would disagree, and say that while Moses may have been divinely inspired, the Ten Commandments weren't something that were suddenly "revealed" to humankind by God. They (and the rest of the Torah) were written by human beings!

As one would expect, over the past few thousand years a huge number of legends and stories relating to the Ten Commandments and Torah have been passed down from generation to generation. Whether or not one really believes in their authen-ticity, they are a lot of fun. One of my favorites deals with the basic question of "Why us?" . . . After all if the Torah and its laws were given to a people by God, why were the children of Israel chosen?

> *Legend has it that God went from people to people, checking out their*
> *willingness to accept the Torah.*
> *"Hey, how are you doing, children of Esau? . . . "*
> *"Pretty good, God . . . "*
> *"Hey, children of Esau . . . Have I got a gift for you!"*
> *"O.K. Lord. What is it, and what's the catch?"*
> *"It's the Torah — and it says No Murdering!"*
> *"No fair God . . . That's how we earn our living! We'll be unemployed!"*
> *"Look, children of Esau . . . that's my Torah . . . take it or leave it!"*
> *Well the Lord didn't have very much luck . . . One nation didn't like*
> *the restriction on stealing. Another was uptight about the prohibition of*
> *adultery. Finally, God came to Israel.*

> *"Hi Israel . . . Can I interest you in my Torah?"*
> *"What's in it God?"*
> *"Oh, only about 613 commandments!"*
> *"Hmm . . . O.K. Lord."*
> *And so it was!*

Another legend says that the Torah was given to the children of Israel only when the people began to live in peace and harmony with one another! We are also told that there was apparently quite a debate between some of the mountains in the Middle East as to which one would be chosen as the spot for the giving of the Ten Commandments. Mount Carmel, Mount Tabor and Mount Hermon were all in the running. Each was quite anxious for the Decalogue to be given at its site! Because these other mountains had been used as places to worship idols, and because they weren't properly humble, the spot that was chosen was Mount Sinai!

Well, the big day arrived for the giving of the law and our traditions tell us that the earth shook, lightning struck, horns were sounded, and there was quite a commotion. There was so much of a turmoil that the earth itself was afraid that the end was near! In fact legend has it that when the Torah was given, God's voice boomed out like a super loudspeaker. Every person, dead, alive or even not yet born, Jew and non Jew alike heard God's comments at Mount Sinai. Interestingly enough the midrash tells us that God made his remarks known simultaneously in all seventy languages of the world. Another story tells us that God made such an awful noise when the commandments were given that all of the Israelites dropped dead from the shock!

80

Well, the Torah wasn't too happy about this state of affairs and complained to God, "Hey God, are you giving me to people who are alive or dead?" God's reaction was "Hmm, you've got a good point there," and revived the children of Israel. If this sounds corny, remember it is only a legend and all kinds of things happen in legends. But perhaps it tells us something; that the laws of the Torah are meant for the living, to follow as part of everyday life!

THE TEN COMMANDMENTS

Well, let's get down to basics. Just what are the Ten Commandments and what do they say? (See chart on accompanying page). The first commandment is a weirdie! "I am the Lord thy God who brought thee out of Egypt out of the house of bondage." — Generally my students first look at that one in bewilderment. After they stare at it for a few seconds, they yell, **"YAY! ONE DOWN NINE MORE TO GO!!!"** If that is your reaction, stop for a second and consider further. First of all a neat midrash (while you rack your brain trying to figure out Commandment One!) All of the letters of the alphabet (Hebrew ones of course) were competing for the opening spot in the Torah! While Beht won the spot (and hence the Torah begins Braisheet — In the beginning) God was quite impressed with Aleph (a humble letter, that didn't go around boasting about what a "Joe-cool letter it was"). As a result when God needed a letter to start off Commandment One, Aleph was chosen. (Anochi, begins with aleph. Anochi adonai elohecha — I am the Lord your God). Moral, **be humble!** — And so ends our midrash about Commandment One!

Well, back to its meaning . . . Give up? O.K. granted, it just seems to be indicating that God is the boss of everything and helped get the children of Israel out of a messy situation! There were many law codes in ancient times (though few are as well known as the Ten Commandments) and many of them started off by proclaiming the magnificence of some King. But note, our Ten Commandments don't start off by glorifying Moses or Aaron! They start off by stressing the importance of God. So while the first commandment doesn't **seem** to be commanding anything, it **really stresses that God is extremely important.**

Now, as I have indicated above, some Jews feel that the Ten Commandments were given to Israel directly by God. Others feel that they are the product of human effort, inspired by God. If the Ten Commandments were written by a

THE TEN COMMANDMENTS

I.   I am the Lord thy God who brought thee out of the land of Egypt out of the house of bondage.

II.   Thou shalt have no other gods before me. Thou shalt not make any graven image, or any likeness of anything that is in heaven above or that is in the earth beneath or that is in the water under the earth. Thou shall not bow down to them nor serve them: For I the Lord thy God am a jealous God visiting the iniquity of the fathers upon the children to the third and fourth generation of them that hate me; and showing mercy unto thousands of them that love me and keep my commandments.

III.   Thou shalt not take the name of the Lord thy God in vain; for the Lord will not hold him guiltless that taketh his name in vain.

IV.   Remember the Sabbath day to keep it holy. Six days shalt thou labor and do all thy work. But the seventh day is the Sabbath of the Lord thy God; in it thou shalt not do any work, thou, nor thy son, nor thy daughter, thy manservant nor thy maidservant, nor thy cattle nor thy stranger that is within thy gates. For in six days the Lord made heaven and earth, the sea and all that is in them, and rested the seventh day; therefore the Lord blessed the Sabbath day and hallowed it.

V.   Honor thy father and thy mother, that thy days may be long upon the land which the Lord thy God giveth thee.

VI.   Thou shalt not kill.

VII.   Thou shalt not commit adultery.

VIII.   Thou shalt not steal.

IX.   Thou shalt not bear false witness against thy neighbor.

X.   Thou shalt not covet thy neighbor's house; thou shalt not covet thy neighbor's wife, nor his manservant, nor his maidservant, nor his ox, nor his ass, nor anything that is thy neighbor's.

Moses who was divinely inspired, then another important function could be filled by this first commandment. It could represent an early form of "behavior modification". If Moses gave the people the Decalogue and just said "Well, folks, here are a bunch of laws that I wrote, – Go and follow them," the reaction would be "Woop dee doo! Who's this character to tell us how to lead our lives?" By attributing these laws to God, and even having the first commandment announce, "I am the Lord your God . . . etc.", people were just bound to take a second look and think twice before breaking these laws. (They sometimes ignored the laws anyway. However, a strong argument could be made that a divine author would have more authority than a human one). At any rate it's a point to consider.

The second commandment deals with the issue of idolatry. Idolatry in its original sense meant praying to something that is not the one true God. It's almost as if you put your favorite chair on a pedestal and started to pray to it. "Oh chair . . . I thank you for all of my blessings!" etc. It sounds kind of dumb doesn't it? Well when this law was formulated idolatry was quite common. People worshipped all kinds of things; the sun, the moon, little statues of all kinds of materials, rivers: you name it and people worshipped it! Some civilizations came up with gods that were almost like comic book superheros, and a number of stories were developed about these various superbeings. They would get into romantic involvements, fight etc. Some of these stories make interesting reading even today. A few of the "gods" that some civilizations came up with were quite bizarre. For example, in India a very strong drink was discovered that would result in hallucinations. This, of course, was pretty impressive to the people at that time. So we find a drink, soma, being turned into a god!

82   Well our ancestors were no fools. They recognized that there must be a God behind the laws of nature. Still this bit of worshipping little statues or trees or rocks seemed stupid to them. Thus the Jewish tradition talks in terms of a God that exists everywhere but cannot be seen. This seems quite obvious to us today; but when this concept was expressed it was quite revolutionary!

What about this bit of God being nasty to children of those who sin and being merciful to the descendents of those that obey the laws? Well there are various possibilities. First of all, perhaps our ancestors really believed that God was like that, and wouldn't tolerate any deviation from the commandments (yet see Deut 24:16). I suspect however that a second more modern interpretation is in order. A student is less likely to cause mischief in class if s/he knows that the teacher will punish any infractions. In spite of the fact that these laws were set forth, people would break them. Perhaps the inclusion of a comment threatening extensive punishment (or reward) would provide a little more incentive to follow these commandments (more Behavior Modification? – Or perhaps it represents a Biblical expression of our earlier comments in Unit IV about punishment).

On to Commandment Three. This one tells us "not to take the name of the Lord thy God in vain". This is the one that parents and teachers use to tell you that it's not nice to use foul language. While there are certain standards that society does set as to what is considered good and bad taste, this commandment has been the subject of a great deal of debate in recent years. Some younger people have argued that foul language is not as obscene as social injustice and other unethical behavior. Others in turn reply that, while that might be true, foul language is still a no-no!

Let's go on and take a look at the next commandment. Consider first if you will, what it would be like if you had a special booth in your home where time stood still. You could get into it and leisurely think things out for as long as you wanted (hours, days etc.). Then you could emerge to find that only a few moments actually went by. In a sense the fourth commandment deals with something quite similar to that booth! No the booth discussed in Commandment Four isn't a physical contraption that can actually suspend time, but rather a time set aside to give us a taste of the eternal. The booth that I am referring to is, of course, the Sabbath. One hundred and fifty years ago when I was a student, when teachers discussed this commandment I generally would yawn, say "Groovy, so they came up with a Sabbath; what else is new?" and dismiss it at that. Yet later when I started to really consider what the Sabbath is and what it's supposed to signify, I became quite impressed! In actuality, the Sabbath represents a cessation of our typical, everyday chores and a time to renew our relationships with friends and loved ones. It's a time when we are supposed to be able to stop worrying about everyday trivia and consider important things (not questions like "who will win the ball game?" but rather "why were we created?", "what should our goals in life be?" etc.)

I like to compare the Sabbath to a soft drink in the desert. Say, Sally Traveler is wandering along in the desert " . . . Gasp . . . Gasp . . . " and she is THIRSTY " . . . Gasp . . . Gasp . . . " Then she sees a little stand in the middle of nowhere with soft drinks" . . . Gasp . . . Gasp . . . " After having a drink she feels better for a while . . . "Ahh!! . . . Burp!" Well, we are all, in a sense, travelers through life. The idea behind the Sabbath is that once a week we make our way through our spiritual deserts and have a drink, thus refreshing and renewing ourselves for awhile!

If you consider it, the Sabbath is almost like a weekly acknowledgement of creation! In our creation story we are told that God blessed the seventh day and sanctified it (Gen II: 1-3). On the Sabbath we refrain from our everyday meddling in the world around us, as we are "re-created" spiritually.

Well, when our ancestors talked in terms of refraining from everyday affairs on Sabbath, **they meant business.** Thus in the Talmud we find a listing of thirty-nine acts which are prohibited on the Sabbath:

Sowing	Dyeing	Salting
Ploughing	Spinning	Skinning
Reaping	Combing	Tanning
Binding sheaves	Weaving	Scraping
Threshing	Making two loops	Cutting
Winnowing	Weaving two threads	Writing
Cleaning	Separating two threads	Erasing
Sifting	Tying knots	Demolishing
Grinding	Loosening knots	Building
Kneading	Sewing	Putting out a fire
Baking	Tearing	Lighting a fire
Shearing Wool	Hunting	Hammering
Washing	Slaughtering	Carrying

It's just incredible how the sages were able to expand and amplify these thirty-nine prohibitions to cover all kinds of "work".

There are numerous rules and regulations concerning Sabbath observance. You may find it interesting to look up some of these on your own!

The idea of a Sabbath is taken for granted today, but when it was first formulated it was quite unusual — the idea that a person should take a day off to groove about God and the universe was quite radical in its day!

Of course whether the Sabbath can really fulfill its function depends on the individual. A midrash tells us:

> *Every Sabbath two angels, one good the other evil, check out each home. If the Sabbath lights are burning, the table set, and the family in the proper Sabbath spirit the good angel will say "May all of this family's Sabbaths be like this one," and the bad angel has to say "Amen". If however, no preparations for the Sabbath have been made, and the family is grumpy and going about as if it's just another weekday, then the evil angel will say "May all of this family's Sabbaths be like this one," and the good angel has to say "Amen"!*

SHABBAT IN LEGEND AND LORE

There is a great deal of folklore and tradition that has grown up around the Sabbath, much of it quite interesting:

— Legend has it that Moses turned some Sabbath breakers into Apes!

— We are told that Sabbath Joy is one sixtieth of the world to come!

— A legend tells us that the seventh day came to God with a complaint "All the other things you created came in pairs! . . . Even the days of the week can be paired one and two, three and four, five and six . . . Why must I be alone?" God explained to the seventh day, that it would be paired with Israel!

— Another story tells us that the dead rise from the grave and praise God, on the Sabbath!

— Each Jew, we are told, receives an additional soul, on the Sabbath.

— Legends say that Moses, Joseph and David all died on the Sabbath.

— Remember Vashti? (Purim story) Legend has it that she was not a very nice lady, making her Jewish servants work. (Guess on what day!) Ironically it is also on the Sabbath that her downfall began!

— The Rabbis suggested that Sabbath night is an excellent time for sex (with one's husband or wife, of course)!

The fifth commandment deals with parents. "Honor your father and your mother." This is a very straightforward commandment. If you consider it, you are who you are because of your parents. This is true of your physical characteristics ("Oh George . . . she has your nose!"). Thus the midrash tells us that when one is born s/he gets a contribution from the various parties involved:

From the father —	*one gets five parts — brain, bones, veins, white of the eye and nails.*
From the mother —	*one gets five parts — hair, blood, skin, the eyes' pupil, and flesh.*
From God *(who isn't going to be left out!)* —	*one gets ten parts — understanding, sense, soul, breath, some senses — (sight, touch, hearing), light of countenance, insight, and the ability to talk.*

BE CAREFUL IF YOU SHOW DISRESPECT!

An interesting story from the Bible concerns one of the Prophets. The Prophets were a bunch of characters with a lot of chutzpah (nerve). They told people, sometimes even Kings, how to behave. This often resulted in bad Public Relations. Anyhow one of the Prophets was named Elisha. We are told (II Kings Ch. 2:23-25) that one day as he went from Jericho to Bethel some (a lot) small kids started poking fun at him. "Get going baldy!" they yelled. Elisha got pretty mad, uttered a few choice phrases and a couple of she-bears came out of the woods to chew forty-two of the kids up. Moral: Show proper respect for older people in general (and don't mess around with bald prophets!)

To be sure, while our ancestors had no detailed knowledge of genetics (as evident above), they still recognized that each parent contributes to his/her offspring. Families are also important as a source of values. We learn from our relatives what behavior is acceptable in our society and what behavior is not. It would make pretty good sense, then, to have a commandment stressing the importance of the family.

The next five commandments have a rather interesting feature in common; **none of them mention God!!** The ancient sages had a neat way of explaining this. The last five commandments deal with such things as adultery, murder and theft. If you were God, would you want your name associated with such activities?

Commandment Six tells us not to murder. This would seem to be good advice! (understatement of the year!) In actuality this commandment underscores the Jewish concern for life. We find the comment made in our tradition that **if a person saves a single soul, it is as if s/he has saved an entire world. On the other hand if a person has brought about another person's death, it is as if s/he has destroyed an entire world.** That's pretty profound thinking!

In our comments about the Sabbath, the point was made that it is a day of rest during which one is not supposed to do common everyday work. It is a significant fact that Jewish law indicated that even the Sabbath can (and should) be ignored in order to preserve life! In fact various religious leaders felt that in general whether it's Sabbath or not, to refuse a cure for sickness or not to take care of oneself because some ritual law may be broken would be unacceptable.

What if an animal fell into a pit (or pool of water) on Sabbath? Our ancestors took the ideal of refraining from work on the Sabbath quite seriously. Still they weren't going to just sit back, groove on the universe, and let the poor beast die!

KASHRUT AND THE SANCTITY OF LIFE

It is ironic that the Jewish concern for the sanctity of life even takes form in the laws for the slaughter of animals for food. Our ancestors were faced with a tough moral problem. It's all good and fine to talk about not killing — but you still have to eat in order to live, and that certainly involves the taking of life. One gets the impression that some common sense concessions were made. (Compare Genesis 1:29-30 with Deut. 12:20-25). While animals may be used for food **strict guidelines** were set forth:

I.   **Permitted foods**: Restrictions were placed on what may or may not be eaten. All fruits and vegetables are allowed. Animals which part the hoof, are cloven footed and chew the cud are allowed. Birds, with certain exceptions (Lev. Ch. 11) mentioned in the Torah, are permitted. Seafood with fins and scales are also allowed.

II. **Method of Slaughter** (She-hitah): The method of slaughter involved cutting the animal's throat with a swift cut of a sharp knife. While this sounds rather gross, this method would result in less pain (than other methods), and would be fairly quick. The Talmud gives us a number of details. If, for example, the slaughter was carried out, in a clumsy manner, causing extra pain to the animal, that alone would be sufficient to disqualify the meat for consumption!

III. **Removal of Blood**: A procedure of salting and rinsing the meat, (coupled with the method of slaughter mentioned above) had as its purpose, the removal of all blood. Blood was the symbol of life and as such, had to be removed. (Look again at Deut. 12:20-25).

Now this is an extremely quick look at an incredibly detailed area. One can make the argument, and justifiably so, that the significance of the Jewish dietary laws goes far beyond the scope of this article. Indeed Kashrut involves such things as health factors, a desire to affiliate as Jews etc. You may want to examine Kashrut in more detail with your teacher.

The point of my remarks here, however, is that the Jewish dietary laws do recognize a difficult moral dilemma. By placing restrictions upon the killing of animal life, in terms of what is permitted, how it may be slaughtered, and further prepared, our traditions provide strong safeguards that would prevent a wanton or thoughtless destruction of animal life.

Thus we find the suggestion in the Talmud that if the animal's life is in danger one can bring pillows and cushions. These will be placed underneath the animal in order to help it get out of its rather nasty predicament.

If on the other hand the animal was in no immediate danger (e.g. of drowning . . .), the law suggests that one feed it, so it won't die of hunger and get it out of the pit when the Sabbath is over. This is a rather interesting situation in which there is

89

Is the hunter morally justified in killing?

conflict between one ideal, (Sabbath rest), and another, (the sanctity of life).

I don't believe that these examples really diminish the significance of the Sabbath. Rather they point out that, as important as the Sabbath is in Judaism, reverence for life is also **extremely** important, and makes strong demands upon the individual's behavior.

"Well, that's all good and fine," you say. "Certainly I have no great desire to go out and kill anyone . . . but what about special situations? . . . For example, what about situations of self-defense? What about wars? What if someone has a very painful disease and wants his/her life terminated? What if there are only a limited number of resources to sustain a large number of lives, and the choice must be made as to who will live and who will die? What then?" These are good questions and tough problems! While they are not discussed in detail in this section we will be dealing with these issues in depth in other sections later in the course!

Commandment Seven is "Thou Shalt Not Commit Adultery". In other words "No Messing Around!" Adultery is something that Adults sometimes do. It means a married person having sex with someone who s/he isn't married to. As I indicated earlier, Judaism puts a great deal of stress on the importance of the family. It's impossible to have a stable family life if people were all committing adultery.

AN X-RATED BIBLE STORY
(Don't read without proper I.D.!)

King David is considered by many to be one of the most illustrious heroes of Israel. He was quite a character. He had great courage, shown by his little run in with Goliath. He was a talented musician. He was a military and administrative genius, molding Israel into a great nation. David was also guilty of committing adultery.

One day while on the roof of his palace, David looked down and saw a cool looking lady taking a bath. David got all hot and bothered and decided to get friendly with the very attractive Bathsheba. In spite of the fact that she was married to Uriah, David got friendly. David got so friendly that Bathsheba found herself pregnant! Frantic, David tried to cover up. He finally had Uriah, who was one of his soldiers, sent into the "hottest" part of the battlefront. Uriah was killed. After Bathsheba's period of mourning ended, David married her.

Incidently don't think David got away with it. He was publically rebuked by the prophet Nathan and was told that for his misconduct, he would have plenty of problems within his own family (which came about!) II Samuel 11-12.

I made many friends while living in Israel. One of these, was an officer in the Police Force. One day, he was disturbed while taking a vacation. Apparently someone had been murdered in Nazareth, and my friend's help was required. His major concern was that a feud shouldn't break out among the families of the various parties involved. Can you imagine what it must have been like thousands of years ago in Moses' time if someone was caught committing adultery? Certainly a situation as personal and as sensitive as this could have had families **really** at each other's throats! It's no wonder, then, that for societal stability a commandment would be found prohibiting any adulterous sexual relationships.

The eighth commandment tells us not to steal. This again seems quite straightforward. Later in the course an entire unit is devoted to a discussion of stealing and cheating.

The ninth commandment tells us not to bear false witness against our neighbors. If you consider for a moment, a great deal of human interaction depends on how we communicate with each other. Communication has many forms, the most common being speech. The Jewish tradition recognized that a great deal of mischief can result from people communicating in a deceptive manner. "Bearing False Witness" can take many forms. It can include gossip. It can involve unsubstantiated statements about a person in news media. We will also be discussing the ethics of communication, a most fascinating subject, in greater detail later in this course.

Commandment Ten is a rather remarkable commandment. That's the one that tells us "not to covet". "So what's so remarkable about that one?" you ask. Well it's significant that this one is the last one! Breaking this commandment can very easily lead to breaking some of the others. First of all a word of definition is important. When we talk about "coveting" something, we don't just mean simply liking or desiring someone else's possession(s). We mean liking or desiring someone elses possession(s) to the extent that that is all you can think of; that you simply can't stand not having it! So let's say a friend has a watch much better than your own. If you admire it, and say to yourself "Myself, I wish I had one like that," and let it go at that, then you are not really coveting. Coveting is when **all you can think about is that watch!** So it's a difference in degree that turns simple desire into coveting. Well I am sure you can see the implications, as our ancestors did. If one starts coveting it can quite easily lead to breaking some of the other commandments. One could end up stealing, killing, bearing false witness or committing adultery to attain his/her goal.

91

613 COMMANDMENTS

We've discussed the Ten Commandments as an example of some of the various laws in the Bible, that provide ethical guidance. But I don't want to give you the idea that there are only ten! In actuality tradition tells us that there are Six Hundred and Thirteen Commandments in the Bible! (Don't worry we won't go through each one!)

> **Three hundred and sixty-five** of these commandments, the same number as days in the year, are negative commandments.(DON'T DO THIS . . . DON'T DO THAT!)

> **Two hundred and forty-eight** of these commandments supposedly corresponding to the limbs of the body (don't ask me how they came up with that) are positive commandments.(DO THIS . . . DO THAT!)

These commandments deal with numerous items. Such topics as donations to the Temple, idolatry, war, family, dietary laws and agricultural laws are discussed. Some of these laws seem strange today. (e.g. "Do not suffer a witch to live," Exodus 22:18) Many, however, are as relevant today in principle and/or practice as when they were formulated!

THE EVIL EYE

The evil eye, or Ayin Hara, in Hebrew is a rather fascinating superstition that goes back many centuries. It is the belief that some individuals can do harm to others simply by staring at them in a certain way. Indeed in our traditions we have popular stories of individuals who could turn other people into bones or burn things up, just by staring at them.

Implicit in the concept of the Evil Eye is the envy of others. In Proverbs we read "He that hastens to be rich has an evil eye . . . " (Prov. 28:22) Later you get the view that envy of someone else's prosperity, etc, can evoke the evil eye. Thus such individuals as important people, bridegrooms, and even children, whose happiness can be a cause of envy to others are especially in danger of the evil eye! But fear not! All is not lost. There is a huge amount of popular folklore giving advice as to how to protect oneself from the influence of the Ayin Hara:

— Bridegrooms can gain protection from the evil eye by walking backwards!

— In the Talmud the following advice is given: Take your thumb of your right hand in your left hand and vice versa, and say "I am ——— of the seed of Joseph whom the evil eye can't touch." (There was a belief that descendants of Joseph were immune to the evil eye!)

— Passover matzah (or salt and bread) would be put into children's pockets.

— Amber beads or rings on an adult's necklace was supposed to provide protection.

— Looking down at the left side of one's nose was also supposed to protect a person from the evil eye!

— A mother should kiss her offspring and then spit (repeat three times)!

92

FOCUS ON: MISHNAH, GEMARA — TALMUD

Well, the Bible certainly presented a large number of laws that dealt with many different issues. Yet various problems still came up. As people considered the actual implementation of various rules and regulations they found that changing times and circumstances made it necessary to reinterpret and expand upon the Biblical material. In addition there were laws in the Bible expressed in rather general terms which really needed further detail. For example we read that you are supposed to cease from work on the Sabbath, and rest. Well that's all good and fine, but what **really** constitutes work and rest? Can't the definitions vary according to the person asked? Isn't it possible that something that one person regards as work, another person will consider as leisure? Moreover, what do you do if two (or more) laws in the Bible conflict with each other? I think you can see the necessity for continued discussion and interpretation of Biblical material.

For a long period of time this process of discussion, and interpretation was carried out and transmitted from one generation of scholars to the next by word of mouth. The vast unwritten collection of laws, decisions and opinions became known as "Oral Law". It seems strange to think of a large amount of material such as this being preserved primarily through people's memories. It is almost as if no one wrote down the laws for your state and lawyers and judges had to rely primarily upon their recollections! To be sure, modern scholars are aware of private collections of notes etc. being in existence, but there was no one uniform guide in widespread use. Why wasn't the Oral Law immediately put into writing? Possibly because the ancient sages distrusted the possibility of something which flowed and bristled with debate and discussion being reduced into a code. It is also likely that they were afraid that should these opinions be written, the resulting books might be considered as valuable or as important as the Bible.

Eventually, however, the Oral Law was committed to writing. The person who gets credit for this is Judah Ha Nasi. Judah was no fool. He could see that entrusting a large amount of important information to the memories of a relatively small group of scholars was dangerous. If a sage was hacked up by an enemy sword in a period of unrest, the people would not only lose a great teacher, they would also lose the library that was in his head! If enough of those sages hit the dust . . . bye, bye tradition! In addition to this, the amount of Oral Law that had developed was enormous. There was a need to edit, and to systematize a huge amount of material.

The result of Judah Ha Nasi's editing efforts was the set of books known as the MISHNAH. The Mishnah was finished around the second century C.E. It's name comes from the word "shanah" — to repeat. It contained the teachings and opinions of the Rabbis who lived from the time of Hillel up until Judah Ha Nasi. We call these people Tannaim. The Mishnah is organized into six Sedarim or Orders. Each of these orders are, in turn, divided into Massechtot or Tractates. There are a total of sixty-three tractates in the Mishnah. Each tractate in turn is broken down into further subdivisions.

The six Sedarim in the Mishnah are:

I **Zeraim** — (Seeds) — which deals primarily with agricultural laws.

II **Moed** — (Season, or Festival) — which concerns various holidays. (e.g. the Sabbath, Passover, Rosh Hashanah etc.)

III **Nashim** — (Women) — discusses such things as marriage contracts, divorce, infidelity etc.

IV **Nezikin** — (Damages) — a section I find particularly interesting, deals with such issues as compensation for damages, inheritance, real estate, court procedure, punishments for crimes, etc.

V **Kodashim** — (Holy things) — This section discusses sacrifices. Also material relating to the proper way of slaughtering animals is found here (kind of gory)!

VI **Tohorot** — (Purifications) — gets into the issue of what is "clean" and "unclean".

PIRKE AVOT

Time and time again you have seen references in this book to a source known as Pirke Avot. The words mean "The Chapters of the Fathers." I have heard others refer to it as "The Ethics of the Fathers." Pirke Avot is actually a small section in the Mishnah. (It is located in Nezikin). It contains all kinds of short and profound statements by about sixty sages. These individuals lived and taught from 300 B.C.E. to 200 C.E. Thus you can see that the sayings in Pirke Avot were accumulated over a period of about 500 years! While customs varied from time to time and from place to place, many communities studied the material in Pirke Avot between Passover and Shavuot. Actually this short collection of ethical insight is really neat!

This is but a quick summary. When you hear discussions about the Mishnah, you will inevitably be told that it includes both Halacha and Aggadah. The Halacha is legal material. Aggadah is non legal material containing explanations, legends etc. (This is, of course, a simplification). Both Halacha and Aggadah are important parts of the Mishnah.

Things didn't just stop with the Mishnah. Discussions continued in Jewish Academies in both Palestine and Babylon. The Jewish sages, who came to be known as Amoraim, examined the Mishnah carefully and continued to analyze and reinterpret. The commentary that grew up around the Mishnah was called Gemara. But believe it or not, because scholars were at work in both Palestine and Babylon, **two** versions of Gemara were developed! These were written down and:

The Mishnah	plus	Gemara developed in Palestine	=	Palestinian Talmud.
The Mishnah	plus	Gemara developed in Babylon	=	Babylonian Talmud

Thus the Talmud is actually the Mishnah plus either the Gemara developed in Palestine or Babylon. Generally when people talk about **THE** Talmud, they are referring to the Babylonian Talmud. The Gemara developed in Babylon was **much larger,** and superior in quality. Interestingly enough neither Talmud has an entire Gemara!

One hundred and fifty years ago when I was a student, I thought that the Talmud was a dull old set of law books that teachers quote to show how scholarly and erudite they are! I was therefore quite surprised when I actually checked out this source of Jewish knowledge. First of all, I had the misconception that these books would just contain a big listing of laws. It was interesting to find that the Talmud was written in such a way that **opposing** views are given. Different subjects are examined from various angles. You still get the sense of debate and of controversy that must have characterized the discussions from which the Talmud came into being. Moreover, the ancient sages were a pretty cool bunch of characters. They liked variety and from time to time would "wander" away from a legal problem and tell a legend, observation etc. In doing so they dealt with an incredible range of topics, from botany to history, from folk-lore to astronomy. The result is an orderly yet disordered mess of brilliance, encyclopedic in scope and profound in its thinking! I always like to suggest to my students to go to the library and to start looking through some of the volumes of Talmud. While the language and style may be difficult (even in English translation), you may be surprised at some of the interesting stuff that the Talmud contains within its pages!

So why am I making such a big fuss about the Talmud and its component parts? The answer is simple. The Talmud contains a great deal of material that deals with virtually all aspects of life. It is therefore an excellent source for Jewish insights about all kinds of ethical issues. Time and again reference will be made to this unique sourcebook of our Jewish heritage!

BY NO MEANS ENDED

Don't get the idea that after the Talmud was completed, all work ceased! Various codes which tried to organize legal material into a systematic and coordinated form were developed. The Mishneh Torah by Maimonides (a rather cool character who was both a Rabbi and a Physician) and the Shulhan Aruch by Joseph Caro are examples of books of this kind. Another body of literature that has grown over a nearly two thousand year span of time has been various "Responsa". As times and conditions changed people would write letters to noted Jewish authorities asking them practical questions as to how to relate Jewish insights to their lives and problems. Today we have around a half a million of these answers ("Responsa") by at least five thousand different authorities! (Recently work has been done to put these Responsa into computers). The point should be clear. There are literally "tons" of Jewish ethical material available to consult!

SUMMARY

In this unit we discussed some sources of Jewish ethical teachings. One very important source is the Bible. The Bible is actually a collection of "books". It can give us ethical advice in three important ways:

1. There are numerous Biblical stories that contain ethical situations (and morals). Several of these were discussed.

2. There are specific sections such as Proverbs and Ecclesiastes which contain actual advice.

3. One way of translating values into action is through various laws. The Bible contains many laws and commandments.

Probably the most famous set of laws in the world are the Ten Commandments. In this unit we took a careful and detailed look at these commandments. In addition we find that tradition counts Six Hundred and Thirteen Commandments in the Bible.

In the "Focus On: Mishnah, Gemara — Talmud" section we noted that a necessity to clarify and readapt Jewish teachings to varied circumstances, resulted in an evolution of Jewish law. Such things as the Mishnah and Talmud came into being.

CONSIDER THIS:

1. The first commandment makes a special point of the fact that Israel was taken out of slavery. Note that it doesn't just say "out of the land of Egypt" but "out of the land of Egypt, out of the house of bondage", as if to emphasize the fact that our ancestors were slaves there. Why do you think the issue of "slavery vs. freedom" was mentioned in the first commandment? Would a people's freedom affect how they would follow other commandments? Give reasons.

2. Bill's big goal in life is to become President of The Corporation. He craves the position and the power, and he will do anything, **anything** to get it!

   Joan has her targets set on money. It is irrelevant to her whether or not she has to be unethical in her business dealings. She is happy only so long as she stays out of trouble and makes as much money as possible.

   Commandment Two says that one shouldn't have any other gods besides the one true God. In your readings we discussed the various gods that many religions have come up with. Now, the big question; do these two individuals have other gods beside the one true one? What are they? Can we therefore say that there is an additional meaning to this commandment? List five modern "idols", and discuss.

3. Is it possible for one "to take God's name in vain" without using foul language? How? Would that justify the use of obscene language? Give your reasons.

4. Mr. Quigley had a very good opinion of himself. As the Manager of J and C. Enterprises, he felt that employees could and should come to him to confer about their problems. He encouraged free thinking and exchange of ideas telling his workers to freely express their opinions, even if they were contradictory to his own. One day Ann Q came to him with a form. "I need a recommendation . . . Would you be willing to fill it out for me?" she asked. "Why of course . . ." he responded with a smile. "Don't worry about a thing Ann!" Ann was one of his top people, but a bit outspoken. He sat down to write "I find Ann to be rather overbearing and too challenging . . ."

   Mr. Quigley hasn't used any foul language, but what do you think of his actions? Is he "taking the name of the Lord in vain?" What makes you feel that way?

5. Discuss what you think to be the connection of the Sabbath to Jewish Ethics.

6. Complete the following statements:
   a. Girls who have sex before they are married are . . .
   b. If it gives you pleasure then . . .
   c. Boys who have sex before marriage are . . .
   d. Sex, in our society is . . .
   e. The effect of sex on family life is . . .

7. Today we have far more effective means of contraception than were available in Moses' time. With such technological advances and changing atti-

tudes, should we still be so concerned with laws governing sexual behavior? Why? Why not?

8. If you were to write three additional commandments to add to the ten, what would you add? Why?

9. Write an ethical situation or story dealing with:
    a. Idolatry — modern forms
    b. Taking the name of God in vain
    c. The Sabbath
    d. Ethics of family living (Parents etc.)
    e Killing
    f. Stealing
    g. Bearing false witness
    h. Coveting — jealousy

(Your teacher will direct you as to how many of these to write. These stories or situations should be at least a page long. Put a lot of thought into them. Be creative and zany!)

10. "My Sons," Dad got up suddenly from the breakfast table . . . "I'm not a very religious man. I seldom go to Temple, and rarely bother with the holidays. Nonetheless I insist that both of you have a Bar Mitzvah ceremony. You must learn Hebrew well so that you can say prayers for me when I die. It's very important that you continue your Jewish studies after your Bar Mitzvah. This is the essence of the commandment to honor your father and your mother . . . Now hurry up. Finish breakfast, get your books and get into the car. I'll drop you off at religious school. It's extremely vital that we get going immediately. I have a very important ten o'clock appointment down at the golf course."

How good is the father's understanding of the Jewish tradition? Discuss the ethics of the situation.

11. John's family seems to be going in all directions at once. His mother is very busy with her job as a volunteer down at the hospital. When she is not there she is either playing bridge at one of her friend's homes, or is occupied with her dramatic club. His father is usually at the office during the day. Sometimes he doesn't get home until nine or ten o'clock at night. On weekends he often goes off with his friends to bowl, a game that the rest of the family never really enjoyed. It seems that John and his sisters communicate with their parents more by notes left on the refrigerator than by any other means.

    a. How can the family be brought together?
    b. Relate this to commandment five.

12. Joanne's announcement hit with all of the force of a cannonball. She had just told her parents that she and John Aldershot were planning to be married. "But dear, he's not Jewish,"exclaimed her father. Simultaneously her mother started to cry. "How could you do this to us . . . How could you?" She exclaimed "Is this honoring your parents?" Joanne turned red with anger. "I can't see why you people are so uptight," Joanne raged.

"For years you have told me that people of all faiths and backgrounds are equal . . . You've encouraged me to make all kinds of friends" . . . "Bring them home to dinner . . . Go out and socialize . . . Don't be narrow" . . ., you've said. "I'm only doing what you've preached at me all my life."

a. What is your opinion of Joanne's parents' reactions? Why?
b. Does Joanne's decision have anything to do with the fifth commandment? Why? Why not?
c. What do you think of Joanne's comments in reply to her parents? Is she justified in her actions? Why? Why not?
d. What advice would you give to Joanne's parents? Why?
e. What advice would you give Joanne? Why?

HEAVYWEIGHT BOUT OF THE CENTURY!

A DEBATE — WHO'S SMARTER
THE OLD OR THE YOUNG? — PUBLIC
INVITED — ADMISSION FREE!

Rabbi Yose ben R.
Judah of Kephar ha Babli:

If one learns from the young, what is he like? — like someone who eats unripe grapes or drinks unmellowed wine from the vat. How about one who learns from the old, what is he like? Like someone who eats ripe grapes or who drinks aged wine.

VS.

Rabbi Meir:

Look not at the flask but at what is within; there may be a new flask filled with aged wine and an old flask without even new wine in it!

1. What is R. Yose saying? Rabbi Meir?
2. Does age guarantee wisdom?
3. Does youth guarantee wisdom?
4. Do the labels "youth" or "aged" carry with them certain preconceived notions?
   Are these notions to any extent justified?
5. Would a young person's having "aged wine" necessarily always be a good thing? Why? Why not?
6. Whom do you agree with? R. Meir? R. Yose? Neither? A little of both? What are your views on the subject and why?

100

unit six

Me, Myself and I - Selfishness

Story I

"Thanks Jack, but I've already got a date to the Prom." Cindy chatted a few more minutes. "Well I've got to go now, bye." Gail looked up from the book she was reading. "Who are you going with?" She asked her sister. "I'm going with Bill," Cindy responded. "I didn't think you liked Bill as much as Jack?" Gail looked puzzled. "I don't," responded Cindy, "But Bill plans to become a dentist . . . Jack, on the other hand, isn't quite sure what he plans to do . . . I figure I'd be better off encouraging Bill rather than Jack."

Story II

The clock read 8:15. Don sat down in the classroom next to his friend Dick. The class wouldn't start for another five minutes. Mr. Gerring the teacher was fair about talking in class. Until the bell rang at 8:20 quiet talking was allowed. "How was your vacation?" Dick asked. "Oh it was terrific." Don thought back over the past twelve days. Instead of vacations coming between periods of school, maybe school should come between periods of vacation. "What did you do during vacation?" Dick asked. "Oh, nothing. I just relaxed and slept late." responded Don. "You did nothing? Well I spent the whole vacation working on our social studies report." said Dick in a loud voice. Mr. Gerring was putting some material on the board. Although he had been close enough to hear most of the conversation, Gerring customarily said nothing. With the last comment he spun around and glared sharply at the two boys.

Story III

The chairman of the board called the meeting to order. The board of directors of the Billings Corporation sat around the long oval table. The hours of strain showed in their faces. The issue seemed clear enough. Information sent anonymously pointed to one of their number being guilty of a "conflict of interest" situation. The Vice-President of the corporation, Jeff Rogers, was accused of being involved in outside business dealings that were contrary to the best interests of the corporation. The board had to decide his fate. It was no easy task, for Rogers' career was on the line. Thirty years of dedicated work could go down the drain, oh so quickly. Jane Mirdrell, one of the board, squirmed in her seat. She knew that the charges against Rogers were false, and had been planted by an outside party intent on removing him from the company. As Vice-President Rogers had been prodding the Billings Corporation to take a stronger and more positive stand in helping to promote the conservation of the environment. This would result in scraping several products that Billings was intending to manufacture. The Hudson Company produced some of the component parts that would have been used in those products. They stood to lose millions if the deal fell through.

In fact, if the Billings account was lost, Hudson could very easily go out of business. Thus, they were frantic to eliminate Rogers. Mirdrell wanted to clear Rogers, but she had a problem. Many years ago when she had started out she had worked for the Hudson Company. They knew a terrible secret from her past! If she tried to get involved she knew that they could disclose her secret.

Story IV

"Well I think that purple with blue dots is a very good color scheme for the entry hall." said Mr. Cogmit. "What do you think Stan?" "Oh yes sir, Mr. Cogmit. It's terrific, typical of your progressive leadership sir!" answered Stan Gelinsky. Actually Stan thought it was terrible. "Wonderful, and how about green and yellow plaid in the waiting room? " continued Cogmit. "Magnificent sir! A stroke of genius!" Gelinsky thought to himself, "If we're lucky maybe our customers will be colorblind. ""And how about metallic green and pink in my office?" "Oh yes," said Gelinsky . . . "It will look exceptional with your chartreuse desk." "Exceptionally bad," he thought. "Gelinsky?" Yes Sir?", answered the boss's assistant. "I feel that we accomplished a great deal in this meeting . . . keep up the good work . . . you'll go far in our company." Cogmit got up and smiled. "Yes sir!" Gelinsky responded as he left the room.

Story V

Harry was on his way to see his girl friend, Ruth. As he walked down the street he noticed that Mr. Linder had just planted a large number of geraniums in his yard. "My, how pretty!" thought Harry. "Say, I bet Ruth would love a few flowers!" Harry figured that there must have been at least one hundred geraniums in the yard, and that Linder would not even notice if a few were missing. "Besides which," said Harry to himself, "Linder is a wealthy man. He can afford to share four geraniums." At that point Harry quickly put his hand within the bars of the fence and pulled out four flowers. "Boy, will Ruth love these." he thought.

Story VI

"Come on lady, what do you think this is . . . a retirement home? I don't have all day, so hurry up. "Mrs. Hasty was shocked. She was rather elderly and slow but the girl at the checkout counter in the supermarket didn't have to be so rude about it! Hasty was livid with anger. After paying for her order and receiving her change, she walked over to the manager's office and complained to him about the way she had been treated. The manager calmed her down and assured her that the girl would be properly reprimanded. The next day when Mrs. Hasty returned to the store to pick up something the check out girl turned to her and said "You've got a lot of nerve reporting me to the manager. I could lose my job!"

Story VII

Rover had been chewing up Mrs. Hasty's house plants, that morning. As a result, that afternoon, he was sick. "You get out of here . . ." Mrs. Hasty chased the dog out of the living room. "If you chewed up the plants and are going to get sick, that's all good and fine . . . but you can't throw up and dirty my Kerman rug."

CONSIDER THIS:

Story I:
1. Why did Cindy decide to go to the Prom with Bill rather than Jack? What was Gail's reaction?
2. What do you think of Cindy's justification?
3. What would you do if you were Cindy?
4. How is this case an example of "Me, Myself and I"?
5. Have you ever heard of other situations where someone chose his/her friends, or made decisions according to such criteria as another person's school, job etc.? What did you think of this story? Was it sexist? Why? Why not?

Story II:
1. What do you think of Dick's actions?
2. What do you suppose he was trying to do?
3. If you were Don what would you do now?
4. How about Mr. Gerring? How do you suppose Dick's comments affected him? Would his conception of Don change? How about his opinion of Dick? Should Mr. Gerring do anything? Why? Why not?
5. How would you evaluate Dick as a friend?
6. How would this be an example of "Me, Myself, and I"?

Story III:
1. If Jane Mirdrell actively gets involved in Rogers' defense she may very well find her secret disclosed. If she does not, Rogers' career is most likely finished. What would you do if you were in her place? Why?
2. Evaluate the selfishness of the following: Rank them in order from the most selfish to the least: Rogers, Mirdrell, Billings Board, Hudson Co. Explain your ranking order.
3. Why is this story an example of "Me, Myself and I"?

Story IV:
1. Is one morally justified in being a "yes-man"?
2. How about people who are nice only to certain people in order to accomplish their goals — are they any different from Gelinsky? Why?
3. Gelinsky wandered in during a student discussion. He said, "Look, I work for the man . . . I only want to make him feel good . . . What's so wrong with that? . . . After all I'm only being polite. Aren't good

manners important?" How would you evaluate his justification? Why?
4. Here are some comments from Pirke Avot:
   "Receive all men with cheerfulness."
   "Dispise not any man."
   Discuss with regard to this situation.
5. How does this case relate to the subject of "Me, Myself and I"?

Story V:

1. Was Harry being selfish? Why? Why not?
2. Why did Harry want to take the flowers?
   Could the fact that his actions were influenced by concern for another person make his conduct seem more excusable? Why? Why not?
3. What was his justification for taking the flowers?
   How would you evaluate it? Why?

Story VI:

1. Why was Mrs. Hasty upset? Would you be upset if you were in her place? Why? Why not?
2. Was Mrs. Hasty justified in complaining? Why? Why not?
3. Who was more selfish — (Rank the three, from most to least selfish).
   a. Mrs. Hasty.
   b. The girl at the checkout counter.
   c. The manager.
   Explain why you have ranked them the way you have.

Story VII:

1. Was Mrs. Hasty justified in throwing the dog out of the room? Write a paragraph defending the affirmative position, and a paragraph taking the negative position. What do you think?
2. Are people who don't have any pets selfish or not? Why? Why not?
3. Compare the relative selfishness of **all** of the individuals in **all** of the stories (I–VII).

KITTY GENOVESE

In the early morning hours Kitty Genovese, a pretty young woman age 28, was returning to her home in Kew Gardens. She was stalked and brutally attacked. Her assailant spent about a half hour repeatedly stabbing her. During this period of time she screamed and cried repeatedly for help. In fact enough noise was made so that many of her neighbors were pulled out of bed and watched the grisly episode. Thirty-eight of her neighbors later admitted to being witnesses to the incident. They heard her scream out "He stabbed me! Please help me! Someone help me!" and more. Some saw Kitty being attacked. Others saw her staggering along the sidewalk trying to hide after she had been stabbed. Kitty even looked up at one of her neighbors looking down from a window and asked by name for help. It was to no avail. No one came out to help her. No one even called the Police until after her assailant left the scene of the crime. The witnesses had seen the event so clearly that they were able to give a good description of the man. He was later picked up and confessed. But that was rather irrelevant to Kitty Genovese. She was dead.

— What are your reactions to this situation?

THINKING FROM PSYCHOLOGISTS ABOUT THE GENOVESE-TYPE CASE

The story of Kitty Genovese is true and really happened! In fact it has been repeated in many variations, in our country. Two psychologists, Darley and Latane were intrigued by this kind of situation and did some interesting work relating to it. In our culture, it's generally considered socially unacceptable to stare at people in public. They suggest that this could, in some cases, hinder people from even being aware that something is wrong. Assuming that one does notice that an event is not as it should be, does that mean that the event is seen as an emergency? Not necessarily. A person could dismiss an incident as not being particularly serious. Some of the witnesses to the Genovese murder thought it was a lovers' quarrel! In addition one would feel awfully stupid if s/he intervened unnecessarily. Darley and Latane also suggested that in an emergency if all bystanders sit around doing nothing perhaps everybody present can delude themselves that the situation isn't all that bad. "Gee if the guy over there isn't getting disturbed over this thing, why should I?" Finally, what about the decision to get involved? Wouldn't you think that the more bystanders present, the more likely it is that the victim will get help? Not so! Darley and Latane suggest that if there are a large number of people around, individuals feel **less** of a responsibility to help out . . . "Let the other guy do it."

An Unusual Event?
Yes — No
An Emergency?
Yes — No
Should I get Involved?
Yes — No
Person Helps Out

- From what you've read, how do you think Latane and Darley would respond to the statement "Anyone who refuses to help out in an emergency is a cold-blooded selfish individual"?

- Would their views totally excuse a person from taking action? Why? Why not?

- How about someone who is aware of the above theories, and then finds him/herself in an emergency situation. Does knowledge of bystander behavior provide **greater** or **lesser** motivation for action? Why? Why not?

BUD'S FRUSTRATIONS

"But Professor Gorkin, the question was ambiguous. It could be answered either way." Bud looked up anxiously at his engineering professor. Gorkin responded, "Yes, but when I asked for the answer to this question I had intended that you should take the numbers through the Himmelschwartz contraction." "But that wasn't stated in the test's instructions, and I did use the Eenitz permutation to get the right answer," persisted Bud. "This man is quibbling over detail." he thought. "Look that's the way it is." responded Gorkin . . . "Anyhow you got a B so what's the big deal about getting an A? . . ." Without giving Bud a chance

to answer the professor glanced at his watch, "Well I don't know about you but I'm hungry. I'm going off to lunch. Have a nice day!" Bud stormed out of the engineering building. It was all good and fine for Gorkin to be carefree about the grade, but getting a B in that course wouldn't exactly help him get into graduate school. Bud had always liked tinkering with mechanical things. He hoped to eventually be involved in the designing of bionic replacements for parts of the human body. He was certain that such replacements would really help people. But before he could develop anything, he needed to get into a special graduate program, which only five schools in the country offered. Getting to the cafeteria he spotted his friend Joe. "Hi Bud! Get anywhere with Professor Gorkin?" "Nah," replied Bud. "He was more concerned about his lunch than about making an adjustment on the grade." "That bad?" asked Joe. "Yeah . . . But you know that's typical in my department." As he silently ate his fish sticks (ugh), Bud thought about the past two years. He had entered City University full of great hopes and expectations. The engineering studies which he had started with such great enthusiasm was one big elimination contest. He could see why. You had to be capable if you were going into human systems engineering. It wouldn't do to make mistakes in technological replacements. After all, people's lives were at stake. Still that didn't make his course of study particularly pleasant. Take that first course that all H.S. engineers were required to have! One hundred and fifty students were in the course. Six received A's. Most did pretty badly. Many of those kids got the hint, and quit the sciences. Maybe he should have quit too. Well from there on it was a constant grind. Most of his free time was spent in the library. If he didn't put in the hours, someone else would. He had to get the A! While those graduate schools talked about how they wanted well rounded individuals, everybody knew that what really counted was high scores! And then there was Gorkin! His department had seven professors. Six of them were great! They were good teachers and fair people. But Gorkin was the department chairman and was a mean character. He graded harder than most. He would give his lectures too quickly or lacking vital information. He would even order insufficient books at the store, which didn't help students any. The problem was that Gorkin ran all of the required courses, so that there was no way of avoiding him. Bud was annoyed. His parents were paying good money for him to receive such a good "education". "Joe," he spoke up, "you're a Sociology Major. How do you find your department?" "Oh I like it a lot." said Joe, "They're pretty nice to us." "I bet!", thought Bud. When Bud was a freshman he had tried to arrange to exchange notebooks in case he or other classmates were absent. But the competition was so tough in Engineering that nobody would compare notes anymore. "Oh, Oh", he thought as he saw Stan, Gus and Nancy approaching the table. They were all in his Thermo class, which had had a test last week. "Joe I'll see you. Between these fish sticks and those three comparing grades, my lunch hour would be ruined. " "Yeah. Hang in there; it's not that bad." smiled Joe. "How could he be so optimistic?" wondered Bud. En route to the computer terminal, Bud passed the library. Some idiot tore the two most important pages out of the article that Professor Mason had put on reserve. All of the copies of that scientific journal that the class needed to use to research their Engineering 105 papers had been taken out, in spite of the fact that Professor Moriarity had asked that they all be left there for everyone to use. "It's absurd." thought Bud. "How can I get into that program and help people if things like that go on?" As Bud passed the school aquarium wrapped up in his thoughts, a girl tripped about ten yards away, dropping all of her books. "To blazes with everyone." thought Bud as he quickened his pace. "If I don't get to that terminal I'll never finish my work." The girl was on the ground still groping at her ankle. Bud entered the computer center and sat down at a terminal. The big problem in his Engineering 729 course was J.B. White.

White was the kid who always was getting higher scores than the others. He kept lousing up everyone else in the process. With J.B.'s high scores, Prof. Mason just couldn't use a sliding scale in marking. Aside from looking strange with a big derriere and funny glasses J.B. never helped any of his fellow classmates . . . "Not that I would if I were in his place." thought Bud. Bud grinned fiendishly! "Let's see if we can wipe that constant smirk off of White's face." In addition to his course work Bud had prepared a "special program". After Bud put this program into the computer, J.B. would be messed up! Whenever J.B. would try to utilize material that he had stored in the computer he would receive dummy data instead! "By the time J.B. figures out that he is not getting his own genuine data, it'll be too late! He'll be so far behind the rest of us that he won't be able to hurt our grades!" smirked Bud. "Gee . . . maybe the day wasn't a total loss at that!"

1. Is Bud really concerned with helping people or is he really selfish? Why? Why not?

2. What would make him seem selfish?

3. What is Bud's excuse for sabotaging White's work? Do you think it's justified? Why? Why not?

4. Could Bud's faults be in part due to his environment or does he take full blame? Explain.

5. If you were to evaluate Bud for the graduate program on the basis of this story would you let him in? Why? Why not? (Assume his grades are comparable to anyone else applying to the program).

6. Write another story concerning the title of this chapter "Me, Myself and I".

ARE WE ALL POTENTIAL SHEEP?

110   "How far will someone go when an authority gives him/her orders that conflict with that person's conscience?" This was the question that Stanley Milgram posed in an experiment at Yale University.

A person is told that s/he is to be involved in an experiment about learning. S/he is to be the "teacher". The "learner" is to be strapped into a chair in another room, and will receive a stronger shock everytime s/he gives a wrong answer. As the "learner" makes mistakes, the "teacher" hears groans, screams etc. as s/he presses the switches administering the shocks. The "teacher" is told, however, to continue. What will the "teacher" do? Will s/he continue to ask the questions and give shocks in response to incorrect answers?

In reality, **no one** was in the chair being shocked. The experiment **really** tested the "teacher" not the "learner". Milgram found that about two thirds of the subjects continued to give large shocks! When the experiment was repeated away from Yale to prevent the prestige of that institution affecting the study almost half of the subjects continued the shocks.

1. What would the results of the experiment imply?

2. How would you relate this experiment to events in Nazi Germany?

3. Would the results of an experiment such as this excuse a person from behaving ethically? Why? Why not?

4. No one was really shocked in this experiment. Milgram took care to have the "learner" and the "teacher" meet and chat after the experiment. He made an effort to reassure and explain the experiment to

the participants and let them know they were acting just as others would under the circumstances. He even sent them follow-up letters later to make sure there were no after-effects. Very few said that they regretted the experiment. In spite of this, and in spite of Milgram's adding to our knowledge, he was criticized strongly by many people who felt that this experiment was unethical. Why would they feel this way? Do you agree or not? Why?

YETZER TOV, YETZER RA AND THE QUESTION OF FREEDOM

Our ancestors had a big problem. They believed that God was a kind of cosmic genius. God knew all the answers and could do anything. If that was so, then why, you may ask, (and they asked) would God create a world in which people are often such **creeps**? After all couldn't God, knowing in advance that some people would turn out that way, have created the world so that everybody would **have** to be nice? Well, our ancestors had a tough time trying to answer that question. It's a problem that no one really knows the answer to. However, that doesn't mean we can't still consider it! When we check Pirke Avot we find the comment "Everything is seen in advance by God but freedom of choice is given." This kind of summarizes a lot of Jewish thinking in this area. No person can escape moral responsibility. We all have the choice as to whether or not we are going to live in an ethical manner. Certainly you feel aware of that ability to choose whenever you face an ethical problem (should I or shouldn't I?).

111

Well, why then do people sometimes do nasty things? This question offers a perfect excuse to discuss one of my favorite concepts of Jewish lore, that of the **Yetzer Tov** — the impulse to do good and **Yetzer Ra** — an inclination to do evil. You know how sometimes, just when you have a ton of homework to do, something inside of you says "Hay you . . . yah you, with the big ears . . . Why are you wasting your time doing that stuff when you could be watching T.V.? . . . Come on . . . life is short . . . and the T.V. is just waiting for you to turn it on! . . . The homework can wait till someday in the future!" Then you hear something else inside of you say "Say, are you going to listen to that Sap? . . . If you don't get going on that assignment now, there's no guarantee you will later . . . Anyhow you know that doing the assignment is really the right thing to do." I'm pretty sure you can figure out which is the Yetzer Tov and which is the Yetzer Ra! (No the first one isn't the Yetzer Tov — wise guy!) Where are the Yetzer Tov and the Yetzer Ra? Well one view put the Yetzer Ra in the left side of the body and the Yetzer Tov in the right side! (Maybe the person who thought of that one just had gas!) Another opinion had the Yetzer Ra being something hovering around outside of a person ready to fall on him/her. (Like a rainstorm?) But the standard opinion was that the Yetzer Tov and Yetzer Ra were **non physical** things that make up part of our personality. If a person does good s/he is following his/her Yetzer Tov. If s/he does evil, s/he is following the Yetzer Ra. Sometimes when caught between the demands of the Yetzer Tov and Yetzer Ra one can indeed feel as if s/he is being squeezed from two directions at the same time. (See p. 113).

In modern times people have been very impressed with Freud, for he was one of the first in our era to really concern himself with the problem of how one's personality is shaped. Yet this business of Yetzer Tov and Yetzer Ra was formulated by the ancient Rabbis many hundreds of years ago!

DO WE HAVE FREEDOM?

Freud believed that our personality is affected by interactions between our
ID — which tries to seek pleasure
EGO — which copes with reality and
Superego — kind of like our conscience.
Much of what one's personality is like comes about due to the interaction of early childhood experiences with one's internal situation. (This is very simplified!)

Here is another view of what shapes people. The **genetic information** that we receive from our parents will contribute to determining many of our traits (hair color, height etc.). This information is coded in a chemical found in our cells known as Deoxyribonucleic Acid (D.N.A.). In recent times the suggestion by some people that such things as intelligence may also be inherited has caused considerable debate.

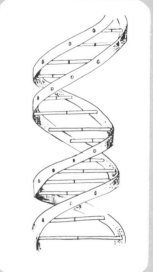

Skinner's interest is in the outside observable forces, the **environment**, which he feels is of primary importance in shaping an individual's personality. If a person is constantly rewarded for a behavior s/he will continue. If a person is constantly punished s/he will eventually stop doing whatever brought about that punishment. Thus one is shaped by the environment.

— What would each of these views imply in terms of our "freedom"? Analyze in detail.

— Do you think that any of these positions would excuse a person from making a moral decision? Why? Why not?

112

What else did the Rabbis have to say about the Yetzer Tov and the Yetzer Ra? Well, one observation that they made was that if one follows the evil impulse it seems to grow in strength after awhile. If you followed your evil impulse, and didn't bother with your assignment you could very well find that the next time you are faced with the same decision, that it will be even easier to follow the lazy course of action. We are told by the Rabbis that the evil impulse starts like a passerby then becomes a lodger and finally becomes master of the house.

There is yet another midrash which is crucial to our understanding of the Yetzer Tov and Yetzer Ra:

> One day the Rabbis decided to get rid of the Yetzer Ra once and for all. They caught it and tied it up! Well, just as they hoped, getting rid of the Yetzer Ra put an end to such nasties as stealing, killing etc. Everybody got along in peace and harmony. But just as some medicines have side effects, so too did the Rabbis' prescription! Everybody was so happy that people started to goof off! No one worked. No one built or did anything. Everyone just sat around grooving about how happy they were! The Rabbis said to themselves "Ourselves, we made a big mistake!" They broke the bonds and released the Yetzer Ra!

And thus we find the recognition in the tradition that, in a sense, the Yetzer Ra is necessary for anything to be accomplished!

Now at this stage you are probably thinking, "Well this psychology — Rabbinic style, is all good and fine, but what does it have to do with the topic of this chapter, namely, "Me, Myself and I"? We have been translating Yetzer Ra as an "inclination to do evil" or an "evil impulse." Yet if we consider it very carefully the Yetzer Ra could also be considered an inclination towards **selfishness**! Selfishness is certainly an example of an advanced case of "Me, Myself and I"! Go back now and re-read all of the comments concerning Yetzer Tov and Yetzer Ra, substituting selfishness for Yetzer Ra!

SUMMARY:

In this chapter we have been considering the issue of "Me, Myself, and I". This points to the whole problem of selfishness. We indicated earlier in this book that while Judaism believes that concern with oneself is important, the individual must also think about the welfare of others as well.

In this section we raised the issue of freedom. Do we really have the freedom to make ethical decisions? Some people would say no. Judaism however holds that one does have the ability to choose between right and wrong. Why then do some people choose to do wrong? The ancient Rabbis used the concept of Yetzer Tov and Yetzer Ra to come to terms with that problem. Yetzer Ra can be considered an inclination to do evil, but may also be considered as an example of selfishness, — which brings us back to the problem of "Me, Myself and I"!

CONSIDER THIS:

1. What is the Rabbinic view of selfishness? Discuss and give your reactions.

2. A midrash tells us:

   After Cain killed his brother, he was questioned by God, "Where is Abel?" Cain's response was "Am I my brothers' keeper?" Cain went on, according to the midrash, and said "Sure I killed Abel; but God, you created the Yetzer Ra in me . . . You permitted me to slay him . . . In effect then, you killed him yourself."

   115

   God wasn't very impressed with Cain's defense. From your knowledge of the Jewish view on moral responsibility can you explain why? What do you think of Cain's reasoning? Why?

MARTIN BUBER'S I – THOU

A fellow named Martin Buber is considered by many to be one of the most important Jewish philosophers (people who sit around thinking and worrying about all kinds of profound stuff) of modern times. Buber was born in Vienna. He eventually ended up in Israel. Here is an interesting story that is told about him. When he first came to Israel his Hebrew was fairly elementary, so people could understand him. After his Hebrew improved, people could no longer figure out what he was talking about! His thinking gets pretty involved! One item that he thought about was "How do people **know** things?" One way that we know about something is by objective study. We measure, test, and examine things. We try to take an item apart and see how it ticks. When someone uses this approach s/he doesn't become personally involved with the object. This is the way scientists learn about things. It's an important approach. Buber calls this an "I–It relationship". A major problem comes up, however, if this becomes our **major** way of relating to everything. Another approach Buber talks about is that of the "I — Thou relationship". This approach is more difficult to describe but it involves active participation, not objectivity. In an "I — Thou" encounter one is giving of one's self to another. It's a kind of sharing. Something for you to consider — perhaps the whole problem of "Me, Myself and I" arises because we sometimes treat others as **objects**, in an "I — It" encounter, rather than trying to relate in an "I — Thou" manner. Think about it, and review this chapter with that thought in mind!

117

118

My bowels, my bowels! My heart is in agony! My heart moans within me! I can't hold my peace because you have heard, O my soul, the sound of the horn, the alarm of war.

Destruction follows destruction, for the whole land is spoiled! Suddenly are my tents spoiled, and my curtains in a moment. How long will I see the standard and hear the sound of the trumpet? For my people is foolish, they have not known me. They are stupid children, and they have no under-standing. They are wise to do evil, but to do good, they have no knowledge.

I beheld *the earth, and lo it was without form and void; and the heavens, and they had no light.*

I beheld *the mountains, and lo they trembled, and the hills moved to and fro.*

I beheld, *and lo, there was no man. And all of the birds of the heavens had fled.*

I beheld, *and lo, the fruitful field was a wilderness, and all the cities thereof were broken down, at the presence of the Lord, and before his fierce anger.*

For thus saith the Lord — the whole land shall be desolate . . . . .

Jeremiah 4:19-27

War

TRADITIONAL COMMENTS

It's when we discuss the issue of war that we get a really good picture of the practical realism of Judaism. Face it, war is an ethical issue. It involves killing people. It's a grimy, dirty, business. And the Ten Commandments say "Thou shalt not kill." As such would we expect Judaism to say, "If you are Jewish, you must be a total pacifist"? No, not so. It's not quite as simple as that. Judaism recognizes that we live in a world where often one must defend his/her own interests. Often to take a completely pacifist stance can be equivalent to committing suicide, not a very practical, realistic or acceptable course to follow. The Jewish view of war is unique in that while taking into account the practical realities of armed conflict, it tries to maintain as high an ethical standard as possible under the circumstances. "Ethics in warfare . . . Isn't that a rather difficult if not impossible objective?" you ask. You bet it's difficult! But let's see how our ancestors tried to deal with that dilemma.

First of all, our forefathers recognized that there were certain specific underlying causes to warfare. Wars don't just happen. They are made. Different countries will declare war for various reasons. In Pirke Avot we read:

> The sword comes into the world
> because of the delay of justice,
> the perversion of justice and
> because of those who make poor
> legal interpretations.

And also:
> If there is no flour (bread), there is
> no law (Torah).

Thus we find the recognition thousands of years ago that various distortions of justice bring about war. We also find that war sometimes comes about because of lack of resources. The above second quotation underscores the point that if there is little food, people aren't going to worry too much about justice, laws, or being nice. This could be expanded. Very often wars break out because one country desires or needs various resources that another nation has (e.g. minerals, population, strategic locations etc.). And of course if one country gets a little frisky, another country is bound to retaliate. Also from Pirke Avot:

> The payment of a good deed
> is a good deed.
> The reward of a transgression
> is another transgression.

Now when we read the Bible, we get a lot of very gory war scenes. (Go and take a look for yourself — you might be surprised!) For example we find the story of Deborah:

119

Deborah was one of the Judges, a boss-person of the Israelites. She was a pretty tough customer. When a Canaanite King Jabin and his general Sisera picked on some of the Israelite tribes, Deborah sent for Barak. "Barak, you will be my general and finish off Sisera's Army." "Hooold it . . . Wait a minute . . . I'm not going out there myself . . . If you come along, I'll go." said Barak. Deborah, always one for the feminist cause, agreed. After all if she went along and they won, it would be her victory! The battle took place and Sisera's 900 chariots and army were completely destroyed, with not a person of that side left alive. Sisera seeing defeat at hand said to himself, "Myself, I've got to get out of here!" And so, when the going gets tough the tough get going – he fled! Sisera came to a tent where he thought he could get help. The woman there gave him something to drink. While Sisera slept she picked up a big peg and a hammer and split his skull. A very detailed description is given in Judges Ch. 4, 5.

Well as you can see there is plenty of "blood and guts" in our history. Of all of the places in the Middle East, did God promise Abraham a nice oil rich country off to one side? No! God promised the land of Israel which is right in the so-called "crossroads" of the Middle East! That means that anyone down in Egypt who wanted to reach some of the countries to the North, or anyone around the Tigris and Euphrates who wanted to conquer down South would go smack dab through "you know where!" It could very well be that because of these historical

120

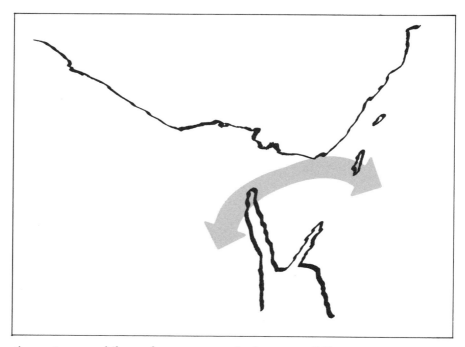

circumstances, while warfare was recognized as a possibility, it **never was really glorified or romanticized in the Jewish perspective, as it has been in other cultures.** Our traditions tell us that King David wasn't allowed to build the Temple in Jerusalem because he had been involved in too many wars, in too much killing. Indeed the ideal of Jewish history was a period of time someday in the future when the following would occur:

But in the last days it will come to pass,
That the mountain of the Lord's house will be
established in the top of the mountains,
And it shall be exalted above the hills;
And people will flow into it.
And many nations will come and say:
Come and let's go up to the Lord's mountain, and to the
house of the God of Jacob.
And he will teach us of his ways,
And we will walk in his paths.
For out of Zion will go forth the law,
And the word of the Lord from Jerusalem.
And he will judge among many peoples,
And will decide among strong nations far off;
And they will beat their swords into plowshares,
And their spears into pruning hooks.
Nation will not lift up sword against nation,
Neither will they learn war any more.
And each person will sit under his fig tree and vine;
And none will make them afraid . . .   *Micah 4:1-4*

"Swords into plowshares . . . spears into pruning hooks." These words have captured humankind's imagination for centuries, as to the kind of world towards which we should work . . .

But what about a situation where it seems war is likely. What then? Well, our traditions list a number of rules and regulations regarding warfare. In reading the following keep in mind that what is to follow is but a **summary** of views that were shaped **many, many years ago!** First of all in the book of Deuteronomy we find a distinction between warfare in Canaan and outside of Canaan. In warfare **within Canaan** (as when the Israelites returned from Egypt), the enemy is to be "utterly destroyed." (This was later softened by Rabbinic decisions). In a war with an enemy **outside of Canaan,** the Israelite is obligated to first try to make peace. If peace is accepted the enemy is to become a tributary. If the enemy decides to fight, and is conquered, the men are to be killed and everything else is to be taken as booty (Deut. 20:10-18). If this sounds rather bloodthirsty, remember two things. First of all war has always been rather grimy (especially in those days) — that's why our ancestors preferred plowshares and pruning hooks! Also this bit about first seeking peace is a significant point to note.

Later the Rabbis discussed the whole problem of war and they came up with two categories: **Milchemet Chovah** — Obligatory War and **Milchemet R'shut** — Optional War. The various characteristics of these two types of wars are summarized in the accompanying chart. As you can see, these two kinds of wars differed in their purposes and goals. The obligatory war would be one that would be fought under three circumstances:

1. It was a war of self-defense.

2. The conquest of Canaan (under Joshua) was classified under this heading.

3. Warfare against the Amalekites who attacked our ancestors was also included in this category.

A JEWISH VIEW OF FUTURE HISTORY

Have you ever wished you could predict the future? Have you ever wondered what it would be like? Well the ancient Rabbis also wondered about such things. The quotation from Micah is but a small part of a lot of stuff looking to the future. While details vary our ancestors looked forward to an age in which war would finally end. They looked forward to an era in which death would cease and there would be spiritual happiness. Poverty would be eliminated and people would live in comfort. The Kingdom of Israel would be restored, and all nations would turn to God. The concept of a Messiah enters here. The Messiah, or "anointed one", was someone who's appearance would signal that these things were about to happen. Many believed that the Messiah would be of the House of David. Throughout history there are rather interesting and bizarre cases of individuals who decided that they would be good candidates for the job! For example: In the mid 1600's a guy named Sabbatai Zevi had many people so excited that a number of them were actually selling their possessions in Europe, and preparing to march to Jerusalem! Do Jews "believe in" the Messiah today? That depends. An Orthodox Jew might. On the other side of the spectrum Reform Jews may not expect a Messiah, but would talk in terms of the coming of a **Messianic Era**, in which many of the positive conditions (e.g. elimination of poverty, war etc.) mentioned above could be brought about, by humankind. In a discussion of ethics, it's certainly worth considering!

122

And there shall come forth a rod out of the stem of Jesse, (David's father) and a branch shall grow out of his roots. And the spirit of the Lord shall rest upon him, the spirit of wisdom and understanding, the spirit of counsel and might, the spirit of knowledge and of the fear of the Lord. With righteousness shall he judge the poor . . . and with the breath of his lips shall he slay the wicked . . .
And the wolf shall dwell with the lamb,
And the leopard shall lie down with the kid;
And the calf and the young lion and the fatling together;
And a little child shall lead them . . .
They shall not hurt nor destroy in all my holy mountain; for all the earth shall be full of the knowledge of the Lord, as the waters cover the sea.

Isaiah 11: 1,2,4,6,9

The optional war, on the other hand, was primarily a war for territorial expansion. Because of the different nature of these two kinds of conflicts, there was variation in how readily the nation could go off to war, and in the allowance of exemptions from battle. A ruler could simply go off to fight an obligatory war and no exemptions would be allowed. On the other hand in the case of an optional war, a decision would have to be rendered by the Sanhedrin and various exemptions could be permitted.

Now let's assume there is a war. What about exemptions from military service? It's interesting to note that this subject was discussed thousands of years ago in the Bible!

The officers will address the people in these words. Is there a man who has built a new house and hasn't dedicated it? Let him go and return home lest he die in battle and another man dedicate it. And is there a man who has planted a vineyard and hasn't yet eaten of it? Let him also go and return home lest he die in battle and another man eat of it. And is there a man here who has betrothed a wife and has not taken her? Let him return home lest he die in battle and another man take her ... And is there anyone here who is afraid? Let him return home or his comrades will be discouraged as he is.

Deuteronomy 20: 5-8

Maimonides (see p. 95) made distinctions between possible exemptions in Optional Wars as opposed to Obligatory Wars. He also comments that some individuals who are exempt from serving should help provide food and water for the soldiers or help fix the roads.

Now some of the comments about battle procedures are really quite neat. For example:

When you are making war and besieging a city for a long time to take it, don't destroy the trees in the area by taking an ax against them. You may eat of them, but you can't cut them down. The trees of the field aren't men that you should besiege them! But you can destroy or cut down any trees that don't give food and use them to build bulwarks against the city that makes war with you, until it falls.

Deuteronomy 20:19-20

123

OBLIGATORY WAR

— Against the Amalekites who unnecessarily attacked our ancestors (Exodus 17:8-16).
— Against the nations that inhabited Canaan in those days. (many, many, many moons ago!)
— A war of self-defense.
— Maimonides points out that the King may set out on an Obligatory War independently and may compel the people to go out and fight.
— Maimonides also points out that in an Obligatory War, no man is to be exempt from battle.

OPTIONAL WAR

— A war for territorial expansion.
— Maimonides tells us that a King may not just go off and declare an Optional War. A decision must be made by the seventy-one membered Sanhedrin.
— Maimonides tells us that in an Optional War, various people may be exempt from battle:
    1. One who's planted a vineyard but hasn't enjoyed its fruits.
    2. Someone who has built a new house but hasn't dedicated it.
    3. Someone who is engaged, but not yet married. etc.
    4. Someone who is afraid and weakhearted.

THE AMALEKITES

We have several accounts of the battle between the Israelites and The Amalekites. One (Deut. 25:17-19) tells us that the Amalekites launched an attack upon the Israelites rear flank, during the trek from Egypt to Canaan. There's a bitter feeling about that unnecessary attack. In Exodus 17:9-13, we get a rather fascinating account of the battle:

And Moses said to Joshua — "Choose us men, and go out and fight with Amalek. Tomorrow I will stand on the top of the hill with the rod of God in my hand." So Joshua did as Moses had told him and fought with Amalek, and Moses, Aaron and Hur went up to the top of the hill. And it came to pass when Moses held up his hand, that Israel prevailed; and when he let down his hand Amalek prevailed. But Moses' hands grew heavy; and they took a stone and put it under him and he sat thereon; and Aaron and Hur held up his hands, one on one side, and the other on the other side and his hands were steady until the sun set. And Joshua discomforted Amalek and his people with the edge of the sword.

In ancient times a standard war procedure was for an army to surround an enemy city. While waiting for the enemy supplies to run out, the besiegers would try to devise various weapons that would either be used to scale the walls or knock them down. As you can well imagine, if the enemy used all of the trees for wood, weapons, fuel etc. there would eventually be a rather desolate and messed up area. After the war the land for miles around the city would be totally useless until more stuff could be planted and grow to maturity! Ecology in the Bible? Why not??

Oh yeah, here is another comment. This one is kind of gross! You know, in those days they didn't have modern plumbing (toilets etc). So you can well imagine that an army of ten thousand or more men must have really been odorous! If the wind shifted, the stench alone would have been enough to cause the enemy to suffer! Well, our ancestors recognized that both the besieger and the besieged wouldn't be too happy with that state of affairs and so:

> With your equipment you will have a trowel and when you squat down outside you will dig a hole with it and turn and cover that which comes from you. For the Lord your God is in your camp and delivers your enemies to you. Therefore your camp shall be holy, so that he will see no unclean thing in you and turn away from you.

> *Deuteronomy 23:12-14*

I bet you never thought you'd be learning that in Religious School! Oh yes, Maimonides went on to make the point that even a soldier in battle must practice cleanliness!

Another point about battle procedure involves treatment of captives. In Proverbs 24:17 we read "Rejoice not when your enemy falls and don't be glad when he is brought down." There are a couple of really cool stories that relate to this:

We are told that when Pharoah's army got caught in the middle of the

124

Red Sea the Angels were ready to start singing. God, however, commented "Stifle yourselves! How can you sing when my creations are dying?"

A later play off on this story was that God said to the Angels "The Egyptians can die by themselves. They don't need to die from your singing."

Regardless of the variation, the point of all this is that while the enemies' misfortune might help bring a war to an end, it's not an occasion to gloat and enjoy, for it involves the suffering of others.

We also read in Proverbs 25:21 "If your enemy is hungry, give him bread to eat; if he is thirsty give him water to drink." In our traditions we find the comment "Who is the greatest hero? He who makes a friend out of his enemy." We also get this advice in Exodus 23:4, 5 —

If you meet your enemy's ox or his ass going astray, you will surely bring it back to him again. If you see the ass of one that hates you lying under his burden, however unwilling you might be to help, you must help him with it.

All of this is rather remarkable when one considers the time period in which this stuff was formulated.

VIETNAM: AN EXAMPLE OF DELIBERATE WARTIME ECOLOGICAL DESTRUCTION.

If you are wondering whether the discussion of Biblical restrictions on ecological damage has any modern application, then consider the War in Vietnam. Modern science has developed extremely effective herbicides — chemicals that destroy plant life. Some of these such as 2, 4, 5–Trichlorophenoxayacetic acid (abbreviated 2, 4, 5 –T), 2, 4–D and others cause plants to grow wildly losing their leaves and/or killing themselves. Others such as fenuron and monuron interfere with photosynthesis so that the plants, in effect, die of starvation. Many of these herbicides were used massively in Vietnam. While estimates vary it seems that at least ten percent of the land area of "South Vietnam" was sprayed. More than 500,000 acres of cropland was also treated in order to deprive enemy troops of food. How do these herbicides affect the ecology of the area?

— They obviously do great harm to plants.

— Many animal populations are hurt, for they rely upon plants for food.

— Some of these herbicides last a short time. Others remain active for many years.

— It's believed that some of these chemicals may result in birth defects (human as well as animal).

— In hurting crops, many innocent people suffer.

— There are many types of soils. About thirty percent of "South Vietnam" is made up of Lateritic Soils. These are fine if covered by a forest, or if constantly irrigated as in a rice field. But if a forest is destroyed, or a rice field abandoned, these Lateritic Soils become very hard and turn into brick, leaving the area barren and useless.

— Other types of soil in Vietnam are very easily eroded after the vegetation is removed — again ruining the land.

— It's pretty obvious that the loss of food, land and lumber has a severe impact on the economy of the country.

— As these chemicals get into the ecosystem, they run off into rivers and oceans, hurting fish and other aquatic life.

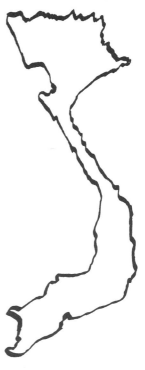

O—CH_2—COOH

Cl

2,4-dichlorophenoxyacetic acid (2,4-D)

126

Incidentally other devices also have hurt the ecology of the area. One bomb of 500—750 lbs can form a crater 30 ft. deep and 45 ft. across. Millions of these were dropped! These leave farmland useless. Large areas of Vietnam were also subjected to "Rome-plows", vegetation cutting bulldozers.

Some might argue that "War is War." "Measures such as these might not sound nice, but war is never nice . . . Moreover by taking actions such as these, the lives of our soldiers may be preserved." This is a very important point. Human life is very precious. Wouldn't a country be unfair to its soldiers by not offering them the greatest amount of support? At the end of World War II, the U.S. used the atomic bomb. Most experts agree that while the use of such a weapon was not nice, that an invasion of Japan by conventional methods would have cost millions of lives on both sides. How do we resolve such a mess? In a wartime situation can the ends justify the means? Is either side justified to use every possible means to victory? What guarantee is there that "the other side" won't try every possible means? What do you think?

FOCUS ON: AN OBLIGATION FOR SELF-DEFENSE:

Item One: Question: If God wanted human beings to be humble, why were the Ten Commandments given on a mountain? Why weren't they instead given in a valley, for valleys are certainly humble?

> **Answer:** God didn't want man to be too proud. But God didn't want man to be too humble either. To be a human being, one cannot allow him/herself to be trodden upon — like a valley!

Item Two: In the Talmud we read that one who pursues after another in order to kill him, must be stopped even at the cost of his/her own life!

Item Three: And it came to pass in those days when Moses was grown that he went out unto his brethren and looked upon their burdens. And he saw an Egyptian hitting a Hebrew, one of his brethren. And he looked this way and that way, and when he saw that there was no man, he slew the Egyptian and hid him in the sand.

Exodus 2:11-12

Item Four: If a man comes to kill you, get up early and kill him first.

Talmud

FOCUS ON: RANSOMING CAPTIVES

This section is included in a unit about war primarily for the reason that just as war is a rather violent event, so too is kidnapping.

In modern times it is not unusual to hear about individuals being kidnapped and being held for a ransom of some sort. Actually kidnapping to achieve monetary or political purposes is nothing new. We find the following comment in the Bible:

> *He who steals a man and either sells him*
> *or holds him shall be put to death.*

Exodus 21:16

It's all good and fine to condemn kidnapping, but what do you do if someone has been kidnapped and you are sent a ransom note. Well, the Rabbis were quite aware of that situation and even developed guidelines to help individuals deal with that issue. Here are a few traditional comments:

1. In the Talmud the observation is made that being killed is a better fate than famine and its suffering. Captivity, however, is recognized as being a worse fate than either of the other two, for a person in captivity is at the mercy of his/her captors.

2. Within our tradition there is also the recognition that redeeming captives is an important responsibility. Community funds intended for other purposes could be used to pay ransoms. In fact, let's say that money had been collected to build a synagogue. The Talmud tells us that those funds could be used instead to redeem a captive. If that money had been used to buy building materials, those materials could be resold to get the necessary funds to pay the ransom. The Rabbis, however, indicated that should the synagogue already be erected, it could not be sold to get money to pay a ransom.

3. What about the amount paid? The Talmud tells us that captives should not be redeemed for more than their value for the good of society (e.g. to prevent abuses).

4. It also indicates that captives shouldn't be helped to escape, to prevent any abuses. Rabbi Simeon B. Gamaliel felt that the reason for this was to prevent any abuses of fellow captives (e.g. those who didn't manage to escape).

5. What if there was a situation where there was more than one captive and a choice had to be made as to whom would be saved first?
   If it was a choice between a man or a woman, we are told that a woman should be rescued from captivity before a man. But if it's a situation where captives could be sexually abused, or both are in danger of losing their lives, the man preceeds the woman.

6. But the tradition doesn't just let it go at that. In the Talmud we are given even more suggestions as to priorities, when trying to bring about the release of captives. Let's say a man, his father and his teacher are all captured. The man, we are told, may first ransom himself and then his teacher and then his father (in that order! — So remember **that** the next time you feel like giving your teacher a hard time). And of course one's mother takes precedence over all of the above!

7. Moreover a scholar takes precedence over a king of Israel. (This is rather suspect — after all, scholars and not kings wrote the Talmud; however, the comment is made that scholars are harder to replace than kings!)

128

CONSIDER THIS:

1. What part of these comments concerning traditional views about ransoming captives do you like the best? Why?

2. What part do you like the least? Why?

3. Do you feel that the comment against helping a captive try to escape is justified? Why? Why not?

4. If you were to help the Rabbis revise their guidelines what might you suggest? Why?

❖◆❖◆❖◆❖

FOCUS ON: CRIME AND SOCIETY

Again, this section is included here in a war chapter, primarily because its subject, crime, sometimes involves violence.

129

The problem of ransoming captives has been with us for many centuries.

Statement from Q:

Sure, everybody is concerned with crime. The current approaches to fighting crime are inadequate. First of all we really need to put our priorities where they should be. Let's face it, punishment doesn't really serve as a deterrent to crime. Rather than concentrating on more and more penalties for criminal acts we should really concentrate on the underlying causes of crime. Perpetrators of crime are really victims of both government and societal attitudes. If a person must resort to robbery in order to make a living, that's because social conditions were such that, that individual was forced into it. I say clean up the causes and you will reduce crime. Certainly a society that could help rebuild Europe after World War II or put a man on the moon has the knowledge and the resources to rebuild our cities!

Statement from J:

I believe that Q is all wet! Q talks in terms of eliminating the underlying causes of crime yet the researchers are still arguing as to just what brings it about. Is crime due to environmental, genetic or social causes? — Even the so-called experts don't know. How can Q suggest that we eliminate a "cause", if it is unclear just what that "cause" is? Moreover it's all good and fine for Q to blame it on society, but what good does that do for an innocent person who is mugged? I say let's crack down on law breakers. The Muslims had the right idea. If somebody stole something his/her hand would be amputated. Maybe we should do the same thing. Penalties like that would bring about some law and order. Let's get rid of paroles and make punishment for breaking laws something to be avoided. Moreover we have a double standard of law in this country. If you're wealthy you can get away with more. I say let's standardize the law throughout the country and enforce it with equal severity. That will encourage more respect and reduce crime!

130

CONSIDER THIS:

1. What was the basic issue discussed by these two statements?

2. What does Q's statement imply? How do you feel about it? Why?

3. What about J's statement? What would that position imply? How do you feel about it? Why?

4. If there was an election who would you support, Q or J? Why? (Assume that you must support one or the other, and that the issue raised above is the only one!)

5. If you were in a position to try to solve the problem of crime in our society how would you go about it? Explain why whatever course of action you suggest would be superior.

SUMMARY:

In this chapter we examined some Jewish perspectives on war. While Judaism longs for an era in which war will be eliminated, it nonetheless recognizes the practical realities of a world in which armed conflict exists. Our ancestors recognized that war doesn't just happen. It is caused. They speculated as to what factors help bring it about. Distinctions were made as to different "types" of war.

Earlier distinctions between warfare inside and outside Canaan were followed by the categories of **Milchemet Chovah** — Obligatory War and **Milchemet R'shut** — Optional War. We noted that even in Biblical times, the issue of military exemptions came up. An area that most people commonly overlook is that of the environmental impact of warfare. Ecological considerations, both in terms of maltreatment of environment, as well as personal cleanliness were discussed. Additional material, relating to Self-Defense, Ransoming Kidnapped Victims, and Crime, rounded off this unit.

CONSIDER THIS:

1. Give some examples from history and/or current events of Obligatory and Optional Wars.

2. Is it possible for a country at war to be ethical? Why? Why not?

3. Which is more ethically justifiable — an Obligatory War or an Optional War? Why?

4. Why do you suppose this distinction was made? Is it a valid distinction?

5. Why do you suppose Maimonides felt that military exemptions should be allowed in an Optional War, but not allowed in an Obligatory War?

6. Why do you suppose that a suggestion would be made that the Sanhedrin be involved in declaring an Optional War?

7. Bill, a student who read this chapter commented: "Anyone who is exempt from military service, but is involved in providing backup services such as food and water is really killing the enemy as surely as if he were on the battlefield." Do you agree? Why or Why not?

8. What were the Biblical exemptions from military service? Were they fair? Why? Why not?

9. Another comment as to the treatment of captives is to be found in the book of Deuteronomy (21:10-14):

> *When you go forth to war against your enemies and the Lord delivers them to your hands and you have taken them captive; and you see among the captives a beautiful woman and desire her, that you would have her as your wife; then you will bring her home to your house; and she will shave her head and pare her nails; and she will discard the clothes she had when captured, and will remain in your house and mourn for her parents a full month; and after that you will go in unto her and be her husband and she will be your wife. And if you have no delight in her, then you will let her go free; you will not sell her . . . because you humbled her.*

Remember that this was written thousands of years ago. Discuss in terms of the earlier comments concerning treatment of captives. In what ways does it seem advanced for its time? In what ways would we agree or disagree with it today?

10. The situation between the countries of Osloff and Berimba has been getting

increasingly tense. The Berimbans sealed off the border, preventing the Trans-national Railroad from running. Osloff does most of its trade by shipping its goods by that railroad through Berimba to a port on the Sea of Water. In the last twelve hours the general of the Osloffian armed forces has received reports of five Berimban army divisions being sent to the border region. In the event of war, the chances are 50:50 that either side would win. You are to advise the Osloffian commander what to do!

☐ = Berimba Military Division

P.S. If Osloff were to launch an immediate attack before the Berimbans did, would this be an example of Milchemet Chovah, or Milchemet R'shut? Why? Why not?

11. Are our ideas about the sanctity of life harmonious with such needs as national defense? Aren't we really being hypocritical when we "arm ourselves for peace"? Why? Why not?

12. Is a person justified to refuse to serve in the military forces, when his/her country is at war? What if this person claimed that the war was unjust? Would that substantiate that person's stance? What exactly causes a particular war to be "unjust"?

13. In this unit we indicated that Judaism recognized that there are various reasons for war to break out. Would such a recognition contain the seeds for the eradication of war? Why? Why not?

14. The Amalekites' attack was considered very treacherous, the epitome of evil. Is it obligatory to fight an enemy who is very evil — because that enemy is evil? (e.g. See Exodus 17:16) Why? Why not?

15. Do you agree with the comments on self-defense? Why? Why not? To what extent should one go to defend him/herself? (Once again, can the ends justify the means?)

16. Maimonides also made the comment that when a city is besieged, it should be surrounded on only three sides. Why do you suppose that course of action is suggested? Analyze in detail!

17. Look up Lev. 19: 17-18 in the Bible. Discuss as it relates to this unit.

132

134

unit eight

Stealing & Cheating

STEALING – A GOODY-GOODY SUBJECT SUITABLE ONLY FOR RELIGIOUS SCHOOL?

Sometimes people have the idea that stealing is such a basic concept, and is considered so universally bad, that the major place to discuss it is in a Religious School class in "goody-goody tones" (e.g. – "It's not nice to steal!"). Yet the stark reality is that stealing of all forms is far more prevalent in our society than we'd care to admit. From time to time, the more bizarre cases get into the news. There was for example, the story of the man who over a period of years walked off with thousands of public library books, or the sales clerk who under rang every sale on the cash register by a penny, thus taking home five dollars extra every day – for twenty-two years! Did you know that in a single year over four thousand Bibles were "removed" from hotel rooms in New York City? Security experts tell us that among other things clocks, typewriters, dishes, furniture, fire extinguishers and even toilet paper are "walking away" in unprecedented amounts. Someone was recently caught trying to steal a plant from a public place. The person's excuse – "I was only trying to give it a decent home." In a study of customer habits, five hundred shoppers, picked randomly were watched. Out of that number, one in twelve stole something! Is the thief a shady character of questionable background? No. Believe it or not, your "average thief" is a nice person, beloved by the boss and the kids who lives in a nice neighborhood and attends religious services! Incidently U.S. Government statistics indicate that businesses lose about **forty billion** – that's right **billion** – dollars a year, in crime ranging from outright employee theft and shoplifting to bribery and frauds. How do we all suffer for this? Consumers end up paying higher prices!

SOAP BOX DERBY

A few years back a rather interesting news item appeared in the New York Times. The story started harmlessly enough. A boy wanted to enter the National Soap-box Derby. His cousin had won it the year before. That's about where the innocence ends. The boy's uncle decided to help out. He persuaded his nephew to install a special electromagnetic device in the car. This device would give his car the added advantage of a faster start! It also was against the rules.

Well the day of the big race came and the boy ended up winning first place! A few days later, the secret of his success became known and he was disqualified. Although no legal action was taken against the boy, his Uncle was taken to court.

While Mr. L. felt that their course of action was an error, he nonetheless said that it was justifiable. He argued that breaking the rules was common practice in the Derby Races and was necessary to win.

CONSIDER THIS:

1. What are Mr. L.'s two justifications for cheating?

2. Do you agree with them? Why? Why not?

3. It has been said — "It's not who wins or loses, but how you play the game." It has also been said — "The only good loser is a born loser." What are both of these statements saying? Which do you agree with? Why?

4. Is winning the most important thing? Why do you suppose people are often so concerned about winning?

5. A fellow named Samuel Butler once made the observation (roughly paraphrased here) that we often hear about the death of a successful person with private satisfaction, for successful people are generally humbugs. Do you agree? Why? Why not? Isn't it possible to be successful and still ethical? Why? Why not?

❖◆❖◆❖◆

WHAT IS "WINNING"?

Even though this chapter centers around cheating and stealing, a basic issue was raised in the soapbox derby incident. What really constitutes "winning"? What really defines "success"? One could make a very strong argument that Judaism has always been in favor of a person trying "to achieve". The Biblical stories of Joseph or David certainly portray people trying to get ahead. A very wise man named Abraham Maslow once indicated that there are various levels of needs that we all have. These are summarized in the diagram below. Self-actualization is an interesting one. It's when a person really kind of grows and becomes more

creative; "really doing his/her own thing". An old Jewish tale kind of sums that one up; Rabbi Zusya was about to die. His disciples asked him for any final words of advice that he might have. Zusya responded " . . . When I die, I won't be asked in the world to come "Why weren't you Moses?" but rather "Why weren't you Zusya?" To me that illustrates a good point. How many of us ever really live up to all that we could be? — to our fullest potential? Could that be "winning"? Could be! But if that view of "winning" doesn't seem satisfactory to you look at

p. 40
p. 122
p. 196
p. 169

and let's see what you can come up with!

Oh yes, one last question to think about. (Oh my aching head!!) If we were all always successful and happy — would those terms have any meaning? Could it ever possibly be so?

THE BOX

Mrs. Andrews put the last bag of garbage into the huge box. "Phew does that stink," said Mr. Andrews as he walked into the kitchen. "Yes it sure does, so get Roger to help you take it out of here." "O.K.," responded her husband. "Hey

137

Roger . . ., Roger." "Yes Dad?" Roger came in from the den. "Roger, your mother wants us to get this box of garbage outside. It's not too heavy but with my weak back I don't want to lug it myself." "It's not bad at all," said Roger as he lifted the box momentarily. "Look Dad, you relax, and I'll put it outside my-self." "Good," said Mr. Andrews. "Say Mom, where is the rope?" Roger looked through one of the drawers. "I'm sorry, we're all out, but here's some ribbon. Maybe that will do," responded Mrs. Andrews. She handed him several long pieces of bright red ribbon. Roger took the ribbon and tied the box up. Having a little extra ribbon left, he even added a bow. The box which originally was used to ship stereo equipment still had all of the advertising markings. "Oh you darned fool." Mrs. Andrew came into the room. "It looks like a birthday gift . . . Enough of being a creative artist. Get it out of here!" Roger lugged the box out into the yard. Before he had a chance to put it in the customary garbage pick-up spot his Dad came to the window. "Roger! . . . Telephone! . . . It's Melinda!" Talking to his girl friend Melinda was far more interesting than putting out a box filled with garbage. Roger left the box in the middle of the lawn and ran inside the house.

A station wagon turned the corner. "Hey Jack," said the passenger sitting in the front seat to the driver sitting next to him. "Look at that; fancy stereo equipment!" The driver stopped the car. "Yeah you're right . . . The box is even gift wrapped . . . It must be a present of some sort . . . Bill, do you see anyone around?" "Nah." His friend quickly glanced up and down the street. "Then let's go," responded Jack. "You mean take the box? . . . What if we get caught?" "We won't if we move fast enough," responded the driver. The two friends dashed out to middle of the lawn and quickly lugged the box to the car. In a flash it was stashed in the back. As the station wagon went around the corner Jack commented to Bill "I can hardly wait to see the look on my wife's face when I let her open this box!"

ENGLISH CLASS BLUES

Linc was fed up. Here his parents were going skiing next weekend, and he would be stuck at home. It wasn't fair! He looked at the clock. "This is the dumbest English Class I've ever sat through!" he thought. "Let's liven it up a bit!" With that in mind, he started to stomp his feet and raise a general commotion. Some of the other kids around him, irritated because his noise prevented them from hearing the lesson, told him to keep quiet. The teacher, distracted because of the commotion, had to stop the lecture.

SALLY

Sally was exhausted! What a pain it was moonlighting. If Mr. Pebbles would only pay her a half decent salary then she wouldn't have to hold two jobs. "Let's see, $2.79, $3.25 and five percent tax; that comes to $6.75." "Hold it" said the customer. "As I see it you are overcharging me by about forty cents." "I'm sorry Sir, you're right. It's only $6.34. Here's your change."

PIANO LESSONS

"Of course you will take piano lessons this season!" Mr. Firble beamed at his daughter Joan. "But Dad, we've been through this before. I'm willing to take some piano lessons, but I'd also like to go into The Peewee Hockey Team." "No," said Mr. Firble. "Just as I said last year, the only extra activity that I will allow you to do is the piano . . . I want you to become a great virtuoso! . . ." "But Dad," protested Joan, "I've tried the piano . . . I'm working at it but I'm just not that good . . . besides I'd like to do other things too."

KARIMA X

Karima is a High School Senior. He's grown up in the Ghetto. There are five children in his family. They live in a three room apartment. Karima's mother is seldom around for she's working. Karima has never met his father. Conditions in the apartment are deplorable. His little sister was bitten by a rat the other day, and despite Mrs. X's best efforts, the family is continually hungry. Karima wanders into another more affluent part of the city, sees a little old lady slowly making her way down the street, pushes her down and grabs her pocket book. The woman is injured and ends up in the hospital. Karima is identified and caught. Because of his age and the fact that it's a first offense the Judge let's him go stating that "it's society's fault."

HARRY

Harry had a good job working at the Yum Yum Candy Company. The owner, Mr. Jones, was a pleasant man to work for, and paid him a good salary. In addition, Harry received a number of fringe benefits that one might normally not expect. In return for this Harry worked extra hard and took on extra responsibilities to make himself even more useful. Then one day Jones hired Sam to work in the same department with Harry. Harry tried to be friendly but he couldn't stand Sam. Maybe it was Sam's constant clumsiness or perhaps his incessant whistling. At any rate within a month Harry was a bundle of nerves. Finally not being able to stand it any longer he marched into Mr. Jones' office and asked for a raise of $2.00 per hour. Harry didn't really expect to receive the raise and hoped that Jones would fire him. At least that way he wouldn't have to work with Sam!

SNOWSTORM

It was the worst winter in the past fifty years. Brownsville had been completely snowed in. When it began it had seemed harmless enough; but one snowstorm followed another. The cleanup crews, normally quite efficient fell behind. Fifty-five inches of snow in a two week period completely immobilized that part of the state. The superhighways were closed. The airports were unable to function. Everything had come to a standstill. State and Federal aid was slow in coming. Bob and Marcy Engel were in a quandary. They had two small children. Their food supplies were just about exhausted. Quigley's, the neighborhood grocer had been closed for the past week. Bob and Marcy slowly made their way to the store and forced open a small window in the back. They filled two bags which they had brought with them with food. It was late at night and they returned to their house seemingly undetected. Unknown to the Engels, they had accidently tripped a burglar device in the store. A special infrared movie camera had recorded their every action.

BAD RECORD

Jeff had made a mistake. Twenty-two years before he and a couple of friends had held up a local liquor store. They were arrested and sent to prison. Because Jeff had never been in trouble until that time, his sentence was relatively light. Within a few years he was out of prison . . . .He never returned home, though. Instead he drifted for a while traveling from one small town to another. Eventually he landed up in Gulcher, a small university community. In Gulcher he made a few friends and found a job in the grounds and buildings department of the local university. He stayed on that job for a few years. During his free time Jeff sat in on some of the university courses, and found that they seemed interesting. This came as quite a surprise to him for he had previously found high school to be so dull that he had dropped out! Although Jeff attended some classes he never bothered to enroll as a student. Eventually Jeff got bored with his job and moved to Cleveland. Trying one job after another, he ended up with a sales position in a big electronics company. Jeff worked hard and excelled. He was finally putting money in the bank! The work was challenging and Jeff was happy! But then, last week Jeff was given some news that made him feel ill. He was going to receive a promotion to an executive position. Not that he didn't want the position. He wanted it more than anything else in the world! The problem was that he had falsified his background when he had first gone to work for the company. The form which he had filled out asked if he had ever been arrested or convicted of a crime. He had denied it. He also had told the company that he had attended college. Jeff knows that the store doesn't really double check the information when it concerns a sales job. However he realizes that the background of candidates for executive spots is thoroughly researched.

BASEBALL AND MATH

Hal is quite upset. He wants to be on the school baseball team in the worst way.

139

His parents, however, have given him an ultimatum. In order to stay on the team he must have honor grades in all of his subjects. In such subjects as english and social studies, Hal finds it quite easy to get top scores. Turn to a math text, however, and Hal quite literally breaks out in a cold sweat. It's not that he is a hopeless case. Hal has been managing to pass math. But he hasn't been able to raise his grade above mere passing. Unless Hal can manage at least a B in the subject, his parents won't allow him to remain on the team. Not only would this be personally frustrating; it would also be a disaster for the team. Hal happens to be the best pitcher they have. Should Hal be forbidden to play, the possibility of the team making the regional finals would be greatly diminished.

Time: One week later.
Place: The Grande School.

Hal sits down to take his math test. This is the test that will make the difference between playing or sitting out the rest of the season. Hal looks down at the exam. Oh no! He goes blank. This is the first time in his career as a student that he has studied something, but is so nervous that he just can't think! A teacher enters the room and talks to Mr. O'Brien, the math instructor. O'Brien gets up and says to the class, "I am going to have to leave the classroom for a short time. While I'm gone you're on your honor." At that point both teachers leave the room.

Hal's best friend Joe is sitting in the next row. Joe is very good at math. He is also on the baseball team. Hal has never cheated before in his life. He looks down at his paper, and then over at Joe.

140   **CONSIDER THIS**:

THE BOX

1. Who stole from whom? Was the Andrews family "stealing" from the two gentlemen in the station wagon or visa versa? Why?

2. Did this story turn out satisfactorily? Why? Why not?

ENGLISH CLASS BLUES

1. Were Linc's actions a form of stealing? Why? Why not? He didn't actually take any physical property. It is possible to steal without removing a physical object? How? Analyze in relation to this situation.

2. We are told that Linc was upset. Would our knowledge of that fact enable us to excuse his actions? Why? Why not?

3. What would you do if you were the teacher? Why?

SALLY

1. Why did Sally make her error?

2. Was Sally's error a form of stealing? Why? Why not?

3. Who was more guilty of stealing: Sally or her boss, Mr. Pebbles? Why?

PIANO LESSONS

1. What is the basic conflict here?

2. Who is "right", Mr. Firble or his daughter Joan? Why?

3. Why would this be considered an example of stealing? (After all, as in "English Class Blues", no physical property is being removed).

KARIMA X

1. Why did Karima commit his crime?

2. What did you think of the reason that the judge offered for letting Karima X go? Did you agree? Disagree? Why?

3. In this example we had **more** than one example of stealing. What were they? Which do you feel is worse? Why?

4. If you were the judge, what would you do?

HARRY

1. Was Harry really trying to cheat or steal from his boss? Why? Why not?

2. Was the reason given for his actions sufficient justification? Why? Why not?

3. If you were Mr. Jones, what would you do?

SNOWSTORM

1. Why did Bob and Marcy Engel burglarize the store?

2. Would their circumstances justify their actions? Why? Why not?

3. If you were the owners of the store what would your options be?

4. If you were the owners of the store what course of action would you follow? Why?

5. Was there any other way that the Engels could have handled the situation? Any that would have been more ethical? How? Analyze in detail.

BAD RECORD

1. What is Jeff's problem?

2. Why do you suppose Jeff falsified the application form that he had to fill out when he first went to work for the store?

3. Was that action wrong? Why? Why not?

4. Is it right for a person to suffer for a mistake s/he made many years before? Why? Why not?

5. Would it make any difference in this situation if Jeff's first crime had involved something like murder (rather than armed robbery)?

6. What are Jeff's options?

7. What would you suggest he do? Why?

BASEBALL AND MATH

1. What are Hal's various **options?** (e.g. cheat, not cheat etc.).

2. What are the **possible outcomes** that may result from following each of the various options that Hal has available to him?

3. Summarize your answers of one and two in chart form as follows:

Option	**Posible Outcomes**
1. – – – –	a. – – – –
	b. – – – –
	c. – – – –
	d. – – – –
2. – – – –	
etc.	

(While this is a fairly simple example, you might find that analyzing **options** and **possible outcomes** in chart form will help you think through other more complex ethical dilemmas, that you may encounter).

142

4. Should Hal cheat? Why? Why not?

5. What might happen if he does cheat? If he doesn't cheat?

6. What would be Hal's reasons for cheating? Would they justify that course of action?

7. How could cheating affect Hal's perception of himself? How could following each of his other possible options affect his perception of himself? (Analyze each one).

8. How could Hal's course of action affect his friendship with Joe? Analyze each option and possible outcome with that factor in mind.

9. What about Hal's relationship with his teacher? Analyze each of Hal's options, possible outcomes, with that factor in mind.

10. What if Hal decided to cheat, but promised himself that it would only be this once under emergency conditions? How do you feel about that justification? Why?

11. Is there any difference between someone who cheats continually and someone who cheats only once in a while or in an emergency? If so what is it? If not, why not?

12. How could additional knowledge (e.g. about Joe, about Mr. O'Brien), affect how you would handle this situation (if you were Hal)?

Felix Weatherby slammed the door of his friend's car. "Thanks for the ride Henry!" "My pleasure Felix. See you tomorrow," replied his friend. The seventy-three Chevy turned the corner as Felix entered the house. Felix was a departmental manager working for the Billings Corporation. He had his own car, but he was forced to admit that this car-pooling system worked out by the company vice-president had its advantages. It saved money, anyhow. "Anybody home?" he called. No answer. His wife Jane was a buyer for a local supermarket. "She's apparently not home yet," he thought. Ajax, their son wasn't around either. "Oh of course," he thought; "with the Zebras in the play-offs Ajax wouldn't be around right now!" The Zebras were the local school ice-hockey team. As the team was in the semi-finals, Ajax spent more time in practice than in the house. Felix picked up the mail from the chute and went into the den. "Now what have we got here?", he said to himself. "Bills, bills and more bills, with a touch of junk mail thrown in for variety." Felix tore open one letter after another. "Wait a minute . . ." Felix had opened what he thought would be a bill from the White Department Store. He had purchased a coffee percolator from them when he had been in Washington on a trip there early in the month. Slam! The door opened and closed. Jane was home. "Hi dear." She came into the den. "Jane, look at this!" he said. "What, White Department Store? Didn't you buy a present for Janice and Bob there when you were out on the West coast?" she asked. "Yeah, but instead of billing me $19.95, they've sent me a check for $175,000." Felix looked sick. He had never seen so much money at one time in one place, and of course it had to go back! "Oh boy," replied Jane. "Their computer really messed up this one!" Felix sat down at his typewriter:

143

> 2020 Mission Lane
> Boston, Ma., 02114

Sirs,

On the fifth of the month I purchased a Zingon Coffee Percolator from your Washington store. Instead of getting billed $19.95, I have received a check of $175,000. Please advise. My account number is 003-279-41098.

> Sincerely,
> Felix Weatherby

"What do we do in the meantime?" Felix asked his wife. "Well I suppose we should put it into a special bank account until the store straightens the mess out. At least that way it'll be safe," she responded.

The weeks passed. Felix followed Jane's suggestion to safeguard the money. The Zebras won the semifinals and went on to become the state champions! Outside of that life went on normally. Although Felix had sent the letter off to White Department Store, he still had heard nothing.

"Felix it's arrived!" Jane ran into the living room. "Two letters from White Department Store." She was still clutching the rest of the mail in her other hand.

"Well it's been a month . . . It's about time . . . Let's see what we've got here . . ."
Felix tore one envelope open and read the contents:

White Department Store
Accounting Department
Washington Branch

Dear Mr. Weatherby,

Our Accounting Department is now automated and is under the expert guidance
of the B.R.P. 150, computer. Please be advised that all of your accounts have been
settled in full and we look forward to your future patronage.

Sincerely yours,
B.R.P. 150.

"I don't believe this," gasped Jane. "Hold it Jane, let's not go into shock . . .
There's a second letter here from White's." Felix ripped open the second en-
velope. Inside was another check, this one for seventy-five thousand dollars.
"Go into shock" he stammered!

2020 Mission Lane
Boston, Mass., 02114

Gentlemen,

I still would like to pay for that percolator, – $19.95 – remember? And where
you've sent us a second check for seventy-five thousand dollars you should have
noticed that you are now missing a grand total of $250,000. Now wake up the
idiot in charge of that department and give us instructions as to how to handle
the transfer of funds back to your company. I want to make certain there is no
slip-up and that the proper authority gets the money.

Disgustedly,
Felix Weatherby.

One Month Later:

White Department Store
Accounting Department
Washington Branch

Dear Mr. Weatherby,

Our Accounting Department is now automated and is under the expert guidance
of the B.R.P. 150 Computer. Please be advised that all of your accounts have been
settled in full and we look forward to your future patronage.

Sincerely yours,
B.R.P. 150.

"I don't believe this," groaned Jane. "Shazaam!" exclaimed Felix. In a second
envelope was another check, this one for $125,000. "Well what are you going to
do?" asked Jane. "I don't know." responded Felix "At this stage I'm almost

tempted to keep the money!"

DECISION!

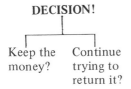

Keep the money?   Continue trying to return it?

1. What should Jane and Felix do? The Weatherby's have received a grand total of $375,000 from the White Department Store. Should Jane and Felix persist in their efforts to return the money or should they follow the impulse to keep the money? Why? What about the interest on the money?

2. Finish the story. Be creative!

SCIENTIFIC ADVANCES

Here's a rather fascinating ethical dilemma for you to consider. Most scientific advances are based on the work of others! For example we commonly think of Marconi as the inventor of the radio, yet the first person to transmit radio waves was a man (from a Jewish family) named Heinrich Hertz! Marconi's work was based on Hertz's! In fact Hertz's work also helped pave the way for the "invention" of T.V. Similarly it was the work of Otto Lilienthal in gliding, that helped the Wright brothers. You are, I am sure, aware of the fact that Alexander Graham Bell first invented the telephone. Wrong! Johann Reis (a Jewish fellow) was the first (by about fifteen years). Indeed the U.S. Government even tried to sue Bell, because the theft was so blatant!

145

Columbus might have discovered the "new world," but the name America came from Amerigo Vespucci! And what about knowledge that is discovered, forgotten and then rediscovered? Columbus supposedly discovered that the world is round. Yet that fact is recorded both in the Talmud and Zohar hundreds of years before Columbus was born! We credit Darwin with the discovery of evolution, yet Aristotle noted variations between generations and increasing complexity in various life forms. In fact there is even material in our Jewish tradition that tells us that humankind originally was created with tails and for a period of time had faces resembling monkeys!

How would you evaluate these various situations? In some "borrowing" is obvious, in others no intentional theft is involved. Is the common scientific practice of building on the work of others really "stealing"? Is it good or bad? Why?

FOCUS ON: JUDAISM AND BUSINESS ETHICS

When we get into the issue of cheating or stealing, there are numerous points which we could focus upon in discussion. One area that has always fascinated me was some of the Jewish thinking about the subject of Business Ethics. Please keep in mind that what is to follow is but a **small** sampling of a huge amount of available material.

The first thing that should be pointed out is that Judaism has always had a very positive conception of work. The comment is made in the Talmud that "Great is work for it honors the person that performs it." Here's a neat story:

> An old man was at work planting a fig tree. The Roman Emperor Hadrian was in the neighborhood and wandered by. "Hey, old man, why are you working so hard? Do you expect to live long enough to eat the fruit of that tree?" As you'll recall from Unit 3 the old man's response was that if he didn't enjoy the fruit of the tree, certainly his kids would. Well, three years later Hadrian wandered by again! The old man was still alive, and was working in the garden. When he saw Hadrian, he filled a basket with figs, identified himself, and gave the Emperor the gift. Hadrian admired the old man's chutzpah, and intestinal fortitude. He had the basket filled with gold and returned to the old man. Well word got around, and a rather greedy woman got a smart idea. "Bernie", (or whatever her husband's name was), "Take a basket of fruit to the Emperor so we can get a basket of gold too." Well her husband did what she "suggested". "Oh great Emperor Hadrian, here is a basket of fruit for you to enjoy." Well the Emperor was no fool. In fact he got pretty annoyed. He had Bernie thrown out, and gave his soldiers orders to pelt him with his own fruit. (A rather painful, not to mention messy affair!) He finally got back to his home. "Well how did you do?" asked his wife. "Oh wonderful dear . . . Had I taken something large like watermelons I would have been killed."

Moral number one: Labor is a yes-yes. But this tale also illustrates another extremely important point.

146

Moral number two: Labor must involve **honesty**. Anything less than honesty such as the attempt at freeloading described above is a no-no. There are some really fascinating stories in our tradition that illustrate how seriously this bit about being honest was taken:

> A Rabbi purchased a donkey from an Arab. He discovered a pearl accidently left in the animal's saddle. He insisted, however, that the pearl be returned to the original owner. When questioned as to why he didn't keep the pearl which was quite valuable he responded, "I bought the donkey . . . not the pearl".

Here's another story, even more intriguing:

> One day a Rabbi met a few people who left a few measures of barley in his care. They apparently forgot about it and departed from town. The Rabbi planted the barley and stored the profits. This went on for about seven years. When the people who entrusted him with the barley finally showed up, the Rabbi made certain that they received their profits.

This thing about honesty underlies much of what will be said about business ethics. But there is something even more basic that is involved; a sense of fairplay. In any aspect of business dealings the Jewish tradition has always worked hard at making sure that all parties involved are treated fairly. Time and time again we read the eloquent words of the prophets condemning exploitation in their day:

For among my people are found wicked men:
They lay in wait, as one who sets snares;
They set a trap, they catch men;
As a cage is full of birds, so are their houses full of deceit;
Therefore they've become great and rich.
They are waxen fat, they shine — yea, they overpass the deeds of the
wicked:
They don't plead the cause, the cause of the fatherless,
Yet they prosper; And the right of the needy do they not judge.
                                                        Jeremiah 5:26-28

And Ezekiel made the comment:

The people of the land have used oppression and have exercised robbery
and have vexed the poor and needy: yea they have oppressed the
stranger wrongfully.
                                                        Ezekiel 22:29

These are but several of the many comments made by the Jewish Prophets. Many
people have the incorrect notion that the prophets were people who could somehow miraculously predict the future. Actually, the prophets were intelligent
observers of society somewhat like members of the news media today who
give editorials, news analysis and personal commentary etc. Because they watched
carefully what was going on, the prophets were able to give educated opinions.
They were a rather colorful collection of individuals (e.g. one of them lay on his
left side for 390 days, then on his right side for forty days — to illustrate a point,
not to get a sunburn! See Ezekiel 4:4-6). They were quite controversial. I like   147
to think of them as the hippies, the rebels of their day! But theirs was the voice of
social justice:

. . . Your hands are full of blood .
Wash yourselves, make yourselves clean;
Put away the evil of your doings from before my eyes.
Cease to do evil; learn to do well; seek judgement.
Relieve the oppressed, judge the fatherless, plead for the widow.
                                                        Isaiah I: 15-17

A sense then, of fairplay, of social justice, characterizes the Jewish approach.

Well then, let's get down to specifics! One thing that Jewish sources insist on is
that neither the worker nor his/her employer take advantage of the other. For
example, in the Mishnah it states:

If one hires workmen and they retracted (pulled out of an agreement),
they are at a disadvantage; if the employer withdrew from an agreement
he is at a disadvantage. Whoever alters the terms of a contract is at a
disadvantage and whoever withdraws from an agreement is at a
disadvantage.

Now that sounds messy, but it really isn't. What it comes down to is that a contract or deal between an employer and his/her workers is mutually binding. The
person who breaks the deal ends up being at a disadvantage in settling. But you
can see neither the employer nor the employee is automatically favored. It depends on who pulled out of the deal, causing the other party extra hassles.

What about time of payment? In the Bible the comment is made:

> *You will not oppress a hired servant who is poor and needy whether he is of your brethren or of strangers that are within your land, within your gates. On the same day you will give him his hire, nor shall the sun go down upon it, for he is poor and set his heart on it . . .*
>
> *Deuteronomy 24:14-15*

In Leviticus 19:13 the comment is made that the wages of an employee shouldn't stay with the employer all night until the morning. In other words these passages point to the fact that when an employer hires people s/he should pay them as soon as possible!

FOUR CHARACTERS

There are four kinds of characters among human beings:

One who says — What's mine is mine, and what's yours is yours — This is the ordinary person.

One who says — What's mine is yours and what's yours is mine — This is an idiot.

One who says — What's mine is yours and what's yours is yours — This is a benevolent person.

One who says — What's mine is mine and what's yours is mine — This is a wicked person.

from Pirke Avot

What other obligations does the employer have? The Mishnah tells us:

> *If one hired workmen and asked them to work very early in the morning or very late at night, he has no right to force them to do so in any area where it is not customary to work early or late; where it is the custom to furnish them with food, he must supply his workers with food; if it is the custom to supply the workers with refreshments, he must do so; everything should be in accord with local custom.*

In the Talmud there is a further comment relating to the problem of length of hours. The Gemara points out that an employer can't force a laborer to work longer than the norm (if s/he doesn't want to) even with the promise of extra pay. (After all the employee could respond that more pay is for better work, but not for longer hours).

Another rather interesting discussion centers around laborers who work in the fields. There was a great deal of farming going on in Israel in ancient times. Naturally that would affect laws dealing with business. The Mishnah makes the comment that a laborer working in the fields can eat from the ripened produce of the soil (fringe benefits!). Now there are, believe it or not, various rules and regulations concerning this particular practice. The comment that I like the best

concerns how much a laborer should eat. Eleazar ben Chisma felt that a worker should not eat any more than the value of his/her wages. The majority of sages however permitted it. Nonetheless they stressed that a worker who is too much of a pig might find that employers won't want to hire him/her.

While our discussion here is of necessity a summary (much could be written about the subject of Jewish business ethics alone), the following story will show you just how "picky", and "detailed" the whole subject can get:

> One day Rabbi Johanan told his son to hire some workers. The son did so and began to make arrangements to provide them with food. When he reported back to his father, Rabbi Johanan was not entirely thrilled. "My son, even if you prepared for them a banquet like one of Solomon's (renowned for high living), you wouldn't have fulfilled your obligation towards them . . . Before they start to work go and tell them, 'You are to work on the condition that I don't have to give you anything more than bread and pulse (beans etc.).'"

Rabbi Johanan felt that it was important that the type of food be specified in advance. After all, unless it was agreed upon before the workmen even began, the food might not be accepted no matter how fancy or elaborate it actually was. This bit about bread and pulse sounds rather gross, but remember eating habits do vary according to the time and place. This particular story discussed above is found in the Mishnah. Interestingly enough another Rabbi, Rabbi Simon heard about what happened and felt that Rabbi Johanan was overreacting, because after all, the entire issue could be settled according to local custom! (Rabbi Simon's comments were also recorded in the Mishnah!)

Just as an employer has certain responsibilities to the people s/he hires, so too does the employee have an obligation to the boss. A worker must not shortchange his/her boss in terms of the amount of work s/he produces. Jewish sources go so far as to indicate that a worker has no right to hold other jobs or to eat less (e.g. in order to feed his/her family) if that will diminish his/her efficiency on the job. In terms of personal experience, I remember once having a teacher who was so busy "moonlighting" on a second job, that as a result his teaching was horrendous except on a Monday (after a weekend) or following a vacation. Perhaps this individual should have read the Jewish laws on the subject! Maimonides makes the comment in his Mishneh Torah that while an employer shouldn't delay a laborer's wages, so too the worker shouldn't "steal from" the boss by wasting time, a little here and there, on the job. (too many coffee breaks!) The Jewish tradition indicates that a craftsperson is liable for damages s/he causes to something entrusted to his/her care. (Yet we also find a demand for leniency on the employer's behalf). In addition Maimonides points out that anyone holding a job of community trust and responsibility who messes it up and can't make good, can be removed from that office.

Just as the employer and the employee hold obligations to each other, so too, is it necessary that a consumer of any goods produced be dealt with fairly. A legend states that when a person dies and comes up before God for questioning, the first question that will be asked will be "Were you honest when you did business?". One important area involving fairness to consumers concerns proper weights and measures. Whenever someone buys something such as food, naturally s/he will be charged according to the amount of whatever is being purchased. Unless care is taken to insure that whatever measuring devices that are used are accurate, consumers can easily be cheated. Thus we find this comment in the Mishnah:

150

> *The wholesaler must clean out his measures once every thirty days and the householder once every twelve months. Rabbi Simon felt that the opposite is necessary. The storekeeper must clean his measures twice a week, rub up his weights once a week, and polish the scales before each weighing.*

TALMUDIC LAWS FOR SELLING

If one has sold wheat to another as good wheat and it turns out to be bad, the buyer can withdraw from the deal.

If it is sold as bad, and turns out to be good, the seller may withdraw from the deal.

If it is sold as bad and it's found to be bad, or good and it's found to be good, neither may withdraw.

If one sold wheat as dark colored and it's found to be white (or visa versa), of if wood sold as olive wood is found to be sycamore wood (or visa versa), etc. either side may retract.

No, the sages weren't being extra sanitary. The reason for all of this cleaning was that if extra crud from liquid measures etc. got onto the scales or weights, then when something new was weighed, there would be inaccurate readings. (See also Leviticus 19:35-6, and Deuteronomy 25:13-16).

The ancient Rabbis even got involved in the issue of "pricing." They had nothing against making a profit but they weren't too thrilled with excessive profiteering. Thus they came up with legislation indicating that either an overcharge or an undercharge of greater than one-sixth the value of an item may invalidate a sale. As with many areas in Jewish law, there's a great deal of detailed discussion on this point (and exceptions to the rule). Maimonides points out that this law should apply to necessities of life, but with regard to luxuries a merchant has the right to make as much profit as s/he desires.

Oh yes, you are I am sure familiar with the term "Monopoly" — when one person or company controls an entire supply of something. In our day we also talk about companies acting as "Oligopolies" — in which a few producers of something control the supply of that item. You might find it interesting to read this passage:

> Woe unto them that join house to house,
> that lay field to field, until there be no room,
> and you be made to dwell alone in the
> midst of the land.
>
> Isaiah 5:8

A TALMUDIC PROBLEM

Samuel's father would sell his fruit early in the season at a modest price. This would encourage others to sell (and keep the prices at the early market price).

Samuel however would hold the fruit until the prices had gone up. He would then sell at the season's lowest price. This would help poor people buy fruit at a low cost when prices were high.

Who is more ethical — Samuel or his father?

SUMMARY

In this section we discussed Jewish views on Business Ethics. Judaism has always had a positive regard for work. In all dealings honesty and fairplay are of vital importance. Judaism insists that an employer deal fairly with his/her employees. This ranges from such issues as time of payment to working conditions. Similarly a worker has the obligation to do an honest job and not cheat his/her boss. While the general subject of the rights of the consumer has been in the public eye only in recent times, Jewish law displayed a concern in this area thousands of years ago. Discussion of such items as fair weights and measures, profits, and monopoly type situations was presented.

FOCUS ON: THE APPEARANCE OF AN ITEM

Here is some Talmudic material that discusses the ethics of changing the appearance of things in order to improve sales:

> Produce can't be mixed with other produce.
> If this is true of mixing fresh items, it's even more true of mixing old with new items. However, it's been stated that it's O.K. to mix strong and mild wines together, because this improves it. . .

The sages were concerned with the whole problem of deception in selling. In this case you can see that while mixing different things together is generally looked down upon, if the result is beneficial to the customer, then an exception could be made.

> If a shopkeeper's wine was diluted with water he must not sell it in his shop unless he informs the customer that it's diluted. Moreover, he must not sell diluted wine to a merchant even if he tells him that it's diluted for the merchant could buy it in order to cheat others. However, in a place where it's common to dilute wine with water they may do so.

This gives us an idea of the scope and breadth of Jewish ethical material. One couldn't sell anything that was less than it appeared to be, unless the customer was well aware of the composition of what s/he was buying. Moreover the sages discouraged selling to another, items that could be used by that other person to cheat a third party. Only if it was standard procedure to dilute the wine, in which case all of the buyers would be aware of the prevailing practice and therefore not be deceived, would it be permissible.

> A shopkeeper must not sift pounded (crushed) beans.
> This is Abba Saul's viewpoint. But the sages allow it.

Crushed beans were a common item of food at that time. Abba Saul opposed sifting the beans, in other words, removing the bad ones etc. from a container because the shopkeeper might then be tempted to charge more. The sages, however, permitted it.

> But the sages admit that one shouldn't sift them only at the top of the container, because that would be deceitful. Utensils, men or cattle can't be painted.

To keep the good looking beans at the top and leave the junky ones below is plainly misrepresentation and as such is a no-no! Similarly one was not allowed to try to "paint" any old item to try to make it look better than it actually was. The Gemara to this Mishnah revealed many ways that this was done, and it was not just limited to "painting". For example:

— Some merchants would brush an animal's hair up, or feed the animal a special broth to make its hair stand on end (Aside-sometimes students coping with school cafeteria food complain about similar symptoms). These practices were done to make the animal appear fatter and in better shape than it actually was.

— Another stunt was to soak meat in water to make it appear larger than it really was.

While the Mishnah states that men, cattle and utensils can't be painted, it's Gemara goes on to tell us that:

— Samuel allowed fringes to be added to a cloak.

— Rab Judah allowed a shine to be put on fine cloths.

— Ravah permitted arrows to be painted.

— R. Pappa G. Samuel allowed baskets to be painted.

The million dollar question: Are these practices that the Gemara records as being allowed, a contradition of the Mishnah upon which it is based? The Gemara answers this question. The remark about not painting utensils etc. refers to old things. These Rabbi's were talking about new goods. While making old items appear new is deceitful, the Gemara indicates that there is nothing wrong with improving the appearance of new merchandise.

CONSIDER THIS:

1. Why were the sages so concerned about mixing things together?

2. Abba Saul was against sifting the beans. Why? Why do you suppose the sages would permit this practice?

3. A discussion in the Gemara pointed to various means of deception when selling items. List and discuss (write in detail about) six modern cases that exemplify this kind of practice.

4. You have probably (and if you haven't you should have) been wondering about the comment about painting not only utensils, but men as well. That referred to the practice of dyeing a person's hair etc. to make him/her appear younger than s/he actually is. This would be done with slaves. Remember at that point in history slavery was quite common. Here are some Biblical references to slavery:

> Genesis 15:3
> Exodus 20:9-10
> Exodus 21:1-11,16,20, 26-27
> Exodus 23:12
> Leviticus 25: 39-46
> Deuteronomy 5:14-15
> Deuteronomy 15:12-18
> Deuteronomy 16:11-14
> Deuteronomy 20:10-11
> Deuteronomy 23:15-17
> Deuteronomy 24:7

Based on these passages write a report on the Biblical institution of slavery. Include in it the answers to the following questions:

> a. How could a person become enslaved in ancient Israel?
> b. How could slaves attain freedom?

     c. What were the slaves' religious duties?

     d. Did the slave have any property rights? How was s/he protected from maltreatment?

It is interesting to note that the Talmud also contains regulations concerning slavery. It makes the point "He who buys a slave sets a master over himself." Why do you suppose it says that?

5. How do you suppose the concept of modern packaging for such products as records or foods would be viewed by the ancient Rabbis?

6. Does it make a big difference whether or not old products are "beautified" for sale? Why? Why not?

7. Let's complicate matters further. In our day considerable money and effort is spent on packaging products to help improve sales. Would you be as willing to buy any given record if it was **not** attractively displayed in a pretty album cover sealed with plastic wrapping? Why? Why not? Many people feel that packaging can contribute significantly to the price that a consumer may pay for an item. Discuss that comment in regard to the above issue.

FOCUS ON: FAIR OR UNFAIR COMPETITION

A rather fascinating discussion in the Talmud concerns the ethics of fair vs. unfair competition:

> *Rabbi Judah feels that it is unacceptable for a merchant to give nuts or burnt ears of corn to children doing errands for their parents. After all this would be unfair to other shopkeepers because the children would always want to go to the shop where they received the treats. But the sages allow it. Nor should a shopkeeper sell below the price (give discounts). But the sages say it's O.K.*

CONSIDER THIS:

1. At the time this was formulated burnt ears of corn and nuts were like candy today. Why did Rabbi Judah object to these things being given to children?

2. Why do you suppose other sages of the day felt it was permissible to give children the burnt ears of corn and nuts?

3. What is the significance of selling something below the market price?

4. Why do you suppose the view is expressed that selling below the market price was undesirable?

5. Why do you suppose the sages felt that it was O.K.?

6. Give examples of either of the two situations described above **happening today!**

7. With whom do you agree — Rabbi Judah, or the sages? Why?

8. Which of the opinions expressed in the Talmudic excerpt would be more consumer oriented? Why? (Hint: this is tricky!)

MORE THINGS TO CONSIDER:

1. A customer came into Miss Nicely's candy store and asked for four pieces of chocolate in a box. Miss Nicely was annoyed for she felt that a paper bag would have been sufficient given the amount that the customer was buying. Rather than taking the smaller sized box, Miss Nicely deliberately picked the larger one, thereby making the candy appear even smaller than it was. The customer looked unhappy and suggested that she buy some more candy to fill the box.
   a. Who is at fault, the customer or Miss Nicely?
   b. Discuss the ethics of this situation.

2. The following situation is discussed in the Talmud:

   A man asks a friend to buy four hundred barrels of wine for him. While the friend stores the wine it turns sour. Who is liable?

3. Look up the following verses: Deut. 25:12-15, Lev. 19:11, 13-18, 35, 36, Lev. 25:14, Psalm 128. Discuss as they relate to this chapter.

4. "The discussion of ethics in business is bunk. The major purpose of business is to make money and nothing more."

   Comment about the above statement.

   What kind of specific standards for ethics in business can or should be set up? List at least five and discuss.

5. Is it ethically wrong for an executive of a company to —
   a. Procure an expense account (in addition to salary) and make sure that it is frequently used? Why? Why not?
   b. Take advantage of inside information that s/he has learned on the job to make a few investments with his/her own money that are **certain** to go up? Why? Why not?

6. An employee of a large corporation has noticed a defect in many of the products that he has been working on. Attempts to bring this to the attention of the management have been ignored. This employee is tempted to go to the authorities, for the defects are a public health hazard. He knows, however, that should he go to agencies outside the company, it could cost the concern millions. He has always considered himself a "company man." What can he do?

CREDIT: BUY NOW, PAY LATER!

One trend in our modern society is the rise of the credit card. A person may get credit, "buy" something and be billed at a later time. How many different credit cards are available? Nobody really knows. One man in California has (at press time of this book) over 800 of them. All kinds of things can be charged: renting automobiles, university courses, taxi rides, art, vacations and even funerals (depending on the place of course). Since 1950 consumer debt has risen to the current $179 billion, (not counting home mortgages), indicating just how much credit is used. Business people say, and rightly so, that easy credit is necessary for an affluent society. If everybody had to pay cash our economy would be poorer with reduced production, goods and jobs. Yet on the other hand, people with credit are tempted to buy on impulse things they normally wouldn't buy if they had to pay cash. About five percent of credit buyers really get into a mess spending far more than they can afford. Discuss the ethics of this situation!

Is graffiti a form of stealing or an artistic expression of social commentary?

Money
and Snob Appeal

ANGIE'S GOOD FORTUNE

Linda held the ball for a second, searching the court to see which of her teammates was clear. Then Angie swooped in. Linda quickly passed the ball. Angie dribbled a few times — then swoosh! — Score, sixty-four to sixty! "Nice shot Angie," yelled Linda. Angie grinned. Darlene took the ball out for the other side. She dribbled a few times and attempted to pass to Rhoda. Angie bounded in and intercepted the pass. "Come on gang" she grunted. "Let's put these snobs on ice." "Twenty seconds to go," bellowed the coach. Angie tried to work the ball closer to the opposing basket. "It was more than just a game. It was a triumph of the little fellow against the strong", she thought. In desperation she tried her hook shot. It went around the rim once . . then plop! Sixty-six to sixty! The shrill whistle was heard! The period was over. Everybody headed for the showers and the locker room.

Nice going Angie! The compliments came right and left from her teammates. "We showed them." "Hey did you see the look on old horse face Darlene when you intercepted that pass? . . . Great!"

The rivalry was nothing new. Darlene and her crowd were the wealthiest kids in the school. Bingston, a city composed of middle class working people, had a large area of very wealthy people. These people called their neighborhood "Rose Meadows." They were too good to consider themselves "Bingstonians" like all the rest. Angie's class was split between the two factions, which vied for power whether it was in the school paper, a sports competition or even a classroom discussion.

"Nice going Angie darling" . . . She turned around and there was Darlene. "Do you intend to try out for the town equestrian competition too?" . . . "Oh I'm so sorry I forgot . . . you don't own a horse do you? . . . poor baby" sneered Darlene. "Take a walk" growled Linda who overheard the comments. "I suppose I ought to" smiled Darlene. "My but this place does smell like a locker room . . ." as she went off.

The rest of the day was typical. Mr. Pileiton the math teacher gave another of his murderous exams. Ms. Putosleep, the english teacher droned on about the finer points of Shakespeare. Angie got hollered at for staring out of the window during those finer points. Finally school was out! Yay!

Angie got on the bus. Her boyfriend Bill helped her with her books. Suddenly she heard honking. It was some of the snob crowd driving by in Rhoda's Ferrari "Boy they make quite a show of it," grunted Bill "Yeah, too much," responded Angie . . . The bus meandered in and out of the streets of Bingston, letting people off here and there. Finally it reached Angie and Bills' street. Both Angie and Bill got off. "Hey, I'll see you later over at Malby's," said Bill. Malby's was the neighborhood ice cream joint where all the Bingstonian kids hung out. "Naturally" responded Angie. Angie entered her house. It was a small split-level ranch house, not too fancy but pleasant. She heard talking within the kitchen. Dad's voice? But Dad was supposed to be at work. Dad was a shoe-salesman. Angie wondered if anything was wrong. She never remembered Dad being home in the middle of the day, with the exception of the time that Grandfather died! She ran into the kitchen. "What's wrong?" she asked. "Nothing's wrong," chuckled Dad. "For once everything is right," smiled Mom. "You know the state lottery that your father has been playing for the last twenty years? Well look!", as she handed Angie the telegram.

Dear Mr. Ethrum,

It is my pleasure to inform you that you have won the top prize in the State Lottery! You are now the recipient of one and a half million dollars! Please give us the necessary information about bank accounts or the name of your investment counselor etc. so that we may make the transfer immediately.

> *Congratulations,*
> *J.C. Money-banks,*
> *Co-ordinator State Lottery*

Dad's eyes glowed. "Now we can get out of this house and move to Rose Meadows! Angie, you're old enough to drive. How would you like one of those fancy foreign jobs with all the trimmings? Of course we'll do those things after spring vacation, during which, we are going to Europe!"

161

FINISH THE STORY

Put some time and effort into it. Write at least three or four pages! Be Creative. Among the items you may wish to explore are —

— How will the money change the family's life style? (Work, leisure time activities etc.)

— How will it affect Angie?

— Will her relationship with Linda and her friends be the same?

— How about Bill? Will he still be in the picture, and in what way?

— And what about Darlene and her crowd? Will they accept Angie? Reject her?

— How will Darlene and her crowd affect Angie's relationships with her friends?

In class: You will all compare stories and see how the plots evolved.

CONSIDER THIS:

1. Evaluate all of the above questions for the story and the varied endings that will be produced.

2. How would you feel if you were Dad or Mom, Angie, Linda, Bill, Darlene etc.?

3. What would **you** do if **you** were handed a check for a million and a half dollars?

4. How do the various plots that you and your classmates write compare? Differ?

❖❖❖❖❖❖❖

CLUBS? – YES OR NO?

John K. is a high ranking Government Official. Recently he has come under criticism in the press for belonging to the Squire Club. The Squire Club is a private establishment near Washington D.C. The bylaws of the club restrict membership to 500 individuals. The families and guests of those 500 are allowed to use the club's tennis and squash courts, indoor swimming pool, and sauna facilities. Only the Walling Library and Bar are off limits to all but members. (Though other meeting and dining facilities are available when members wish to entertain relatives and guests). While the club has no written constitution barring any social or ethnic group, it is standard club policy to be very careful about admissions procedures. In recent years the club has admitted a few token blacks and Jews to appear progressive. It will not give full membership to women claiming that it's facilities (restrooms etc.) are simply not adequate.

CONSIDER THIS:

1. Does an individual such as John K. have the right to join such a club? Why? Why not?

2. The members of the Squire Club claim that they have the right to associate with whomever they want to in private. Moreover, they say, a great deal of

private personal business is negotiated in the club setting. How would you react to these comments?

3. Is there any difference between the Squire Club and any school clubs you know of? How about honorary organizations such as Phi Beta Kappa?

PROFILE OF A UNIVERSITY

Stuffnose University on the banks of the James River in Mulberge enjoys an international reputation. Founded well over a century ago, it has grown, prospered and is extremely affluent. A citadel of learning, Stuffnose's faculty are often more aware of Zambian culture than about socio-economic conditions in Mulberge. Administrators at Stuffnose are proud of how cosmopolitan their University is. The student body is likely to include representatives from most locales except Mulberge. Stuffnose University takes pride on transforming their competitive student body into gentlemen, although most of its lower functionaries and secretaries are both rude and inefficient. An education at Stuffnose is considered to be an experience, and many of it's alumni even emerge with an accent. Stuffnose people are quite arrogant about the magnificence of their school. Legend has it that the school has lost out on some excellent gifts because of that arrogance. Occasionally events that occur at Stuffnose (such as a student cheating or a graduate turning out to have falsified his credentials to get in) even make the news!

CONSIDER THIS: 163

1. While Stuffnose University is fictional, can attendance at certain schools be prompted by snob appeal?

2. Many people feel that the excellent education provided by such schools is important. Others feel that just the diploma or degree with a name is the important thing for career advancement. Evaluate these comments.

3. Can educational excellence be provided without arrogance? Why? Why not? Does it make any difference?

TRADITIONAL COMMENTS

Now, I suppose that at this stage you are probably thinking "Well I bet he's going to tell me something about the Jewish view of materialism that's really goody goody!" Well the Jewish view of material wealth is not really "goody, goody" but quite practical.

Some religions make a positive virtue out of giving up all of one's physical possessions and going off to find spiritual enlightenment. Not so Judaism! As we mentioned earlier, Judaism believes that one should live in this world and enjoy its benefits:

An old Jewish legend tells of a man who came to a great Rabbi and told him that for spiritual reasons he drank only water and put nails in his shoes. The Rabbi pointed to a horse tied up nearby. "Look, "said the Rabbi. "It drinks only water and has nails in its shoes, but it is still only a horse!"

Thus Judaism comes out positively for material pleasures. In the Talmud the comment is made that "poverty is worse than fifty plagues". And then there is the quite valid recognition that "if there's no meal, there's no Torah." Face it, (as was indicated earlier) if someone is hungry, nothing else is very important to that person, until s/he is fed! And from our traditions we receive the knowledge that "If I don't labor — I won't eat."

But the ancient Rabbis balanced their view of wealth. While acknowledging that wealth and material pleasure is good, our tradition abounds in stories and sayings showing that desire for wealth shouldn't be overdone; that it isn't the **only** or most important goal in the world. There is, for example this old tale:

*Once there was a man who was offered a lot of money for an item in his possession. His answer to the potential buyers was "My father is sleeping in the room where I keep that item and I can't wake him up." Thinking the answer was but an excuse to get a better price the buyers kept offering more and more money. Still the man refused to "disturb his father." Later when the buyers came back to try again the man sold them the item but would take no more than the original price they offered. It turns out his father **really was** sleeping in that room. The man not only didn't wish to disturb his father, but refused to make an excess profit from the situation.*

164

And indeed there is the saying that you can have all of the food and drink in the world, but they're not worth anything if there is no peace. One of my favorite legends shows how peace was considered more important than snob-appeal:

Once there was a big shot Rabbi. People from miles around came to listen to him. Well, one guy got pretty mad. He said to his wife, "You're spending too much time going off to this big shot Rabbi's lectures and not enough with your family." The wife however persisted, and the husband threw her out of the house. "I'll let you back in when you spit in the Rabbis eye!" he sneered. When the Rabbi heard what happened he had the lady spit in his eye more than once to help bring the family back together again.

Pretty gross, huh? And maybe the wife even spit into the wrong person's eye! It does however show that in spite of the fact that the Rabbi was an extremely important person, he valued peace over snob-appeal. Then of course in Pirke Avot there's the tale of a Rabbi from a town of great intellectual resources who's offered a lot of money if he'll go to live in another place. He turns down the offer, not wishing to live somewhere that is "not a place of the law." Also we find the rather interesting observation (also in Pirke Avot):

If love depends on some material thing, if that thing is removed so too will love be removed . . .

If you're thinking "Ho, Hum . . . rather far removed from me." think twice! All of us at one time or another are put into situations where we have to choose

ADVERTISEMENT:

The more flesh one acquires — the more worms.

The more wealth   The more headaches

The more wives   The more witchcraft

The more maid-servants   The more wickedness

The more man-servants   The more stealing

BUT

165

The more Torah study   The more life

The more education   The more wisdom

The more counsel   The more understanding

The more charity   The more peace

One who has a good name has really acquired something for himself!

One who knows Torah has acquired life for himself in the world-to-come.

Pirke Avot

This has been a free, public service Advertisement on behalf of the friends of Hillel committee. Opinions of and reactions to any of the above points, are welcomed.

between one course of action which we might feel is "right" and another which might be more to our advantage, from the aspects of prestige, power or wealth ... There are many people in our society who given the choice will go into a certain career, choose a marriage partner or make a decision choosing primarily on the basis of material gain.

SNOB APPEAL

Money is however one aspect of a far larger area of snob appeal. There are all kinds of snobs in this world:

There are money snobs who evaluate people by material wealth — address, car, clothes.
There are pedagree snobs who evaluate people by family or ethnic group. ("Oh yes, she has blue blood.")
There are intellectual/creative snobs who judge people by their academic achievement ("Oh wow. S/he must be smart. S/he has a Ph.D. from Stuffnose University).

Not from the Talmud; From Rittner!

Judaism has fairly clear guidelines with regard to this issue. It is written in Psalm 128, verse two, "you will eat the labor of your hands and you'll be happy and it'll be well with you." There's nothing wrong with being pleased with yourself and your accomplishments. But if you strut down the street:

"Here I am, Joe Cool Magnificient — The great, majestic and supreme; God's gift to the world; the unique one!"

Well, that's not so good (according to Judaism). Not many people strut down the street calling themselves "God's gift to the world"? You'd be surprised. There are numerous people with egos that are pretty inflated for one reason or another. Even King Solomon had an ego problem:

In legend Solomon owned a flying carpet and, like the U.S. President flying around on Air Force I, was able to travel all over the world. Well, one day he was flying along and happened to zoom over a valley of ants. The queen ant saw his carpet and told all the other ants to run to safety for Solomon was around. Solomon heard the order and wondered why his public relations were so bad. He landed to discuss the matter with the queen. She refused to talk to him until he picked her up in his hand. He did so. Then in the course of conversation he asked her "Queen, Queen hear my sound, can there be any greater than I in town?" Well, Solomon almost went into shock when the Queen ant said "Yes, I am greater than you." Solomon, still thinking he was Joe Cool asked "Queen, Queen how can that be — You are about the size of a flea?" The Queen answered "The fact that God brought you here to hold me on your hand shows that you're not so important."

Another midrash tells us that fruit trees are asked why they don't make a lot of noise. Their response is "Our fruits tell it all for us". The point being, there's no need to go around acting like a "Joe Cool". (If you really are outstanding in some regard, it'll be evident in and of itself). Have you ever wondered why in the creation story only a single person (or couple) was first created? Well even if you haven't some of the old Rabbis did! Their comment in the Mishnah was that it was done so that no one could get snobby about a so-called "better" ancestry.

Another midrash, one of my favorites, talks about the composition of the human body. As you know we are all made of chemicals. One hundred and fifty years ago when I was a student, teachers would even put the dollar and cents value of all of the chemicals making up our body on the black board. It was only a few dollars, though with inflation it's probably somewhat more now. Anyhow, this midrash tells us that when God created Adam he took dust of different colors from **all** four corners of the earth. Moreover humankind was created **last** so that if anyone got snobby s/he could be reminded that even the simpliest insect was created earlier.

In the Zohar the point is made that fools judge by the outer appearance of a person. It's a wise person who judges what's inside. There is also the saying that when a person destroys one human life, it's almost as though s/he has destroyed an entire world; and when a person saves a human life, it's as if an entire world has been saved (see p. 86). This can be taken on many levels. When someone is snobby to someone else s/he is, in a sense, killing that person in a psychological way.

SUMMARY

Judaism **does not,** by any means, take a negative view of material wealth. On the contrary, our traditions state quite clearly that it is far better to be prosperous than poor. Nonetheless Judaism insists that possessions aren't the **major** thing in life, and shouldn't be the prime motivation for all that one says and does. Now, you might be considering this, yawning and saying "Yeah, right . . . sure." Nonetheless, I'll never forget the comment once made by a lawyer friend. "You wouldn't believe it . . . the things that I see . . . nice close knit families . . . then someone dies . . . some of the haggling and ill will between close relatives over possessions . . . Wow!" The issue of our attitudes toward material things is a real and quite valid one.

167

Allied to this is the whole thing about "humility" and "ego trips." Our tradition abounds in numerous comments and legends telling us to "be humble." While that in itself might sound corny consider it for a minute. When individuals are off on "ego trips" and each takes the position that s/he is "Joe Cool — center of the universe" obviously other people are going to be affected, and not in a very positive manner. Various forms of snob appeal, feeling superior for reason A or reason B, obviously will do little to promote good relations.

CONSIDER THIS:

1.   The Hebrew word for rich is עָשִׁיר (ashir). To be sure, we often don't realize how "rich" we are in just having good health. If your

עֵינֶיךָ eyes,
שִׁנֶּיךָ teeth,
יָדֶיךָ hands
רַגְלֶיךָ feet

are in good shape, then you are indeed עָשִׁיר !

(Note how the first letter of each word combines to spell ashir). Have you ever been in the hospital, broken a bone? etc. If so discuss with regard to the above.

2. In Pirke Avot it is also written:

> *Who is rich? He who is happy with his lot.*

What does that mean? Can you find any connection between that statement and the 10th Commandment? What is it?

3. Another Rabbinic definition of a rich person is someone "who enjoys his/her wealth." Is it possible for someone with a lot of money to be poor by this definition? Why? Why not?

4. Is it possible for someone with little financial resources to be "rich" by the above two definitions? By your own definition?

5. Another comment from Pirke Avot (you get a lot of those in this book) is:

> *Be not like servants who serve a master for the sake of a reward, but rather be like servants who serve a master without the condition of a reward.*

   a. Does that sound like a very practical course of action in our society today? Why? Why not?

   b. Insert the word teacher in place of master and grades in place of reward. Now re-evaluate the same question (above).

   c. Don't you sometimes do or learn things without the condition of grades (rewards)? Are there any other kinds of profit and reward besides money? Explain.

6. There is a midrash in which a man dies and leaves his money to all of his children. The youngest, however, gets little money but receives instead a letter of recommendation to the man's friends. These friends end up helping the boy. As a result he becomes very wealthy.

   a. What's the moral of this tale?
   b. How can having money affect friendships?
   c. How can lack of money affect friendships?

7. Dr. Cohne has a very difficult problem. He has decided that it is about time for his family to join a synagogue. He has narrowed his choice down to two congregations, both near his home:

> **Congregation A:** This congregation is a fairly small one. It has a Rabbi who is very intellectual, a fine religious school for his children, and also seems to have a very pleasant atmosphere.

> **Congregation B:** This congregation is enormous. It has an outstanding reputation in all regards. Dr. Cohne notes that a larger congregational membership could result in more friends and could thereby benefit his practice to a larger extent than congregation A.

Which should he join? Why?

8. Jack and Bill went into a store to buy something. Jack immediately asked the salesperson for the item he had in mind. When the salesperson brought it, Jack appeared dissatisfied and asked for something else. This procedure went on for about five minutes. While the salesperson was off looking for the most recent request, Bill turned to Jack. "Why are you giving the guy a hard time?" he asked. "I'm really not trying to." responded Jack. "If I am spending money, the salesperson is supposed to cater to my likes and dislikes."

    a. Do you agree with Jack? Why? Why not?
    b. How do you suppose the salesperson feels? Why?

9. Hal Bewine drove into the driveway of the new home that he had just purchased. He was driving the dilapidated pickup truck that he used in his business. Noticing a man trimming a hedge next door, he got out of the truck and went over to him. "Hi!" he said. "I'm Hal Bewine your new neighbor." The man looked at Hal, who was dressed rather shabbily at the time, and looked at the old truck. He sniffed as if the air smelled bad and turned and walked away.

Several days later, Hal was returning home from work in his own personal car, a Rolls-Royce. The same neighbor was mowing his lawn. He glanced at Hal's car and the suit that Hal was wearing, and came over to Hal. "Hi I'm Harvey Maxwell. Welcome to our neighborhood."

    a. How do you suppose Hal felt the first time he tried to introduce himself?
    b. Why was Maxwell initially unfriendly? Why did his attitude change?
    c. What would you do or say if you were Hal? Why?

169

STATUS SYMBOLS – GOOD OR EVIL?

We all have the need to be liked, respected or admired. One way that many people try to fulfill that need is through "Status Symbols." Status is a difficult word to define but everybody pretty much understands it as one's "standing." "rank," or "position." The King of a country might be said to have a lot of status (unless there's a revolution!). People often try to show that they have status in numerous ways. It can be displayed by an address in a fancy neighborhood or by comparisons between homes.

People often judge others by some of these additional means: Profession, amount of education, automobile, knowledge of so- called "in" sports or games, schools attended, one's travels and whether that travel experience was "deluxe" or "by bananna boat," furnishings in home, art collectables, clothing etc. Different geographic locations and even age groups sometimes have different status symbols!

1. A status symbol is generally something that would be **desirable** as well as **scarce.** Let us say that color T.V.'s were once a status symbol; as more and more people buy them will they remain such? What would that imply about status symbols in general?

2. Find seven items you feel are symbols of status. (e.g. Mulharry beer, Splinter Skis etc.). Ask your parents for seven. How is your list similar to your parents? How does it differ? Why?

3. Is the search for status a justified one, worth the time and effort? Why? Why not? Do you suppose that there will always be an effort to "keep up with the Jones"? Why? Why not?

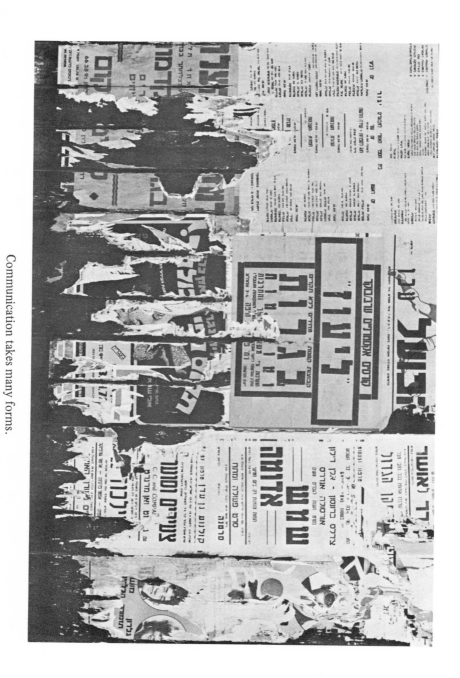

Communication takes many forms.

170

The Ethics of Communication

TRADITIONAL COMMENTS:

A midrash:

> *One of the ancient Rabbis sent his servant to the market with the rather general instruction, "Buy the best thing there that one can eat!" The servant returned with a tongue. Later the Rabbi asked him to go back to the market to buy the worst thing that one could eat. The servant again came back with a tongue. "Hey, what's with you?" asked the Rabbi. "Here I've asked you to buy both the best and the worst, and you came back with a couple of tongues!" "That's true," responded the servant. "After all can't a good tongue be one of the best things in this world and an evil tongue be one of the worst?"*

Normally when we think about the subject of ethics we think in terms of one's actions towards another, and whether those actions are right or wrong (e.g. should I do this or that). Yet ethical issues can even extend to our communication patterns. Our society is based on the ability to communicate. When you learn stuff in school like reading, writing, and even math, you are really learning the tools necessary to both understand messages that others may send you, and send out your own. When you go to the supermarket the various labels on the cans communicate their contents. The writing on money communicates its accepted value. Traffic lights are a form of communication in which both drivers and pedestrians are given information as to whether they should stop or go. Even when you are watching T.V., you are, in effect, receiving communications. (Next time your parents tell you to "Quit watching the T.V. and do your homework" you may suggest to them that you are involved in the important task of receiving communication transmissions – at your own risk of course!!) But just think for a second; if you were not able to express your thoughts, ideas and desires to others (and also receive communications from others) it would be very difficult for you to survive. Indeed, what a mess it would be if no one was able to communicate with one another. In fact one of the messages of the story of the tower of Babel (you remember, that's when some people tried to construct a Biblical Skyscraper – see Genesis Ch. 11) is that problems do result when communication breaks down.

Anyhow as mentioned earlier, ethics is a very broad area, and can even apply to situations involving communication between people. Probably the most basic form of communication that people use is speech. In the midrash at the beginning of this unit we find the opinion expressed that just as one can use his/her tongue for very positive things, so too can an "evil tongue" be one of the worst things around. Here is another midrash:

One day a King came down with a rather exotic disease. His doctors told him that the only thing that would cure him was some milk from a lioness. Well, the King gave the task of getting the milk to a man in his court. This man, traveled far and managed to get the milk. On the way back to the court, however, an argument broke out among the various parts of the man's body: "Boy am I Joe Cool," said the hands. "Without me, we would never have gotten the milk." "Hey, wait one minute," said the eyes, "I am the most important . . . the rest of you would be lost without me!" Then of course the feet and the rest of the parts joined in the argument. When the tongue spoke up, all of the others told it to keep still. "O.K." said the tongue. "I'll show you!" And so when the man finally got back to the King and presented the milk, the tongue spoke out "Here it is . . . the milk of an antelope." Well the king wasn't too happy and was ready to chop the man's head off. The tongue made a deal with the other parts; it would save them provided they all recognize that it was the most important part of the body. They agreed, and the tongue explained to the King that there was an error; the milk was really from a lioness. The king tried the milk and was cured. The man lived happily ever after and the tongue was acknowledged the most important part of the body.

Again the moral is clear. One's tongue can be very useful and can also do a great deal of harm.

Well, what can a tongue do that's unethical? A great deal. The power of an individual to do harm through communication is so great that it is even discussed in the Ten Commandments. Commandment No. Nine says "Neither shalt thou bear false witness against thy neighbor." That's a pretty definite statement. If one "bears false witness" s/he is certainly wronging another person through communication. But that is like examining only the tip of the iceberg There are numerous ways of wronging others through communication. First of all one can simply be a "wise-guy." I'm reminded of the story about an old Rabbi. He's approached by this young fellow who says to him "Say, Rabbi, the Talmud says that someone who studies gets smarter with age, yet your recent books aren't half as good as the writings you did when you were younger." "Maybe so," responded the Rabbi, "But it also states that ignorant people get dumber with age . . . You've got to be smart to understand my most recent books." . . . (Put down!) . . . I think you can see that **everyone** (even Rabbis) **can use words in a rather sharp manner!** Indeed do you remember our earlier discussion about Hillel and Shammai? (see p. 41). Well, legend has it that they were at it again, arguing over some point of Jewish law. The disagreement this time went on for three years! (That's perseverance for you!) Finally the legend tells us that a huge voice was heard that proclaimed "Both the position of Hillel and the position of Shammai are the word of God, but go along with the School of Hillel." Well the scholars weren't just going to let it go at that! "Why was Hillel favored?" they asked. The answer "Because Hillel and his followers are very polite. They even examine the opposing position before their own!" Thus legend tells us that because Hillel and his school were more pleasant in their manner of communicating, their position concerning the particular issue at hand was favored! Indeed in Pirke Avot the comment is made, "Be friendly towards youth and receive all people with cheerfulness."

THE POWER OF THE TONGUE

Proverbs 18:21 — Life and death are in the power of the tongue,
And those that love it will eat the fruit thereof.

Proverbs 12:18 — There are (those) who speak like the piercings of a
sword; but the tongue of the wise is health.

Proverbs 26:28 — A lying tongue hates those who are afflicted by it;
and a flattering mouth works ruin.

Proverbs 17:4 — A wicked doer gives heed to false lips; and
a liar gives ear to a naughty tongue.

Proverbs 18:8 — The words of a talebearer are as wounds, and
they go down into the innermost parts of the belly.

Proverbs 15:1 — A soft answer turns away wrath, but grievous
words stir up anger.

Proverbs 13:3 — He that guards his mouth, guards his life; but
he that opens his lips wide will have destruction.

Proverbs 20:19 — He that goes around as a talebearer reveals secrets;
therefore don't meddle with him that flatters with his
lips.

Proverbs 29:20 — Do you see a man that is hasty in his words? There is
more hope for a fool than for him!

There are other aspects of the issue of wronging through communication. How about embarrassing someone in public? Here's another neat story that deals with that subject:

> *Rabbi Judah Ha Nasi was once giving a lecture when he smelled garlic in the room. Boy was he mad! The idea — someone coming into his lecture with bad breath! He announced, "Will the person in need of mouthwash please leave" (or words to that effect). At any rate Rabbi Hiyya left. Hiyya was very popular and so all of the other students accompanied him. Later Rabbi Simeon, Ha Nasi's son bumped into Hiyya. "Hi ya, Hiyya . . . What's this I hear about you and my dad?" Hiyya told Simeon that he really wasn't the garlic eater. Hiyya had walked out knowing that the rest of the students would also leave. Doing that, he explained to Simeon, would avoid bringing strong embarrassment to the actual offender.*

A pretty smelly story, but an interesting way of solving the dilemma. Incidently another Talmudic legend has it that the Second Temple was destroyed due to a chain of events that started with a person being embarrassed in public! The Talmud describes an embarrassed person as one who has turned pale from shame and expresses the view that one who publicly shames another is like a person who has shed blood! It comments that one shouldn't give anyone a nasty nickname, or persist in calling someone by such a nickname even if that person is used to it!

The tradition takes a pretty strong negative view of slander in general. Here is a rather strong comment from the prophet Jeremiah about his society:

> Oh that I had in the wilderness a lodging place of wayfaring men; that I might leave my people and go from them for they are all adulterers; an assembly of treacherous men. And they bend their tongues like their bows; lying, not truth is strong in the land, for they go out from evil to evil and they don't know me, says the Lord. Be on your guard against your neighbor and don't even trust a brother, for every brother will supplant a brother and every neighbor will walk with slander. And everyone will deceive his neighbor and will not speak the truth . . .
>
> *Jeremiah 9:2-5*

And in Leviticus (19:16) the comment is made "Thou shalt not go up and down as a tale-bearer among your people." Our traditions even go to the extent of analyzing the harm that slander can do. We are told that slander harms three parties; the **speaker** and the **person spoken to** — in addition to the person **spoken about!**

174

These are but a few examples of wronging through communication. In this unit you will be given an opportunity to explore other issues concerning the ethics of communication.

GOTHIC HORROR

"Just wait until you see it honey!" Mr. Jackson rubbed his hands together with enthusiasm. "Look it's all good and fine that you decided to buy a house, but shouldn't you have at least let me take a look at it?" Mrs. Jackson was annoyed. "Well, I didn't think you'd object to it; it's beautiful! It has three spires, a long porch and a garage next door . . . You'll just love it!" he burst out. Mrs. Jackson wasn't as certain but she promised herself that she would keep an open mind. Well, the next day the two went over to see the building. It was, to be frank, dilapidated. The building had been in a state of disrepair for years. "What a gothic horror", thought Mrs. Jackson. "Well honey, what do you think? Do you like it?" asked Mr. Jackson.

AUNT CLARISSA

Aunt Clarissa was normally a very cautious driver. It therefore came as quite a shock to the family when they received the call from the hospital. "Are you the Pipins family?" "Yes this is Charles Pipins speaking." "We have a woman down here in intensive care, with identification of Clarissa Pipins . . . Your phone number was in her wallet." "Oh my God", responded Mr. Pipins "What happened?" "Bad traffic accident" responded the orderly. "We'll be right there." Mr. Pipins and his daughter Betsy rushed to the hospital. They were greeted by a doctor. "Doctor, how bad is it?" asked Mr. Pipins. "Extremely bad" responded Dr. Meltz. "We've done our best but it will be another few hours before we really know whether or not she will survive . . . she's conscious now. If you'd like, you can see her for a few minutes." As Mr. Pipins and Betsy began to enter the room, they heard Pipin's name being paged on the loudspeaker. Mr. Pipins turned to Betsy. "Go along in, I'll be with you in a few minutes." She continued into the room. Aunt Clarissa lay there in the bed. "Boy did she look awful", thought Betsy. "Hi Betsy", murmered Aunt Clarissa. "Well, I guess I must look like I'm half dead, don't I?"

AUTO SHOP

Donna Bradberry sipped her coffee as she read the morning paper. All at once her normally large appetite vanished. She read the article about that smash up on Hudson St. Three people had been killed. One of them was a lady she knew — Ms. Pipins. Donna was in a tumult. Just yesterday Ms. Pipins was in the auto repair shop where Donna was employed. Pipins had needed some work done on the brakes of her car. Bill Malone had been assigned that job. Donna knew that Bill sometimes was sloppy in his work, but as a rule Malone was never **that** sloppy. Still Donna couldn't shake the feeling that Bill's workmanship must have somehow contributed to the accident. Donna didn't really know what to do. The owner of the shop was her brother-in-law. She felt that she should report her suspicions. On the other hand, she knew that her brother-in-law disliked Bill intensely and was looking for an excuse to fire him. Donna and Bill have been friends for fifteen years and have worked on many cars together. Bill had a wife and seven kids, and found it difficult to make ends meet. When Donna came into the shop her brother-in-law greeted her. "Hi Donna, how are you this morning? Is everything going smoothly?"

175

NEW PLAY

Frances was very excited. "The Purple Tent" had just come to town. The reviews for this play were incredibly good, and Frances wanted very much to see it. She hadn't yet made any plans. Then suddenly the phone rang. "Hello." She heard her mother answer. "Yes, . . . Wait a second I'll get her for you . . . Frances, telephone." Frances got on the line "Hello?" "Hi Frances, it's Jerry." "Oh, hi Jerry, how are you?", "Fine . . . Look Frances I've got a couple of tickets to "The Purple Tent" . . . Would you like to go this Friday night?" . . . "Oh, sure Jerry." . . . "Great. I'll pick you up at 7.15." They chatted a while and then hung up. The next day Frances saw Harry at school. "Say, Frances" began Harry . . . "Would you like to see that new play that just came to town?" Frances didn't know what to say. Given a choice between Harry or Jerry, she would much prefer to go out with Harry.

DEAR MYRTLE

Dear Myrtle,

I am writing to you for some advice. I have two very close friends whom I will call "Joe" and "Fred". I have known both of these guys for twenty years. Joe is not the most reliable sort. He is a happy-go-lucky type of person, and gambles a great deal. Fred on the other hand is a very conscientious, honorable sort of person. While I have known both for a long time, neither knew each other until they met at a party at my house last week. Joe and Fred apparently hit it off and became instant pals. Here is my problem. Joe has apparently talked Fred into investing in one of his "get rich quick" schemes. If my past experience is any guide, I believe that Fred is making a horrible mistake. I don't want to interfere in matters that are none of my affair, but if Fred loses money in this deal, I'll feel responsible. After all, I introduced them to each other. Don't get me wrong; I think they're both great guys and don't want to hurt anyone's feelings. Suggestions?

Sincerely yours,

Unhappy Matchmaker

STEIN'S CLASS

Mr. Stein had a great unit planned for his Temple B'nai Levi Religious School class. He had spent many hours researching and planning it. A large aspect of his lesson dealt with areas in which there is distinct disagreement between Judaism and Christianity. He felt that the unit would be very instructive to his students and give them greater knowledge and perspective of their Jewish traditions. As he stood in front of his class one of the students came up to his desk to introduce a friend. It seems that this student had brought a non Jewish friend to class that day. "Oh Oh," thought Stein. "What now?"

SIN CITY

Hal was pretty proud of his looks. He was a rather large person. No, he wasn't stout by any means, but he was large for his age. Also when he combed his hair in a certain manner he looked a lot older. One day he was walking by a local movie theatre. He noticed that a new movie had just come to town. Taking a careful look, he noted that it was called "Sin City" and was rated X. Hal was rather intrigued by the name of the film, not to mention the interesting pictures displayed outside the theatre. Hal knew that he was too young to be allowed into an X rated film. He also knew that the theatre seldom checked I.D.s and that his older appearance could fool the usher.

BORROWED CAR

Bill had a date that Thursday night with Cindy. He had been looking forward to it for they were planning to go to "The Purple Tent" which had just come to town. Bill really liked Cindy a great deal and wanted her to like him too. He left the house and got into his old, beat up car. Brrum . . . Brrrum. The engine finally started. The car had been on the road for twenty years and Bill constantly had to play with the engine to keep the old hulk going. Then suddenly he had an idea! Hey! Why not take his father's car? Sure . . . He knew that his father and mother had gone out to dinner, but they had been picked up by friends. Dad's fancy Maserati was sitting out in the driveway, just waiting for his use!! Well, to be sure, his Dad and Mom were unavailable to give permission, but he knew where the spare set of keys were kept. So back he went into the house!

Vromm . . . Vromm. The powerful engine of the Maserati sounded like music to his ears. Bill put his foot on the gas pedal and shot out of the driveway CRASH!! In his eagerness to give the car gas Bill had forgotten a post that was on the other side of the street. He had backed up into the post. Looking at his watch he realized he was already late, so he hurried on to pick Cindy up.

The night turned out to be a real bust! "The Purple Tent" was overrated, and Bill couldn't really enjoy the show worrying about the dent which he knew he had put on the car. Cindy, it turns out, had a delicate stomach and was car sick. He was lucky to be able to pull over to the side quick enough before she became ill. When he finally came home he noted that his parents were still out. Quickly he pulled the car into the driveway and entered the house, putting the keys back into their standard place.

The next morning Bill came down to breakfast. Dad and Mom were sitting there. "Morning Dad, morning Mom." "Hi Bill." came the response. "H. .h. . How was your evening folks?" asked Bill nervously. "Humph . . . The evening was fine but I noticed a large dent on my car, when I got back . . . Just wait until I get into J and C's Garage where I leave it when I'm at work . . . Leroy Jones over there always parks it in a special spot for me so that sort of thing supposedly won't happen . . . Well apparently they were negligent and somehow damaged the back of the car. I intend to go over there and discuss the matter!" Bill drained his glass of milk and put the empty glass down.

COUNTRY CLUB WOES

Bertha and her parents were members of the Green Valley Country Club. They enjoyed the club and it's facilities a great deal. Her Dad made ample use of the golf course and both Bertha and her Mother liked to play tennis over there. It was no wonder then, when her family decided to celebrate a raise that Mom had received on her job, that the family would go out to have dinner in the Club's restaurant. As they sat there they heard a commotion coming from the other side of the room at the Bar. "Why look," exclaimed Bertha, "There's Mr. Stein, my teacher from religious school." "SWEET LOVE OF MINE . . . YOU ARE DIVINE . . . " Stein was twirling around on the bar seat singing at the top of his lungs. Dad looked up and said to Bertha "Well if he's your teacher, he's awfully drunk at the moment."At that point two husky fellows came over to Stein and quietly said something to him. "I WILL NOT LEAVE . . ." Stein shouted. "AS A CEMBER OF THIS MLUB . . . I CAN STAY AS LONG AS I WANT TO . . ." At that point the two men lifted Stein up and carried him out of the door.

177

CONSIDER THIS:

GOTHIC HORROR

1. Was Mr. Jackson "right" in buying the house without first consulting with his wife? Why? Why not?

2. If you were Mrs. Jackson, how would you answer Mr. Jackson's question (when he finally showed her the house)? Why?

3. If Mr. Jackson had not yet purchased the building would it affect what you'd say? How?

4. Analyze this situation from the viewpoint of both Mr. and Mrs. Jackson.

5. How is this an example of ethical problems in communication? Discuss (write) in detail.

AUNT CLARISSA

1. What are Betsy's options in this situation? Analyze in detail.

2. If Betsy were to tell Aunt Clarissa that she really looked fine, then she would be lying. Haven't we all been taught that lying is a "no-no"? Discuss. (write) in detail.

3. If you were Betsy, what would you say? Why?

4. Have you ever been in a situation like this? What happened and what did you do?

5. Can there ever be any circumstances that make lying "right"? Discuss (write) in detail.

6. What if it hadn't been a situation where a severely injured person had been involved? What if it was simply a situation such as the following:

   Harriet had just picked up a new dress for the prom. She was quite proud of it. Elissa looked at it and thought that it was the most gaudy display of bad taste she had ever seen.

   a. Should Elissa say anything? Why? Why not?
   b. Is there any difference between this situation and the one involving Aunt Clarissa? Between this situation and the one describing the Gothic Horror? Compare all three.

7. What was Aunt Clarissa really asking Betsy? If you were Aunt Clarissa, how would you have wanted Betsy to deal with you? Why?

8. How is this situation (Aunt Clarissa) an example of the ethics of communication? Discuss (write) in detail.

AUTO SHOP

1. If you were Donna what would your options be?

2. If you were Donna, what course of action would you follow? Why?

3. Would it be wrong for Donna to talk to her brother-in-law about Bill? Why? Why not?

4. How is this situation an example of the ethics of communication? Discuss (write) in detail.

NEW PLAY

1. What is Frances' dilemma?

2. How would Harry feel if Frances turns him down?

3. How would Jerry feel if Frances tried to change their plans?

4. Is there any "graceful" way for Frances to back out of the date with Jerry? Is there any possible way to turn Jerry down, now that the date has been made, without hurting his feelings?

5. Would it be fair for Frances to go out with Jerry?

     a. Would it be fair to Jerry? Why? Why not?
     b. To Frances? Why? Why not?
     c. To Harry? Why? Why not?

6. What if Frances went to the play with Jerry and then ran into Harry there? What could (should) she say to him? (and visa versa)?

7. How would you feel if you asked someone to do something and later that person called and cancelled, telling you that something better had came up. Is "honesty" or "tact" more cruel? Why?

8. In this situation couldn't the story of what happened get around to other friends? How would that affect how the problem might be resolved?

9. Is it important to keep promises and commitments? How important?

10. What do you think Frances should do? Why? What would you do in a situation such as this? Why?

11. How do "boy/girl relationships" exemplify moral problems involving the ethics of communication? Explain.

179

12. Write three more examples of "boy/girl" ethical problems. Make sure all three are different and unlike the "New Play" situation here. Each should be at least a half a page in length!

DEAR MYRTLE

1. Why does the Unhappy Matchmaker feel responsible? Both Fred and Joe are old enough to take care of themselves. Should the Matchmaker feel responsible? Explain.

2. How do you think Fred would feel if the Matchmaker said anything to him? How do you think he'd feel if the Matchmaker said nothing to him (and he lost money later)?

3. If the Matchmaker talked to Fred, how could that affect his own friendship with Joe?

4. What could the Matchmaker do (if anything) to save his friendships with both Joe and Fred?

5. How does this situation represent an example of the ethical problems involved with communication?

6. O.K. Myrtle . . . What would you suggest? (outside of a change of name).

STEIN'S CLASS

1. Stein actually only wanted to cover points in which the two religions disagreed. Would a visitor make that much of a difference? Why? Why not?

2. How would you handle the situation if you were in Stein's place?

3. How is this situation an example of ethical problems in communication? Explain.

SIN CITY

1. What is Hal's dilemma?

2. Would Hal be justified in trying to sneak into the movie, primarily on the grounds that he could get away with it?

3. How would the attitude of Hal's parents affect the "right" or "wrong" of the situation?

   a. If Hal's parents didn't object to his viewing X rated films would it be "right" for him to sneak in?
   b. If Hal's parents objected strenuously to X rated films, would it be especially "wrong" (as compared to a) for him to sneak in?

4. If Hal should sneak in, he might not have to **say** a word. How would this situation be an example of an ethical problem in communication?

5. What do you think Hal should do? Would it make any difference if he was three years short of the acceptable age as opposed to, say, six months short of the acceptable age?

BORROWED CAR

1. Was it right for Bill to take his father's car? Why? Why not?

2. We received the impression from the story that Bill wasn't able to contact his parents even if he had wanted to. Would that excuse his original act of taking the car without permission? Why? Why not?

3. How does Bill's experience relate to the material we discussed earlier about one's being "punished" for his/her misconduct? Explain in detail.

4. At the end of the story Bill isn't saying anything one way or another. He certainly is not lying. Is he doing the "right" thing? Why? Why not?

5. Is it possible to wrong through communication without saying a word? Give additional examples and examine in detail.

6. Take this story from where it has stopped, and write your own conclusion. Be creative!

COUNTRY CLUB WOES

1. Stein realizes that as a member of the community, it is possible for his students

and/or their parents to see him in the Country Club. Moreover, he holds a position of responsibility as a religious school teacher. Should he have taken this into consideration before going out on the town? Why? Why not?

2. Does a person's job really affect what s/he can or cannot do in his/her personal life? Evaluate in detail.

3. If an individual is perfectly capable in his/her job, is it fair that that person be judged for matters that have really nothing to do with his/her occupation? Why? Why not?

4. What if Stein occasionally got drunk — but did it only on vacations and in other cities? Would that make any difference in your evaluation of this situation?

5. What should Bertha do? Would she be ethical if she told anybody about what she had seen? Would she be ethical by being silent? Why?

6. What about Bertha's parents? What are their responsibilities in this matter? Why?

7. What if Bertha and her parents became aware of extenuating circumstances that had caused Stein to go out on the town (e.g. He was unhappy because he lost money in the stock market, had a fight with his daughter etc.)? Would that affect their evaluation? Yours?

FOCUS ON: THE ETHICS OF T.V. IMPACT

When discussing the ethics of communication, the subject of T.V. comes to mind. "T.V. an ethical problem?" you ask. Yes! Oh it's not the T.V. itself, that box that people sit and stare at with blank faces, that raises ethical discussion. It's the programs that are put on the T.V. and the possible effects they have on people that are generating a great deal of debate:

> One area of concern centers around the very nature of the media. Face it T.V. is fun and painless. You just sit there like a vegetable and let it entertain you. Some people have suggested that perhaps the very fact that one just passively absorbs could mean that people who are "addicted" to T.V. may tend to become observers in general, rather than active participants.

> Some studies have indicated that too much T.V. can reduce creativity in young kids. After all, it's easier to get suggestions from T.V. than to think of new ideas and approaches.

> Some educators complain that T.V. complicates their jobs in several ways. First of all how can a teacher possibly compete with fancy camera techniques, animation and slick writing that students are quite used to on T.V.? Others complain that students watching a lot of T.V. get used to seeing problems solved quickly and therefore expect instant solutions in real life. A typical T.V. show runs only thirty or sixty minutes, so naturally problems are solved rapidly. In reality, however, it often takes considerably longer to work out solutions to dilemmas.

One of the strongest charges leveled against T.V. concerns violence on the tube. While it may be fun to watch cops, robbers, wars and violent shows in general, there have been a huge number of studies concerning the effect of this kind of programming on viewers. Most studies have indicated that violence on T.V. tends to produce aggressive behavior in young people. Even now research is starting to emerge that would indicate that when people see a great deal of violence on T.V., they get so used to it that they are more willing to put up with it in their everyday experience.

For most American children, T.V. serves as a primary source of information about our society and how it functions. Yet critics feel that the view of life that is presented on the tube is often distorted.

CONSIDER THIS:

1. The above discussion about T.V. focused on some of the criticisms leveled at the media. Why would these criticisms be of ethical concern?

2. While it is quite easy to criticize T.V., one could also give arguments concerning the positive aspects of that media. What would some of those arguments on the positive side be? (Which are stronger — Pro's or Cons?)

3. Watch T.V. for one week, as you normally would, but record your observations on a chart with the following columns:

Name of Show	Occurrence of a Violent Scene	Occurrence of vocal threat	Occurrence of physical violence	Other comments, observations
I. Joe Cool	1. – – – – 2. – – – – 3. – – – –	1. – – – – 2. – – – –	1. – – – – 2. – – – – 3. – – – – 4. – – – –	Yuch!

Keep a careful record of the occurrence of violent scenes in each show. Break that number down into vocal threats and physical violence (e.g. any use of force including use of guns, judo etc.). Write down any comments, or observations including whether you felt the use of force in each instance was justified. Bring your results into class for discussion.

4. Is the violence on T.V. true to life? When we see a simulated violent event on T.V. isn't it really cleaned up? (e.g. How often do you see someone's guts hanging out, arm torn off, eye gushing blood etc?) Would it make any difference if the violence presented was "less clean"? How? (Would violence be as much "fun"? Why?)

5. What if people like and want violence, of the type that is shown on T.V.? Can't one take the position that T.V. is merely a business operating in a buyers' market, with ratings and profits in mind?

    a. Argue "T.V. — a business" vs. "T.V. — social responsibilities."
    b. What is your own opinion? Why?

6. Studies are now indicating that criminal acts in real life sometimes are inspired

by shows on T.V. For example after the T.V. airing of a film called **The Doomsday Flight** which involved a bomb being placed on a plane airlines received, **in one week**, double the amount of bomb threats that were received in the **entire month** before the broadcast. Discuss the ethics of the situation. Can a show be made realistic and exciting without eliciting this kind of response? Should T.V. be more heavily censored? Why? Why not?

7. The same kind of situation can turn up in News Coverage. In a U.S. Government report the observation was made that before 1961 no incidents of airplane hijacking were reported in the U.S. However, from 1957 — 1960 hijackings from Cuba to the U.S. occurred and were given a lot of coverage in the news. It was after this coverage, in 1961 that an American plane was first hijacked.

Freedom of the press is extremely important for a free society. Reporters have the right to cover such events as hijacking, terrorism, assassinations etc. Consider these questions:

   a. To what extent does the news media **shape** the news?
   b. Is it possible to report news without setting off events that could result in "new" news?
   c. Is it desirable?
   d. Can the freedom of the press be maintained while avoiding turning news into a sourcebook of ideas for criminals?
   e. How would you feel if your news was censored?
   f. How is the situation discussed in this question (No. 7) similar to Question No. 6? How is it different?

8. Take one particular news event. Find **three** news reports of the same story that each present it from a different perspective. Discuss in detail. How does each differ from the others?

9. **Write** three news articles dealing with three different controversial news items or issues. Make sure that you give them a bias towards a particular position. (In order to do this effectively, try to be subtle).

FOCUS ON: ADVERTISING

Advertising is nothing new. Naturally individuals offering a product or a service to the public want people to know of its availability. If you ever travel to the Middle East and wander through an open air market you may see people displaying their wares and occasionally even proclaiming their presence. The open market style of attracting attention (displaying wares and possibly shouting to get attention) is even recorded in the Bible:

> *Ho, everyone who thirsts, come ye to the waters,*
> *And he that has no money; come ye, buy and eat;*
> *Yea, come buy wine and milk without money and without price.*
> *Wherefore do you spend money for that which is not bread, and your labor for that which doesn't satisfy?*
> *Listen diligently to me and eat what is good and let your soul delight itself in fatness!*

Isaiah 55:1-2

Of course in this passage Isaiah wasn't trying to peddle shoes or other objects. Rather he was using the same techniques of the marketplace to gain attention for his prophetic message. (What was the message you ask? Read the Book of Isaiah! Sneaky advertisement, huh?)

Well, times have changed since Isaiah. Modern mass media has allowed individuals and companies to reach millions of people with messages to promote sales. Modern mass production has resulted in a huge quantity of items all competing for the average person's dollars.

As a result, numerous companies would like to make certain that people know about their products. Thus in 1972 alone the American public was exposed to about 23 billion dollars worth of advertising. I have seen various estimates of the number of ads that the average individual is exposed to per day. They range from about 500 to well over a thousand. It is clear that when one is exposed to that many ads in such a short period of time, a much smaller number than the maximum to which one is exposed, will be noticed.

In order to insure maximum impact of these ads various techniques are utilized:

1. The Use of Jingles — Very often a company will use a catchy tune on T.V. or Radio to help sell its products. You may find yourself humming these tunes even at other times and places. If you have younger brothers or sisters, you have probably heard them enthusiastically praising various products as they periodically sing the jingles. Pretty sneaky . . . The company trying to sell it's goods doesn't have to pay them for the advertisements!

185

2. The Mindless Statement — Sometimes commercials will make seemingly solid statements of fact about something. When these statements are really analyzed carefully they might not hold up. For example:

— Bigger is better!
— The more you buy at our store, the more you will save!
— Shop at ————, where quality is the name of the game.
— You can depend on us!

3. The use of Motivational Research And Psychology — In the effort to gain maximum effectiveness in advertising a great deal of work has gone into researching what motivates people to buy. Many advertisements make use of people's needs and/or secret desires to promote their products. Just look through a magazine at a few of the ads. A company may be trying to sell soap. Soap is very important for personal cleanliness, health etc. Yet what the ad might really be selling is **beauty**. An automobile is a nice form of transportation, yet an ad selling cars may really be selling **prestige**. A toothpaste ad isn't just selling a personal hygienic product. It may also be selling **sex appeal**. Here are but a few of the common needs/desires that many ads use to sell their products:

A. Sex — Using sex is probably one of the most common tactics. I recall one ad in particular where a cute girl was swinging back and forth in a tire. The company was trying to sell tires . . . or were they? A rugged, outdoorsy type he-man is puffing on a cigarette. The fact that he may eventually get cancer etc. is not that important. After all a beautiful girl who loves the smell of cigarette fumes is hanging onto his arm . . . . The use of sex in advertising is not at all unusual.

B. Status — Have you ever heard advertising using the cliche "Be the first on your block . . . "? If so, you were hearing an appeal to status. I am sure that you can easily think of several cars that are considered signs of status. But the use of status to sell is not limited to automobiles. Numerous items have been sold using the appeal to status. (See p. 169).

C. The Appeal to Conformity — Sometimes an ad will include something like this: "Millions of satisfied customers have used Dupso headache pills . . . You should too!" After all if they used it and were happy, then it **must** be all right, (or so the company would like you to believe).

D. The use of an Authority — This tactic is similar to the last one. Very often you will hear such statements as:

- Tests at a leading hospital indicate . . .
- Doctors recommend . . .
- In a recent University study it was shown that . . .

Again, the typical individual may automotically react, "Well gee, if they say so, then that product must be good." Another common form of this kind of approach is to have your typical John or Mary Doe try out a product or compare several products and (amazingly enough) prefer the one that is being advertised.

E. Ego trip — This type of ad plays on the individual's high opinion of him/herself. It may proclaim:

186

- You deserve . . .
- I know **blob** is costly — but it's nothing but the best for me!

Face it, are you going to argue with an ad that tells you, you're great?

F. The Young, Healthy and Clean Syndrome — We have a "thing" in our society about being young and acting young. Many ads will capitalize on our desires to look and act young and upon our desires to remain physically fit. Coupled with this is a concern about cleanliness. God forbid you have a ring around your collar or don't use an effective deodorant!

G. Excitement — Everybody likes a little excitement from time to time. Some ads will try to appeal to our sense of adventure:

- Come on, get away from it all . . .
- Time to put a little spice in your life . . .

This is particularly effective when promoting various forms of recreation, travel or vacations!

H. Something For Nothing — No person is going to ignore a bargain. Some ads try to cash in on that desire. You know — "Act before such and such date and get a free **yuch**." Sometimes a small sample of some item will be offered at low cost to get you to try it. Or a contest will be run with the real intention to produce more sales.

Well these are but a few of the approaches using Psychology that are utilized. There are other methods as well.

CONSIDER THIS:

1. Is there anything wrong with the desire to advertise? Why? Why not? Is the money spent on advertising justified? Why? Why not?

2. Do you think that the use of the various techniques discussed above is ethical? Why? Why not? Is it harmful? Why? Why not?

3. A student made the comment "Why the big fuss? . . . I know that these various techniques are used and I take that into consideration when I see ads . . ." Would awareness of the techniques used affect the ethics of the situation? Why? Why not?

4. How does advertising shape our perception of the world around us? of business? of goals in life?

5. Watch T.V. for a week as you normally would but keep a record on a chart:

Name of T.V. Show When Ad was Shown	Product Advertised	Technique Used To Sell	Comments

Your chart should include the name of the show when the ad was broadcast, the name of the product, what technique was used to sell the product (there could be more than one technique in an ad, and there may be techniques used that were not discussed in this unit), and any comments that you would like to include about the ad. (e.g. funny, liked it or not etc.).

At the end of the week figure out the total number of commercials you have seen, and the amount you saw for each T.V. show. Bring your chart and results to class.

6. Go through several magazines and tear out advertisements. Bring to class for discussion.

7. Write 3 **different** ads for **each** of the following:

      a. Soap or toothpaste.
      b. A soft drink.
      c. A household utensil. (any of your choice).
      d. An automobile.
      e. A charity.
      f. A house.

Out of each set of three commercials pick the one which you feel is the most ethical. Write down why you believe it to be more ethical than the other two. (Do this for all six items A–F) — Bring your commercials and written comments to class for discussion.

8. Evaluate the following according to the comments made above:

Are you tired? Run down? Have the feeling that life is passing you by? Then try G.R.N. G.R.N. is energy spelled backwards. Tests at the Dooby Clinic indicate that nine out of ten people who have used G.R.N. have found a new lease on life. Come On! Start to live again. You'll be glad you did!

Hey, tired of being the one left out of the fun at parties? I sure was! Then I tried new DISSOLVE the mouthwash with a kick! DISSOLVE isn't just one of those tasty, soda pop type mouth washes. DISSOLVE is serious medicine. Like an army on the march, DISSOLVE seeks out germs and utterly annihilates them! It leaves your breath clean and desirable, and isn't that the name of the game — to be desirable, yourself? Next time you are in the drugstore buy a bottle of DISSOLVE . . . Extra bonus*; buy two bottles before the end of the month, send the labels to us, and we'll put your name in our Fifty Million Dollar Sweepstakes . . . Thousands of prizes available . . . So act today!

*Void where prohibited.

9. What is "Propaganda"? Is there a difference between propaganda and advertising? Why? Why not?

10. Is it possible for a T.V. show, movie or book to "propagandize" How? Give examples.

11. Do you feel exploited by advertising? Why? Why not?

12. Can advertising really be effective if it doesn't appeal to one's emotions? Why? Why not?

13. Mr. Quigley read the above paragraphs and commented: "I don't see what all the fuss is about . . . If advertising helps get people to buy, that's good for our economy. If our economy is strong, then we all benefit! It is obvious that the final result justifies the use of ads."

    a. What is the meat of Mr. Quigley's comments?
    b. Do you agree? Why? Why not?

14. You are the advertising department of a company that manufactures items of high quality. You have a new product that you feel is really beneficial for children. In order to sell it, you would have to advertise on T.V. during childrens' shows. Discuss the ethics of the situation.

15. Look up in the Bible Zephaniah 3:13, Lev. 19:11, 13, 14, 16, Lev. 25:17, and Psalm 34:13, 14. Discuss these in relation to this section.

CENSORED   CENSORED   CENSORED

Miss Fargo is outraged. It seems that she cannot escape smut anywhere. When she goes to the newstand, she notices obscene magazines, with pictures of people in various degrees of nudity. When she goes to a movie she hears swearing deliberately injected into the script. In addition, she notes many movies make a point of working plenty of violence and sex into their plots. Pure sensationalism! Then she tries to sit and enjoy reading a novel! What happens? She finds more sex and violence, not really necessary for the plot, but added for commercial reasons! Miss Fargo is disgusted! If she had any say in the matter, there would be **strict** censorship laws in this country!

CONSIDER THIS:

1. What **exactly** makes something obscene? Give examples.

2. What do you think of Miss Fargo's situation and opinions?

3. Is censorship ever justified? In what circumstances? What kind of restrictions should be set forth (if any)? Why?

4. What if a minority group decides that in order to maintain its standard of ethics, censorship must be imposed? How can such a group accomplish its aims in our society? How far can it, and should it go?

5. List some general arguments **in favor** of censorship laws. Discuss.

6. List some general arguments **against** censorship laws. Discuss.

7. Who ultimately should make decisions concerning censorship? Why?

190

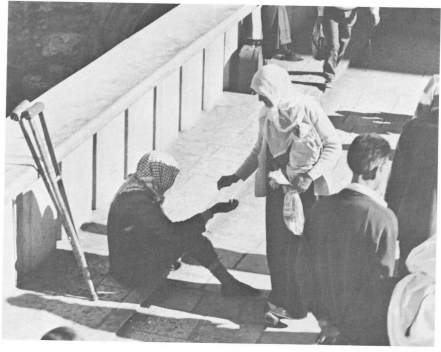

Charity

MERRYBLOB'S WING

J.P. Merryblob originally came to this country as an immigrant, a refugee from Hitler's Europe. While his family had attained some degree of wealth in the old country, it had all been lost in the Holocaust. J.P. and his sister were the only two of the family to escape with their lives. They were lucky to just get out! J.P. found work in this country as a messenger boy in the Stock Exchange. He kept his ears open and his mouth shut and learned as much as he could. After a few years he managed to scrape some money together and invested in some stock. He was extremely lucky as the stock became very valuable. Merryblob took his profits and put them into real estate. He began to build what eventually would become an empire of slum tenements. Merryblob concentrated on the cheapest and junkiest buildings in the sleazier parts of town. He spent little money on them, finding it more economical to pay off various city safety inspectors. At the same time he charged the highest rents possible, mercilessly evicting those who didn't honor their contracts. Merryblob also paid off various bank officials, who in turn, helped him gain control of more properties. What began as two small buildings on Jason Street has in forty-five years grown to its current size of twenty-five hundred dilapidated and rundown buildings. Merryblob's properties have suffered numerous fires. Some have been of suspicious origin, and Merryblob has profited greatly from his insurance. Other fires and accidents have occurred simply due to the property being so badly neglected. A few deaths have even occurred! Merryblob doesn't particularly care about his tenants. He has fought efforts to impose a limit on rents that he can collect. When questioned five years ago by a newspaper person from The Daily Blab as to his feelings about his tenants, Mr. Merryblob went on record as saying "Who cares?"

J.P. Merryblob is getting a bit older, and recently has been reported in failing health. A confidential source tells us that J.P. is becoming increasingly concerned about his future. Merryblob, according to this source, said the following: "I know I've sinned in my life, but I've always gone to Temple every Rosh Hashanah and Yom Kippur. That sort of evens it up. But, I'm not taking any chances. . . I want to make sure I get to Heaven! Maybe if I donate some money to some good cause, I'll get there faster!" Last week The Daily Blab reported that J.P. Merryblob intends to donate a new research wing to the Urban Hospital. The Merryblob Wing will be a valuable contribution to the medical system. Work done there will very likely save many lives.

Yet there is growing opposition to this donation from many quarters. A stream of people, — former and current Merryblob tenants, students, and even people from the health care system, have been parading up and down Main Street, in front of Urban Hospital in protest. Some of their signs read:

"Merryblob Bleeds The Poor!"

"Put A New Wing On Your Own Buildings"

"You Up Our Rents To Pay For Your Charity"

"Custer Died For Your Sins, Merryblob"

"You Give Gifts To Take Off On Your Taxes, J.P.!"

The Hospital Administration is in a quandary. While they would like the gift, they are uncertain as to whether or not they should accept it under the circumstances.

CONSIDER THIS:

1. What do you think the hospital should do? Why?

2. Is it acceptable for a worthy cause to take money from a shady source? Why? Why not? Would it make any difference as to what the motives of the donor are if the cause to which s/he is giving is a good one? Why? Why not?

3. Merryblob might justify his business dealings on the grounds that he was a victim of the Holocaust and it's a dog eat dog world. "After all" stated Merryblob in his interview in The Daily Blab, "The real world isn't like a religious school . . . You've got to be tough to survive."

   What do you think of these justifications? Why?

192

4. What about Merryblob's opinion about going to High Holiday Services to "even the score" for his sins? What do you think about this? Why?

5. Do you feel that Merryblob's contribution to the hospital will "even the score"? What will?

6. What are valid ways to "even the score" for one's sins (any sins)? Why? Evaluate this problem carefully and in detail.

7. Are the people picketing the hospital ethical in their actions? What if Merryblob changed his mind as a result of the demonstration and simply decided to give nothing? . . . Would the protestors be "morally clean"? Why? Why not? Does that mean they shouldn't picket? Why? Why not?

8. Are you aware of any situation similar to the above one? If so what? Discuss.

DONNA'S FATHER

Donna is a hard working student. She always puts into her lessons far more work than what is required. As a senior in High School she longs to go on to State University to study Journalism. There is, however, a problem. While her mother supports her plans, her father is lukewarm to them. He had once commented "All a girl needs to do is to find herself a husband." Moreover her father claims that he doesn't have the money to pay for her education. In the last family "battle," Donna angrily pointed out that he had six thousand dollars in a special account. Her father acknowledged the existence of the money, but told her and her mother that he was intending to donate it to the Fireman's Relief Fund.

CONSIDER THIS:

1. What is your reaction to Donna's Father?

2. The Fireman's Relief Fund is an extremely worthly cause. It benefits many families that have lost someone in the course of duty. Is Donna's father selfish or generous? Why? Why not?

3. And what about Donna's Mother? What should she do?

4. What should Donna do?

5. How does one go about evaluating how s/he should give to charity? What criteria could/should one follow? Why?

POLITICAL INTRIGUE

"Aha. Just look at what we've found here," said the Private Investigator as he handed the file to his client. James Ras glanced through the file's contents. "Boy you sure did your homework . . . It's all there . . . affidavits, documentation . . . everything. It certainly seems that Senator Clarke was a busy fellow. He's married, yet he's been involved with Ms. Sticky, the wealthy socialite. He was on the Committee that arranged the sale of his own land to the Navy . . . This stuff would be disastrous to his political career, should it leak out . . ." "But you won't leak it, will you?" asked the Private Investigator. "It depends" said Ras. "Senator Clarke has been blocking Bill 538 which calls for increased welfare payments to the poor and sick. He feels that it may just lead to increased inflation which, he says, will further hurt the poor. I don't agree. I intend to use these files to persuade him to change his mind!"

CONSIDER THIS:

1. What would you call a situation like this?

2. Do the ends justify the means?

3. Would you consider a situation such as this a very lofty form of charity? Why? Why not?

4. Who is worse — Senator Clarke who refuses to increase welfare checks or James Ras who is trying to force the issue?

5. What would you do if you were Senator Clarke?

IRVING GROCERY STORE

"No Way," growled Mr. Irving. "I won't have any more of this freeloading." Irving looked up from his records and gave Johnson one of his "killer looks." Johnson sighed and quickly occupied himself straightening out some shelves.

Irving wasn't being fair, he thought. It was true that Irving Grocery Store wasn't the wealthiest one in town, but what was to be done about the Smith Family? The father had been killed in an auto accident six months ago. The mother who had been struggling to support the family was sick. Johnson, taking pity on the Smiths had been extending them credit. They paid their bills although, due to their circumstances, they were always somewhat behind. Irving, however, didn't like giving credit at all and Johnson wasn't looking forward to a major clash. Looking out of the window Johnson saw one of the Smith kids, Sandy, coming towards the store.

CONSIDER THIS:

1. What might happen if Johnson continues to help the Smiths? What would happen if he stops aiding them?

2. What would you do if you were in Johnson's place?

3. Is there any way that Johnson can change Mr. Irving's mind? How?

4. If their credit is cut off what could the Smith's do?

5. Mr. Irving might justify his actions on the grounds that it is his store and no one has any right to tell him how to run it etc. Do you agree? Why? Why not?

6. Would it make any difference if you were told that Johnson and Irving were partners? How would this affect your answers to the above questions?

❖-❖-❖-❖-❖

ANALYSIS: TRADITIONAL VIEWS

Today we take such things as "welfare ", "Government subsidies " and "Community self-help" for granted. Yet the Jewish view of "charity" was revolutionary in its day! It might be useful to quickly take a look at some of the "quaint" customs that were occurring elsewhere in the world while the Jewish tradition was developing social ethics.

In many places around the globe if a man died his wife would be strangled or expected to commit suicide to attend him. In ancient Assyria, people would get their jollies by watching captives being tortured, or children blinded in front of their parents. Another popular way of dealing with enemies by Assyrian (and even a few Persian) leaders was by cutting off their tongues. Later the Ancient Romans enjoyed watching prisoners killing each other or being killed by animals. In the Arena interesting stories were sometimes even "acted" out with "players" enjoying such roles that might result in being burned alive or mutilated in various ways. (Ugh!)

It was, against the background of this very vicious and barbaric world, that our ancestors pioneered various humane rules for dealing with their fellow human beings. The Jewish tradition has long recognized that **every individual is an important entity**. Thus, in the Mishnah the comment is made:

All human beings are similar to the first man, yet there is not one in-

dividual exactly like his fellow. Therefore each person must say "For my sake was the universe created."

Yet the tradition also recognizes that **no person really lives in total isolation.** We are shaped by our environment and we in turn shape it. How do we shape it? By our interactions with others, we have a strong effect upon how pleasant life will (or won't) be for all of us. Thus while there is much in the Jewish tradition giving us individual guidance as to what the sages felt constituted good behavior, most of this was formulated with a careful consideration as to the interactions between the individual and others. From Pirke Avot:

> *Keep far from an evil neighbor and don't associate yourself with the wicked.*

> *He in whom the spirit of mankind takes delight, in him the spirit of the Omnipresent finds pleasure, but he in whom the spirit of his fellow creatures finds no pleasure, in him the spirit of the Omnipresent takes no delight.*

> *Separate not thyself from the community.*

When I was university undergraduate, a very popular concept and expression was "Doing your own thing." It meant doing something in such a way in order to express your own individuality – an ultimate expression of the importance of the individual! I'll never forget one particular professor of mine who would occasionally make the comment:

> *"Do your own thing, kid . . . but not on* **my** *floor."*

That was his way (slightly gross, but memorable) of expressing the fact that often one's actions can (and do) have an effect upon others.

Within the Jewish tradition there is the constant recognition that humanity is, in effect a team, where all members have something important to contribute. A midrash:

> *One day a well digger happened to meet an important Rabbi along the road. "Hi important Rabbi!" "Hi well digger!" "Guess what important Rabbi? . . . I'm just as great a person as you." "Oh? Really?" asked the Rabbi. "Well you may tell people how to use water according to our traditions, but I'm the one who has to make that water available!" responded the well digger.*

If you consider it, much of Judaism's teachings on such things as business ethics, the ethics of communication etc. aren't concerned with a person's actions in private, but rather with **individuals' interactions with others.**

As such it should come as no surprise that an individual's own personal value system contributes to the general ethics and values found in society as a whole. "Huh, What's that, again?" you ask. Yes, the values and ethics that every person holds, contributes to the general values and ethics of our society. If for example no individual put a strong value upon the importance of life, murders might be **very, very** commonplace. While sometimes the individual feels that his/her impact on society is very small, a huge number of individuals taking a particular stance on some subject really can influence the direction that society will go. Thus your own personal values and ethics are important in a wider societal sense:

Individuals' attitudes towards laws ⟶ can affect whether or not laws will be enforced.

Individuals' attitudes towards stealing or cheating ⟶ can affect the general way that businesses operate, for individuals both run businesses and are consumers as well.

Individuals' attitudes towards cleanliness as well as personal convenience ⟶ can affect how clean our environment may be.

Individuals' attitudes towards charity, fellow human beings, and personal pleasures ⟶ could ultimately determine whether or not poverty will ever be eliminated.

It is this concern with both the individual and how s/he interacts in society that led to the Jewish concept of charity. The concept of charity wasn't even called by that term. It was (and is) known as Tzedakah. Tzedakah is a concept that is far more encompassing and comprehensive in its scope than the English word charity could possibly suggest. Charity has its roots in the Latin word caritas which means "love" or "affection." The implication is, of course, that charity is something done to or for another from that motive. The translation of the Hebrew word Tzedakah is "righteousness." It suggests justice. It implies that community responsibility is not merely a matter of good will. Rather, it is a necessary part of existence; that it is the proper, right or just thing to do. This way of looking at community or individual care for others contrasts strongly with a world in which an Assyrian ruler might erect a monument made up of slightly "rearranged" corpses.

The Jewish concept of Tzedakah followed from the Jewish concept of the universe. Just as something or someone is responsible for the creation of a chair or table, so too did our ancestors believe that something (or someone) was responsible for the creation of the universe, of the world, and of living things. Regardless of whether we may or may not accept the creation — Adam/Eve story of Genesis as literal truth, nonetheless we still affirm that there must be something behind all reality. That something we call God. Furthermore our ancestors recognized, that we are all but a small part of nature, a part of the cosmos. If you think of it, we are all, in a sense "star children." We are made of chemicals from the earth, which were derived from the particles that formed our universe. It is interesting to consider that humankind is really the "eyes of nature" looking back on itself! We are all the universe's atoms and molecules put together in such a unique way, that we in turn, can observe nature! Pretty remarkable and profound stuff! Well this leads right in to the Jewish view of Tzedakah. Because we all **are** a part of God's world, everything that we have is therefore in a sense, "on loan." Tzedakah to another of "nature eyes," is humankind's way of returning the favor! Thus we find the comment in Pirke Avot, "Give to Him from what is His, for you and what you have are His."

Well, Tzedakah is not just a hit or miss affair. A great deal of tradition grew up around its mechanics and procedure. Here are some Biblical comments relating to this concept (p. 198):

The eyes of nature.

197

WHY DOESN'T GOD GET INVOLVED?

In the Talmud we read that Turnus Rufus once asked Rabbi Akiba "If your God loves the poor, why doesn't he support them?" Akiba answered "So that by our being charitable we may be saved from the punishment of Gehinnom." "No way," replied Turnus. "The fact that you support the poor is what will condemn you to Gehinnom . . . Let me put it to you this way . . . Let's say a King is displeased with a servant for some reason and has him locked up with orders not to bring food or water. If you gave the prisoner those things, wouldn't the King be angry, if he found out?" Akiba answered, "It's more like a King who, angry with his son, carries out the sentence you've mentioned. If someone disobeyed orders and gave him food and drink, don't you suppose that the King, would end up sending that person a present?"

> *When you reap the harvest of your land, don't reap to the very corners of the field; nor should you glean (gather) stray ears of corn. Don't pick your vineyards bare or gather up any fallen grapes. You should leave these for the poor and the stranger . . .*
>
> *Leviticus 19:9—10*

> *When you reap the harvest in your field and forget or miss some, don't go back to pick it up; it should be left for the orphan, widow or stranger . . . When you beat your olive trees (to get the olives down), don't go over them again; what's left is for the stranger, fatherless and widow . . . When you gather the grapes from your vineyard, don't go over it again; it will be for the stranger, fatherless and widow.*
>
> *Deuteronomy 24:19—21*

And:

> *For six years you may sow your land and gather its fruits; but every seventh year you'll let it rest and lie still. Anything that grows there, the poor can have, and what they leave wild animals may eat. Do the same with your vineyard and olive yard.*
>
> *Exodus 23:10—11*

It would be common sense that some of these early comments would be expressed in agricultural terms. (Remember modern manufacturing as big business is a relatively recent development). Yet one can't help but be amazed at how advanced these statements were for their time. In a sense they contributed to a "Biblical Anti-Poverty Program." Note the above comments weren't just mere handouts. Rather the poor person's dignity was as much as possible, upheld in the sense that s/he had to work for his/her benefits. (It should also be noted, however, that there were other means — e.g. a system of "tithes" by which the poor also benefited — see Deut. 14:22-29).

As time went on, the ancient sages developed more detailed ideas about charity. A first question that would naturally come to mind would be, "Who should give charity?" An answer is found in the Talmud. We are told that everyone, even one who is not the best off financially should give to those more needy than him/herself. Another issue that was raised was just how much one should give to charity. Estimates varied but an accepted limit was that no one should give more than one fifth of his/her wealth. After all it wouldn't make sense for a person to become poor, possibly requiring community support just because s/he gave away too much of his/her own valuables. Just how much should be given to a needy person? That's a difficult question. We read in the Bible:

> *. . . You shall not harden your heart, nor shut your hand from your poor brother; but you shall open your hand wide to him and shalt surely lend him sufficient for his need . . . You shall surely give him and your heart shall not be grieved when you give to him . . .*
>
> *Deut. 15:7, 8, 10*

Yet what do you do if someone from a wealthy family finds him/herself poor? Maimonides makes the point that if the person was used to riding with a servant running in front of him, then both a horse and servant should be found. (How often this was actually literally carried out is speculative; but it does demonstrate a concern with what different people would perceive as their needs!) Maimonides, however, points out that one is not obligated to make such a person rich! Another relevant question comes up as to whom should be the recipient of charity when there are many needy people in many places. Maimonides suggested some guidelines to follow. He felt that a person should first help a relative before helping anyone else outside of the family. Next in line were the poor of one's town and after that, the poor of another town. Moreover he also suggested some procedures to protect donors. For example he believed that one shouldn't even try to collect from an overgenerous person who might donate more than his/her finances allow. He also felt that no person should be embarrassed into giving charity. Maimonides commented that should a poor person ask you for charity and you have nothing to give, then at the least speak nicely to that person, so as not to make him/her feel even worse than before.

FOUR TYPES OF ALMSGIVERS

1. One who wishes to give — but not that others should give. (He begrudges others the satisfaction of doing good deeds and is primarily concerned with his own glory).

2. One that wishes that others would give — but he himself won't give. (He's cheap!)

3. One that gives and would like others to give as well. (A pious fellow).

4. One that won't give and doesn't care if others give or not. (A wicked character).

Pirke Avot

Tzedakah is like a suit of armor — Each small part contributes to the whole —
Talmud

What about the person who doesn't really need charity but is taking advantage of the system? (There have always been freeloaders). Well first of all our traditions make it quite clear that one should go out of his/her way to avoid being supported by others. Many of the ancient Rabbis made their livings, not by being Rabbis, but by other forms of work. One, in fact, was a gravedigger! Maimonides suggested that if one got into the habit of pretending s/he needed Tzedakah, s/he might end up actually requiring it! On the other hand, a person who **really needs** charity, but is too proud to accept it is not to be admired, for such a situation could well be suicidal.

To give you an idea of just how much our ancestors considered the entire issue of Tzedakah, I'd like to briefly mention Maimonides' famous **Eight Degrees of Charity**. These are really neat! One hundred and fifty years from now when you are old and "establishment" like myself you might not remember everything that you studied in Religious School. But you will **always** remember that you heard about Maimonides' Eight Degrees of Charity! Here they are:

1. *The highest degree of charity is when one helps a person by giving him/ her a loan or a job, or even giving him/her a business partnership. This enables the person to support him/herself. It's a good way of protecting the person's feelings.*

2. *The next highest way, is to give charity, but to do so in a way so as neither the donor nor the recipient know each other. Maimonides goes on to tell us that this is similar to a system used in THE TEMPLE (you know – the biggie in Jerusalem), where there was a special room where people would leave money and others would take it incognito. Many community funds operate this way and Maimonides cautions us to make sure that the people who run such a fund aren't crooks!*

3. *The third best degree of charity (working down) is when the donor knows who received the charity but the recipient doesn't know who the donor was. Maimonides tells us that some of the Rabbis of past years would do this. He feels that this method is good if the people running community funds have questionable ethics.*

4. *The fourth degree is the opposite of the last one. The donor doesn't know the recipient, but the recipient knows who the donor is.*

5. *After that is when both know each other (Thank God, after those last two!) and one hands it to the other without the donor being asked for the donation.*

6. *A worse form of charity is when one person gives to the other; but the donor had to be asked for the aid.*

7. *Even worse than that, is when a person gives less than he should but does so nicely and cheerfully.*

8. *The worst form of charity is when the donor has "fed lemons to his cat" – in other words, gives with a* **sour puss!**

Tzedakah has been taken seriously throughout Jewish History as theory has been translated into deed. Tzedakah was not just an individual endeavor, but rather a

Two sheep went across a river —
    The one that was shorn passed safely.
    The other one, heavy with its wool
                        S
                        A
                        N
                        K
                        — TALMUD

community responsibility, and various procedures and organizations have been set up throughout the ages to help translate religious ideals into reality. Today Jewish teachings and concerns in this area stand as a model for charitable works and institutions, the world over!

A WIDE RANGE OF ACTIVITIES

The range of self-help activities that Jewish Communities have been involved in are truly remarkable. They have included such things as organizations for burial of the dead, ransoming captives, visiting sick people and prisoners, (no connection between the two intended!), and providing for poor brides. Orphanages, hospitals and even inns for travellers have been among the areas of community concern for many, many years.

Gemiluth Chasadim

Incidently you shouldn't get the idea that charity, is just a matter of distribution of resources. Our ancestors spent a lot of time and effort on the entire issue of "gemiluth chasadim." Gemiluth chasadim can be considered as deeds of loving-kindness. These are actions someone does for another — good deeds. A Talmudic comment is that gemiluth chasadim is superior to the mere giving of alms in three ways:

1. One gives alms only to the poor — Gemiluth chasadim can be displayed to everybody.

2. One gives alms to the living. Acts of loving-kindness can be shown towards the dead as well.

3. Almsgiving involves money. Gemiluth chasadim can involve money but also entails personal service.

Various activities were considered particularly noteworthy. One was **hospitality** to travellers and/or strangers who need help. Legend has it that Job (you read about him on p. 65) had a house with four doors! Now granted the Middle East is a hot place. True, they didn't have air conditioners in those days; but Job didn't have all of those doors just to keep cool! He had them to make it easier for poor people, or even strangers passing through to enter his home and partake of his hospitality. Abraham was another Biblical personality who was renowned for being hospitable. One hundred and fifty years ago when I was a student, the teachers always talked about how Abraham would invite people into his home. First they would wash their feet and later eat. (e.g. see Genesis 18:1-6). That always struck me as rather strange. After all, I couldn't see anybody eating with their feet. Then for awhile I wondered whether Abraham had a particularly strong sense of smell, or whether he was simply trying to tell his guests something! But then, if you've ever worn sandals in a hot desert climate, I think you can see that being invited to wash one's feet would be very pleasant form of hospitality! Anyhow being hospitable is one noteworthy aspect of gemiluth chasadim and Abraham and Job are particularly famous for displaying this trait!

Another admired activity that is a sign of loving-kindness is **visiting the sick**. While that doesn't sound like much, consider it for a second. Generally people

are never overly enthusiastic about this activity, and sometimes even get rather squeamish about sickness or disease. I'll never forget one of my friends, a medical student, worrying over whether or not she had bubonic plague (rather rare in our day) after simply studying about the symptoms! Yet the Rabbis had keen psychological insight. In the Talmud recognition is made of the fact that people who visit the sick can help make them feel better. The sages recognized that a simple visit to a sick person can really do wonders for that individual's morale. Quite often morale can play an important role in a person's recovery.

Other areas considered admirable examples of gemiluth chasadim would include **helping a bride** (get a dowry etc.) or taking care of **orphans**. One area that is considered an extremely fine example of a deed of loving-kindness is any **service performed for the dead**. Face it, if one helped out in a funeral etc., there was little likelihood that the dead person would be in any kind of position to return the favor!

Now gemiluth chasadim is by no means limited to the above activities alone. These are but a few particularly admired approaches. I think you get the idea. Being charitable, . . . righteous . . . involves a great deal in terms of personal action. I'd like to close this discussion with a story:

> *A Rabbi was rushing to synagogue to run the services. As he passed a house, a sleeping baby was awakened and began to cry. The baby was all alone, as its mother had already gone to the synagogue. In spite of the fact that the Rabbi was late, he stopped and cared for the baby. Members of his congregation, concerned because the Rabbi was so late, found him there.*

To me examples such as this from our tradition demonstrate the highest qualities that can be involved in charity and deeds of loving-kindness.

SUMMARY

In this chapter we concerned ourselves with the concept of charity. The Jewish concept of charity goes beyond that mere title. It is Tzedakah — righteousness. What makes the Jewish views of Tzedakah so exceptional is that our ancestors were formulating them at a time when such humane concepts were the exception rather than the rule. The point was made in this chapter that the Jewish concept of Tzedakah followed from the Jewish view of the universe. This is God's world. All that we have is, in a sense, "on loan" from God. Therefore being charitable is a responsibility in which we show our gratitude by our actions to other of God's beings! A great deal of thought was given to the procedures involved in giving charity. "How much should be given?", "To whom?" and "In what manner should it be given?" were some of the basic issues that naturally arose. One of the most famous and most interesting approaches to charity found in any culture on earth is Maimonides' discussion of the **Eight Degrees of Charity**, and we examined those. Also we took a brief look at the concept of gemiluth chasadim — or acts of loving-kindness. Charity isn't limited to the distribution of physical items. It can involve a great deal more. Some acts of loving-kindness that have been particularly noted and praised include providing a bride with a dowry, helping an orphan, being hospitable, visiting the sick, and doing something for the dead. But these aren't by any means the only ways by which loving-kindness can be displayed. The number of good deeds that one can do is limited only by the imagination!

CONSIDER THIS:

204

1. Discuss the terms "Charity," and "Tzedakah." How are they similar? Different?

2. What were some of the issues that came up with regard to Tzedakah? What were some of the guidelines suggested to deal with them? What do you think of these guidelines?

3. Analyze the Biblical passages on p. 198. What were they saying? Read the story of Ruth in the Bible, and relate it to these passages.

4. Mr. Mahoney plans to donate some money to the Cedarcrest Nursing Home. He insists however that the building that will be erected using his gift be called "The Mahoney Rehabilitation Center." Is there anything wrong with this practice? Why? Why not? What if he wanted the name to be "The Grace Mahoney Center" after his wife — would that be ethically sound? Why? Why not? Why do you suppose that people would want such projects named after them? Why do you suppose that institutions would condone such practices?

5. Is the practice of Tzedakah and Gemiluth Chasadim practical in the modern world? Write paragraphs pro and con.

6. Is there a qualitative difference in the way charity can be given? Can one form of charity **really** be better than another? Discuss (write in detail) in relation to this unit. What do you think is the **best** form of charity? Why?

7. Look up the following passages in the Bible. Analyze in relation to this unit:

   a. Psalm 24:1
   b. Lev. 25:35-43
   c. Gen. 1:27 **and** Deut. 10:17-19
   d. Proverbs 3:27-28

A THIRSTY PROBLEM

Two men are traveling through a desert. Only one, however, has a flask of water. After awhile the sun is really beating down hard. It becomes obvious that they both are in need of a drink.

If one person drinks the flask that person will survive — the other will never make it to civilization!

If both drink from the flask — neither will survive the desert.

WHAT SHOULD THEY DO!

(This is an actual Talmudic problem. Consider it with your classmates).

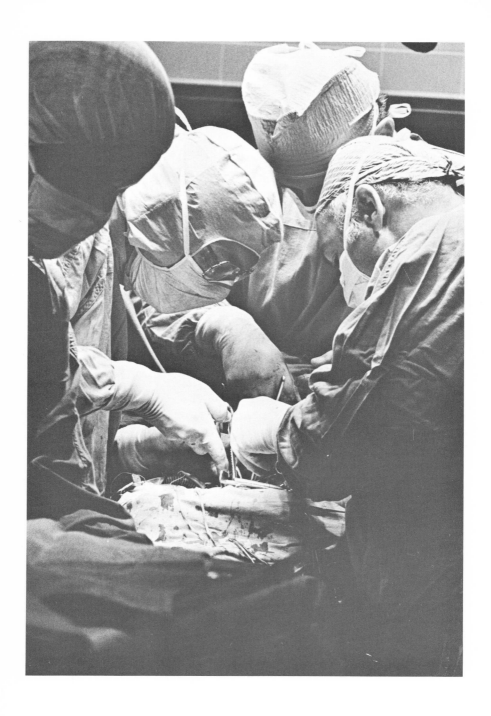

Some Biomedical Ethics

L. A. Y. V. IV — SIMULATION

To Be Carried out in Class.

The class is to be divided into groups. There should be no more than five to six people in each group. The individual groups should analyze and solve the problem set forth below. (Your teacher will give you a specific amount of time in which to work). The entire class will then come together as each group presents its decisions.

PROBLEM

It is the year 2053. In an outstanding feat of engineering accomplishment Dr. J.H. Hiro has developed an artificial heart, — the L.A.Y.V. IV. The L.A.Y.V. IV surpasses all previous attempts to produce an artificial heart. The computer simulations indicate that it will function perfectly and ultra-efficiently. There is however a problem. Due to the high costs and extremely delicate craftsmanship required there are only three models currently available. The central clearing computer indicates nine people who are in desperate, immediate need of the device. Because the six people who do not get it will die the choice as to whom will receive L.A.Y.V. IV is a particularly difficult one. U.N. law No. 6025.3978 indicates that in situations such as this a panel of randomly chosen individuals are to assemble to make the decision. You are on that panel. Some brief biographical data has been assembled to help you in your choices. Take your time and give this plenty of thought. Good luck!

207

CONSIDER THESE QUESTIONS:

1. Whom did you (as a group) choose? Whom didn't you choose?
2. Why did **each person** in your group choose specific individuals (reject individuals) from the assembled data? What **criteria** did you apply when you made your decisions? — How did each person go about deciding who should get L.A.Y.V. IV, and who shouldn't? (e.g. "I thought X was cool ... while Y was a nerd").
3. How did your group as a whole go about reaching a consensus of opinion as to the decisions that had to be made? (e.g. "voted," "Charlie yelled the loudest" etc.).
4. Later each person should write a report discussing the conclusions of his/her group, taking into consideration
   a. Questions 1, 2, 3 above.
   b. Your own reaction to your group's decisions. Was there any person about whom your group made a decision that you disagreed with? Why?

Name:	Jane Abdinton
Age:	33
Address:	1335 25th Avenue, Brewston-Boswash
Occupation:	Physician
Education:	Broderick Grammer, Harlem High,
	B.S. — Metropolan University
	M.D. — P.D.Q. University

Profile:

Jane's father is a powerful representative to the U.S. Congress from Black Harlem. He is proud of his brilliant daughter, but she is often a source of embarrassment to him. It's not that he disagrees with many of her humanitarian principles, — but it's her methods! Like the time she was involved in that shutdown of all the hospitals in Boswash (the city that covers part of the Eastern Coast) in protest to governmental involvement regulating births! He feels that she is too much of a radical activist in her crusades. Jane, has stated publically that "means are justified by the ends."

Ms. Abdinton is single. She lives in a commune. She enjoys Skiing, Judo and Tennis, and is a very active person.

Also in her file: Character Recommendation:

Jan. 26, 2053

Sirs,

Jane Abdinton is one of the finest human beings, I have ever met. She is a compassionate person who takes a real interest in people. She is a champion of human rights and has the courage to stand for her convictions.

Sincerely yours,
Jack B. Merriweather III
Director-Metco Hospital.

Name:	Walter Forson	Mary Forson
Age:	70	65
Address:	235 Gasony Road, Comoben	
Occupation:	Both were executives in Zinsat, the company that manufactures the Zinmore Circuit. (The Zinmore circuit was invented in 1999. It enables computers the size of a wristwatch to contain all of the knowledge of The Library of Congress). Mr. and Mrs. Forson are now retired.	
Education:	B.A. — Comoben University	B.S. — Comoben University
	M.A. — Folsan University	PhD. — Chad Institute

Profile:

The Forsons met at Comoben University. It was love at first sight, and marriage shortly thereafter. Although Walter's interests were in public relations, and Mary's in research they both ended up at Zinsat, where they enjoyed satisfying and challenging careers. The Forsons have since retired. Mary keeps busy by being

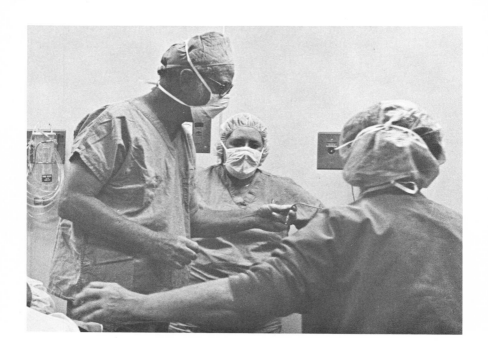

210

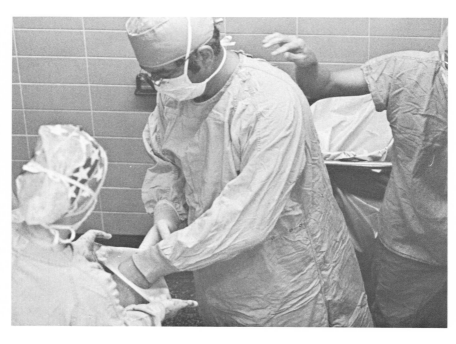

active in the Temple Sisterhood. Walter doesn't find much meaning in Religion. He likes to coach a local hockey team and read. They have two children and five grandchildren, and look forward to their occasional visits. Walter and Mary have enough money from their pensions and government subsidies to live. They worry, however, that the government health insurance may not be sufficient should they require extensive medical care. They are very proud and would rather starve than accept money from their children.

Name:	Joyce Upshill
Age:	40
Address:	175, Level three, Martian Colony
Occupation:	Videobeam engineer
Education:	North Cicero Grammer
	Jackson High
	Scatoor Technical School

Profile:

Joyce always liked tinkering with mechanical devices. When she was a kid she constantly took things apart and reassembled them. When she was in high school a freak accident in the school shop cost her, her right hand. Showing remarkable determination and courage she persevered. Learning to rely on her left hand*, she eventually became a videobeam engineer. For a period of time she serviced 3-Dimensional video consols. (3-D.V.C. is a 3-dimensional color T.V.). Eventually she became bored with the job and applied for duty in the Martian Colony. She encountered some initial discrimination, due to her handicap but eventually attained her goal**. She has performed admirably on her job and her exceptional skill and alertness in manning the videobeam sensors saved the lives of many of her fellow crewpersons.

211

Joyce has two children. She was married, but got a divorce when her husband disapproved of her proposed change of career. She has few interests outside of her technical work. She likes to watch 3-D.V.C. especially if the show features a lot of violence.

  * Because of the limited availability of Bionic replacements, Joyce was given a Bionic hand only last year.
 ** There have been allegations in the tabloids that her successful transfer to The Martian Colony was brought about by unethical means.

Name:	Johnny Hero
Age:	18
Address:	39 Mulbrum Lane, Yiakstown
Occupation:	Student
Education:	Lipenview School
	Pilgrim High — member of Senior Class.

Profile:

Johnny Hero has always excelled in sports. He has been on the track, baseball and football teams, of Pilgrim High, where he is now a senior. Johnny has never been much of a student. He barely gets by. He is, however, considered to be one of the

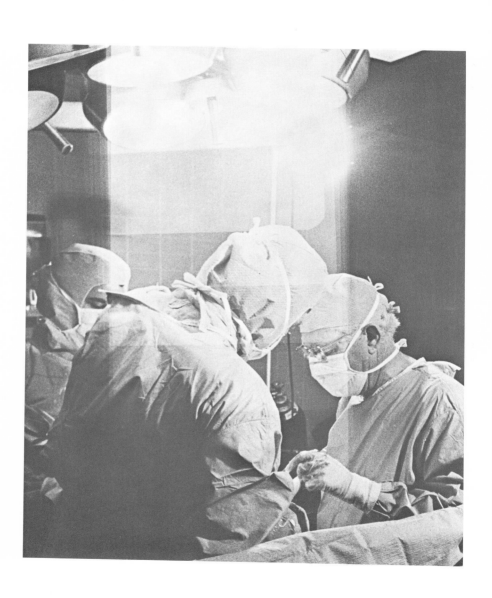

finest athletes the school has ever produced. Johnny is well liked by not only his teammates, but even by kids on the other teams against whom he competes. "He not only knows how to win, but even when his team loses, he displays good sportsmanship," states the captain of a rival team. Johnny is patient and even-tempered. The only troubles to which he has ever been linked have been two minor cheating incidents at school. The teachers involved gave him an opportunity to make the work up so that he would still be eligible for the teams.

Johnny's favorite activity after sports is watching 3-D.V.C. His mother frequently gets annoyed at him for leaving his room sloppy and forgetting (sometimes on purpose) to take the dog out. Johnny has a younger brother, and sometimes the two boys and their parents go off on camping trips.

Name: Bill Adams
Age: 53
Address: 27 Exclusive Road, Wellbury
Occupation: President Insurance Company
Education: Wellbury Elementary School, Mede Jr. High,
             North High School, B.S. — University of Wellbury,
             M.B.A. — Stillings University

Profile:

Bill is a self-made man. He came from a poor family and worked his way through   213
college. At the same time he maintained a high scholastic standing and was admitted to a prestigious graduate school. After joining Shady Mutual, he gradually
clawed his way to the top. Bill has been ruthless in his dealings with business
opponents, and is responsible (and blames himself) for another top executive's
suicide. He is however a family man and has three children. Not only does he
provide them with all the material things they want, but he also works very hard
at spending time, and being active with them. His wife died three years ago in
the tragic accident that wiped out Undersea Colony III in the Atlantic. Bill
is a member of the local Church and both he and the kids attend frequently.
He is quite wealthy and donates a great deal of money to the Church. Bill is
quite conservative politically. When the public voted by computer on question
seven (a law favoring brainwashing of criminals), Bill voted in the affirmative.
He also feels that the people in the Martian Colony have a perfect right to limit
immigration to Mars to certain ethnic groups, if they should so desire.

Name: Evance Jerinsky
Age: 50
Address: 272 Biar Lane, North Clip, — Boswash
Occupation: Accountant
Education: Snerkins Elementary
             South-West Jr. High
             Titanic High School
             B.S.B.A. North — South University

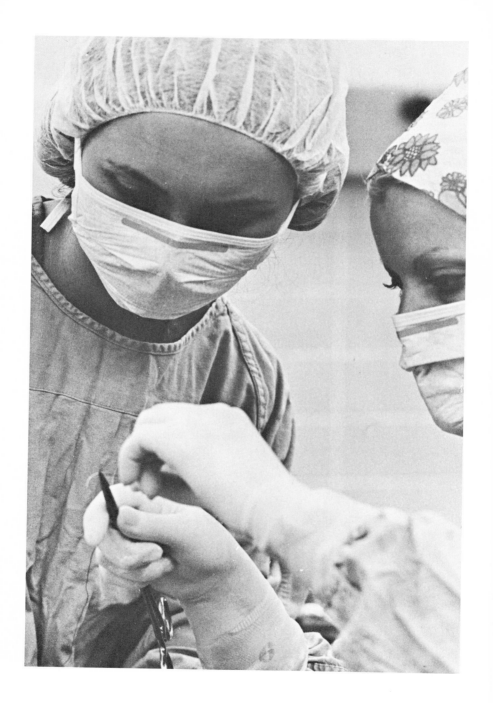

Profile:

Evance is a typical citizen. He has had a typical educational background. His intelligence and aptitude profiles are all average. The amount of money his family spends on leisure, charity, food etc. all closely conform to the national norm. Evance lives in an average sized dwelling. He lives a quiet life and has never been involved in any infraction of the law outside of an occasional parking ticket. He is married and has two children. He lives a very orderly life and neighbors report that "You can set your watch by his comings and goings. Everything is done at precisely the same time, each day, each week." Outside of that they know little about him. Mrs O'Hare a little old lady who lives across the street reports — "They (the Jerinskys) live quiet lives . . . We never hear hide nor hair of them . . . However I dislike their dog who sometimes romps through my prize winning zinnias."

Name:	Darlene Glamorous
Age:	38
Address:	743 2nd Level, Pacific Colony III
Occupation:	Opera Singer
Education:	Billings Grammer
	High School through special tutorial arrangements.

Profile:

Darlene is known to millions through her many appearances on stage and video. Born Sara Levi, she was discovered by the voice trainer, Rodney Bombast when he frequented the malt shop in which she was employed. Comments Bombast, "I heard her vocal range when she sang as she brought me my chocolate malt . . . I knew right then and there that she had great talent." Bombast changed Sara's name to Darlene Glamorous and personally coached her. From that time on her career seemed destined to reach the top. But the sailing was not all that easy. In spite of her spectacular success in the opera, Darlene couldn't find stability in her personal life. Her sixth husband was tragically killed when a studio light accidentally fell on him. Darlene went into seclusion and tried to drown her sorrows in Rocket Juice. Her career plummeted. Her manager Joe Optimist managed to get her off the juice, after repeated attempts. A mere shadow of her former self Darlene began to take a new interest in life. Eventually she made a comeback and her public popularity rose to a level far surpassing her earlier standings. The strain and stress apparently left its toll for she collapsed at an appearance at the Mercury.

215

Name:	Danny Helion
Age:	46
Address:	2053 Tecret Avenue, Bolton, – Floriand
Occupation:	Grave-digger, Ex-Con.
Education:	Dropped out of Botton High, – Senior year

Profile:

Danny Helion has been in trouble with the law since his youth. At first it was minor offences such as speeding, ignoring traffic signals etc. Getting bolder as he grew older, Danny was arrested for numerous crimes ranging from auto-theft to assault with a dangerous weapon. He has served several terms at Grimey State Prison. While serving his latest term for robbing the Cincinnati-Curvis bank, he was granted parole. In the past year Danny has enrolled in night school to finish up his high school training and he plans to go on to Weribether Institute. He is employed during the day digging graves in New Rochelle. Informed sources say that his desire to become a useful citizen has been prompted by one, Jacqueline Zermat, with whom Helion has been romantically connected.

Helion comes from a broken family. His parents were divorced when he was six. His mother who "raised" him spent most of her time at the local bar. His aptitude tests show him to be of average intelligence; but a high aptitude for artistic endeavors was detected.

The dilemma posed by the Artificial Heart Simulation dramatizes but one of the ethical problems that have surfaced in the health sciences. In this simulation you were faced with a lifesaving device available only in limited quantity, and had the very difficult problem of deciding who should benefit, and thereby live and who should not, and thus die. A fictional situation? Not really. This kind of situation is repeated whenever there is a human organ available for transplant, and two or more people in need of that organ, or whenever there is a complex piece of machinery available to only a few individuals. As you probably noted in the simulation, making the choices was not very easy.

216

EUTHANASIA

Another related Bio-ethical problem concerns the issue of "euthanasia." What exactly is euthanasia? Well one definition may be — the act of painlessly putting to death (or allowing to die) someone suffering from a painful and/or incurable ailment. The simulation dealt only with the problem of who should live utilizing a limited resource. As you can see the topic of euthanasia is even more difficult. A few examples of situations that raise this dilemma are in order:

Case I: *A woman was suffering from extreme pain. She has leukemia and has at best only a few more days to live. She had tried to commit suicide and not succeeding in that attempt, was begging her son to kill her, to relieve her suffering. Should he?*

Case II: *Jeanne Schwen was a sociable, and charming girl. She seemed to have everything going for her. She was academically at the top of her class. She was pretty, had a great sense of humor and was quite active in student organizations. Then one day she borrowed the family car to go to the local shopping center. Another car driven by a driver under the influence of alcohol went out of control and crashed into her vehicle at an intersection. While the other driver sustained only minor bruises and cuts, Jeanne's injuries were much more severe. Her parents rushed to the hospital. The physician who met them appeared grim. "I feel terrible having to break this news to you," he said. "There's been extensive brain damage . . . We have her on machines that are helping her breathe etc., but there's no real hope that she will ever feel or experience anything again or be able to exist on a higher level than a vegetable." The Schwens would like the hospital to turn off the life-support systems*

WHY ARE PEOPLE SO UPSET WITH DEATH?

Death is a subject that disturbs many people. Have you ever noticed that often great pains are taken to avoid dealing with it? For example people talk about someone "passing away" rather than dying. People attend a "service" rather than a funeral. It's a very emotional subject that people wish would just "go away." Here are some reasons why:

1. **Love** — We care for our friends and family. No one wants anything to happen to them. When someone dies we feel a personal loss in our lives. Someone who meant a great deal is no longer around.

2. **Fear** — While we may see the difference between a living object and a nonliving one, we really have no idea what it's like to be dead. When someone doesn't really understand something s/he is often quite liable to be afraid of it.

3. **The Great Cover Up** — As was indicated above, people aren't exactly thrilled about the topic of death. Yet the practice of trying to ignore it or to "underplay" it does nothing to lessen people's anxieties about the subject.

4. **Helplessness** — Death is a frustrating event! Everyone must sooner or later die. People get quite uptight because death just can't be prevented. Although we are far more sophisticated scientifically speaking than ever before in our history, we still don't have all the answers.

WHAT HAPPENS WHEN WE DIE?

The truth is we just don't know. While there has been some speculation on this subject, Judaism has generally been more concerned with problems dealing with living people! "That's all good and fine," you say, "but what are some possibilities?" One that you've probably heard of is **Heaven or Hell**. During Biblical times there was the concept of a place called Sheol where dead people were thought to go. If we check later Jewish Folklore, we find very imaginative descriptions of a heaven and hell (which make for good bedtime reading). A second concept is the **Immortality Of The Soul**. This view maintains that while a person's body might die, there is a part of us, a soul, that will exist forever. Interestingly enough there have been studies involving people who were thought to be dead and then were revived. Some of these people underwent similar experiences such as hearing themselves pronounced dead, being pulled through a dark tunnel, or even feeling like they were outside of their bodies, observing what was happening to their physical selves. Does this prove the immortality of the soul? Not necessarily. Various physiological, biochemical reactions in the brain could account for these experiences. The simple fact is we just don't know. Research in this field is in its infancy. Another possibility is **Reincarnation** — the idea that when someone dies his/her soul will be reborn in another body. "Eastern" Religions (e.g. Hinduism) are most famous for this approach although, believe it or not, it has appeared as a belief in Kabbalistic (Jewish Mystical) and Hasidic thought. Does reincarnation occur? Again, while we don't know for sure, occasionally we read about individuals who "remember" past lives and are able to speak in languages, tell us details etc. that we wouldn't expect them to be able to give

WHAT CHARACTERIZES LIFE?

a. Mobility?
b. Reproduction?
c. Awareness — brain?
d. Growth?
e. Metabolism etc?

that are "sustaining" their daughter.

When confronting this issue we find that there are various "kinds" of euthanasia. **Active Euthanasia** involves the performance of some act whereby death is brought about more quickly (e.g. giving a drug, shooting etc.). **Passive Euthanasia** is a situation in which treatment is withheld, thus also bringing about death more quickly.

The problem of euthanasia has been around for many centuries, but it has never been such an urgent nor such an acute area of concern until modern times. Why? Well only a few years ago, it was pretty clear cut if a person was dead or not. If someone's vital life processes such as breathing or heartbeat stopped then that person would be considered dead. (Jewish traditional sources state that the absence of breathing indicates death). But in our day that approach alone is painfully inadequate. Modern medical technology can now prolong breathing and circulation (in cases where the individual can't do so on his/her own). Thus, for example, we find situations where people who can no longer think or reason are maintained often for years on machinery. This has brought about a shift in the entire concept of death. A Harvard Medical School Committee in 1968 talked in terms of "brain death" in which such guidelines as:

1. No brainwaves on an electroencephalogram over a 24 hour period.
2. A lack of spontaneous breathing.
3. Fixed and dilated pupils.
4. No response to externally applied stimuli.

were suggested. This approach of "brain death" is gaining increasing acceptance. But the issue can get even messier. There have been recorded situations where an individual may exhibit spontaneous breathing and not necessarily be "dead" according to the four guidelines, yet still be in a vegetative, non-conscious state. In that kind of a situation the problem is not necessarily whether a person is dead or not, but rather if there is any possibility that the individual will ever experience a meaningful life.

But there is an even more basic ethical dilemma involved here. Does one have the right to choose to die? Does one have the right to decide when and under what circumstances to terminate his/her own life? And what if someone assists a person in that endeavor? Is that person guilty of murder or manslaughter?

What is the legal status of euthanasia in the U.S.? A mess. In considering the "mercy-killing" type of euthanasia case we find verdicts ranging from first degree murder to acquittal (in a number of cases that are quite similar). Current laws have just not managed to keep up with the social pressures brought about by modern medical technology.

What about physicians? What do doctors do who have to decide? Again it varies.

There are no standard set guidelines, and no two situations are identical. Interestingly enough, in a survey of 250 Chicago doctors, sixty-one percent of 156 respondents indicated that physicians sometimes do practice passive euthanasia although about seventy percent don't feel it should be legalized.

Thus individual physicians faced with a rather unpleasant problem try to follow their own consciences. It's not easy with an absence of clear-cut legal guidelines. Yet on the other hand some physicians are against any attempts to legislate medical procedures due to the great variability of circumstances and constant advances in technology etc.

Well then, what are some arguments **against euthanasia?** First and foremost there is the fact that life is very precious. No matter what way you look at it euthanasia involves the taking of life. (Look back to page 86). Physicians have a duty to preserve and protect life. Another point to be made is that there can be errors in a diagnosis. While this is rare it does occur. It's a horrible thought that euthanasia in a situation such as this would be needless and senseless. An additional argument against euthanasia involves the motives of an individual seeking it. Many people who desire death may actually change their minds when faced with it. What might motivate a person to request euthanasia? Financial woes to the family? Acute pain? There is the question of whether a person who desires euthanasia is actually responsible for his/her actions. Was this request solely from the individual, or was it prompted by family neglect and/or suggestion? — After all an incapacitating illness can put emotional and financial strain on families. Very often a person seeking euthanasia will ask another person to help bring about death. Does anyone have the right to impose that kind of burden on any other human being or on society? Another argument against euthanasia would go as follows: euthanasia is often sought as a relief against pain. But aren't there many drugs available that can also alleviate suffering? And even if the amounts of those drugs necessary may as a side effect, shorten life, is that really the same thing as deliberately trying to bring life to an end? Then there is the issue of general reverence for life. Let's assume that euthanasia becomes acceptable for the incurably ill. What is to prevent the popularization of euthanasia for mentally incompetent people (with the accompanying problems of what exactly makes one incompetent, and who is to decide) or for someone who is just very old, or simply physically unattractive? Could it be that by encouraging such a course of action in certain cases, our reverence for life could diminish and the same approach too easily spread to other situations as well?

219

Well those are some of the arguments against euthanasia. But true to form as a "sticky" ethical dilemma there are some strong arguments **favoring euthanasia** as well. One, for example, concerns the individual's personal freedom. Let us suppose an individual learns that s/he has an incurable disease. As long as that person's actions don't infringe upon others, shouldn't that person have the right simply to refuse treatment? Another argument in favor of euthanasia would say that living in great and constant pain or as a vegetable is a fate worse than death. Just as a physician has a duty to preserve and protect life so too does s/he have an obligation to try to relieve pain and suffering. Earlier we mentioned the burden on the family. The financial costs of medical care are staggering. It is not unusual for families to completely use up their savings to pay for medical bills. Does the extra time that the use of extraordinary measures brings justify the cost, particularly if the patient is in constant pain or is unaware of reality? The same question can be asked not only in terms of financial cost to the family but in terms of the emotional cost as well. Then, there is the entire issue of individual needs vs. societal needs. A great deal of time, money and effort has been put into develop-

ARGUMENTS CONCERNING EUTHANASIA

AGAINST

A. Life is sacred. It is suicide or murder.

B. Physicians have a duty to preserve and protect life.

C. There could be errors in a diagnosis.

D. Would this person change his/her mind at the last minute?

E. What motivates the person?

F. No person has the right to burden anyone else with a request for euthanasia.

G. Many drugs are available to alleviate pain.

H. If euthanasia became very acceptable in some cases, would this cheapen our regard for life and spread the practice to other situations?

FAVORING

A. Life is sacred. Living in constant pain or as a vegetable etc. is a fate worse than death.

B. Physicians have a duty to relieve pain and suffering.

C. The use of extraordinary measures to prolong a patient's existence has a high financial and emotional cost. That cost may not be justifiable.

D. If a person's actions don't infringe on others shouldn't s/he have the right simply to refuse treatment?

E. Much time, effort, and money is put into developing and maintaining life support systems for the critically ill. That time, money and effort might be applied far more effectively in other areas.

ing and maintaining life support systems for the critically ill. Is it worth it, or would those resources be applied more effectively in other areas of medicine?

The problem of euthanasia is not an easy one to resolve. As you can see there are strong arguments on both sides of the question. Yet this dilemma is typical of some of the ethical problems to be confronted as we enter the 21st Century.

TRADITIONAL INSIGHTS

Believe it or not Judaism even has discussions relating to the problem of euthanasia. A person who is about to die is called a gosses. According to the Jewish tradition a dying person is to be considered and treated as alive. The sages insisted that even when a physician knows that a person is going to die s/he should still give the patient instructions as to what to eat or drink (or refrain from eating or drinking). **Any actions which could hasten the person's death are strictly prohibited.** These actions can even include psychological stress. For example: one may not close the eyes of a dying person, or make any kind of funeral arrangements until the person is indeed dead. After all a dying person aware of such actions would not exactly be thrilled and indeed could even be adversely affected. Thus our traditions would seem to be against any kind of active euthanasia.

On the other hand let's say that there was something such as a constant noise or "salt on the dying person's tongue" (which in the past were believed to hinder or delay a person's death). According to tradition these things could be removed because these actions did not actively try to speed death but rather removed an impediment to it. Pro-passive euthanasia? Possibly. Even though some authorities feel that the discussion of the gosses involves only the last three days of life, the intent could possibly be consistent with the longer periods of time that a terminal illness may involve due to modern technologies. It's a debatable point.

CONSIDER THIS:

1. What do you find more convincing, the arguments in favor of euthanasia or against it? Why? Take each argument and analyze in detail.

2. What is the difference between active or passive euthanasia? Can either be more "ethically acceptable" than the other? Why? Why not? Can euthanasia ever be morally justified? Why? Why not?

3. Who should make the decisions as to who should live and who should die? Why? Should it be the decision of one person, more than one? Why? Why not?

4. What about a situation in which a baby is born severely deformed? Discuss the problem of euthanasia as it relates to this case. How is it similar to someone dying of an incurable and/or painful disease? How is it different?

THE ETHICS OF HUMAN EXPERIMENTATION

Here is a very tricky ethical dilemma for you to consider. I am sure that you've seen T.V. commercials proclaiming such things as "In special tests, people using Gupso toothpaste had 41% fewer cavities." That's all good and fine. But what about the people who didn't use Gupso and thereby have 41% **more** cavities? This raises the whole issue of experiments using human beings. Some people argue that experiments are necessary in order to advance medical knowledge. They might say that while experiments using animals are useful to a point, there is no guarantee that what works on an animal will work on people. Therefore human beings must eventually be subjects in experiments. An additional factor is that often experiments of this kind are carried out in institutions such as prisons, and mental hospitals. Are the people involved always well informed as to the possible consequences? Are they always enthusiastic non-coerced volunteers? Examples of some abuses:

— Live cancer cells were injected into patients to study immunity to cancer. The people involved weren't told that the injected cells were cancerous.

— Various situations documented where given a large number of people ill with a disease, only part of that population would be treated. The remaining part would be given something worthless, thinking it was a remedy.

It should be pointed out that the abuses are not widespread. Both the Medical Profession as well as the Government have been quite concerned with the ethics and regulation of human experimentation. But the basic ethical problems remain:

1. Is human experimentation really necessary? Are the possible unknown benefits worth the unknown risks that a person is subjected to?

2. Who should be the human guinea pig? Prisoners and mental patients? Middle class people? How should this decision be made? Could people be happy to volunteer? How? Should they?

3. What rules and regulations could be enacted to protect people in experiments? Make some kind of a list, and discuss the various points in it.

Incidentally this entire issue is a very sensitive one to us as Jews. Some of our brethren were abused through various "experiments" by the Nazis during the Holocaust.

THE ETHICS OF GENETIC ENGINEERING

The basic unit of most living things is the cell. Our bodies are made up of billions of cells, all descended from one ancestor cell, the fertilized ovum. (You know "the birds and the bees!"). That one cell multiplied, and the various cells that emerged began to specialize — take on special jobs. So eventually some cells came to be skin, others nerves etc. Now that's what happens in complicated organisms like people. There are also some very simple organisms that are only composed of one or a few cells.

Well, in each cell there is a chemical known as deoxyribonucleic acid (D.N.A. for short). D.N.A. is pretty remarkable stuff. It contains in coded form the instructions for whatever a cell is supposed to be doing. Even more remarkably, every cell contains within its D.N.A. an entire "blueprint" for the body, — and that's a lot of information!

222

Through experimentation, scientists have been learning a great deal about D.N.A. They now have the ability to take small pieces of D.N.A. and insert them into longer strands. This has been done in simple organisms. Because the D.N.A. controls what a cell can do this research in effect produces new and different life forms.

Is it good or bad? That's hard to say. While this work is but in its infancy, there are numerous possible future results. For example:

1. There are many diseases that are hereditary (passed down from generation to generation). Genetic engineering could perhaps eventually cure such diseases.

2. Possibly simple organisms could be designed to eat up pollutants. (Of course we have no exact idea what effect these organisms would have on the environment — they could go off gobbling everything!)

3. Certain rare and useful chemical substances which are made by simple organisms could be made more readily available if specially designed organisms were grown in large numbers on a commercial basis.

4. The plants and animals that we eat are, in many cases, the products of selective breeding. Genetic engineering could enable us to even further improve some species. This could be crucial in providing food for the world.

5. The same knowledge and techniques of genetic engineering could also be applied to humans as well.

6. Cloning — in which many exact genetic copies of an organism could be produced from a single cell may become possible, in animals as well as humans.

Position A:

I believe that all genetic research should be completely and utterly outlawed. There are too many possibilities for abuse. For example even research on simple organisms such as bacteria is dangerous. A scientist could accidently create a new disease, or even worse render an old one invulnerable to our drugs. While scientific knowledge may be hard to come by it is by no means hard to apply. Do you remember how hard it was to develop the Atomic bomb? Yet recently it was shown that a college student with just a few courses and proper materials could design one. What's to prevent some petty tyrant, kook, or terrorist from abusing genetic engineering knowledge? Genetic engineering applied to humans would be indecent. It would be used by governments to control people. It would threaten the sanctity of human life. And then there's that cloning business. One hundred or one thousand copies of someone walking around — Sheer Poppycock! That would destroy family life. And think of all of the identity problems that would result. "Who Am I?" . . . "What's my function?" Yich! Who needs that? I for one say it's time to stop these scientists before they go too far. Outlaw genetic research now!

Position B:

My friend "A" is over reacting. First of all, some of the possibilities he's suggesting such as genetic engineering applied to human beings are **far beyond** our current knowledge. The scientific community recognizes the dangers involved in uncontrolled research of this kind, and super secure labs where all possible precautions are being taken are being set up. Simple organisms are weakened so that they can't survive outside the labs. Face it, research of this kind is going to occur — if not in our country, then elsewhere. Don't you think that it would be much wiser to at least proceed with adequate safeguards and controls here in our country, than to just leave it up to uncontrolled tinkering abroad? Moreover the benefits that this research will have are enormous. The knowledge of how to control cells' molecular machinery could provide a cure for cancer. We will be able to eventually eliminate many diseases. Perhaps we will even be able to extend the human life span, and increase human intelligence. An ability to regrow and rapidly replace lost limbs may be gained. While these things are beyond our current abilities, we may never be able to bring them about unless we continue our research in this area. There have always been critics of technological advance. My friend "A" displays such a narrow point of view. No, by all means, genetic research must go on, but under proper controls.

Analyze position A and position B. If forced to take a side, with whom would you agree more readily? Why?

SUMMARY:

In this chapter some of the ethical dilemmas in the Biomedical sciences were presented:

1. Who should live and who should die? What should be done when there are only limited resources for a large number of individuals?

2. *The issue of euthanasia was set forth. As Jews we believe that life is sacred. Can euthanasia be acceptable in any form? What are the pros and cons concerning this problem?*

3. *What about experiments with human subjects? Are they necessary? How can such experiments be controlled?*

4. *A new and exciting area of research involves genetic engineering. What are the positive aspects of this research? What are the possibilities for abuse? Should work in this area be continued?*

These are but four representative issues. There are many others which could have been raised. You can see that the modern physician is really facing some very difficult dilemmas as s/he strives to help humankind. The four issues raised in this unit give a good idea of the seriousness and importance of some of the ethical problems constantly coming up in modern Biology and Medicine.

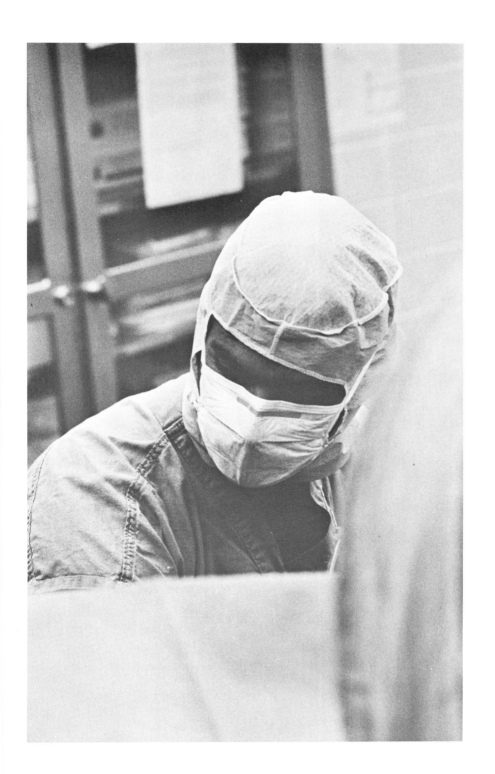

226

Ecology

Believe it or not we are all astronauts, you and I, your parents and even your pet canary! Our spaceship is called Earth! Spaceship Earth is truly an engineering marvel. While scientists have spent millions of dollars setting up the means to transport a few human beings to the moon for just a few days, Earth has self-renewing life-support systems that can handle the needs of billions of creatures for millions of years. Yet our life support systems have been badly treated and continued abuse could bring devastating results upon all of our spaceship's inhabitants!

In this chapter the area of ecology will be discussed. Ecology is the science dealing with the interrelationship of organisms and their environment. The entire ecological mess on Earth is a complex one. First let's try to pinpoint some of the problems.

POLLUTION

One large aspect of the problem is pollution. If you consider it for a second pollution can be viewed simply as a matter of garbage disposal (but on a large scale). There are various kinds of pollution.

Air pollution is one scourge. To give you an idea of how bad a problem it is, modern air pollution can cut the amount of sunlight reaching cities by large amounts (e.g. Chicago by as much as 40%). In fact there are recorded instances of "killer smogs," when air pollution became so bad that many deaths resulted. There are many sources of air pollution ranging from automobiles, to various industrial plants. In the late sixties automobiles alone gave off 86 million tons of junk (various chemicals) per year into the atmosphere we breath! All of this of course, has a cost. Pollution damages crops, corrodes things exposed to it, and findings continually pour in as to how it contributes to various respiratory diseases. Moreover, air pollution is not a local affair. Wind blows the crud everywhere. Thus it is no surprise that high lead concentrations from both industrial as well as older automobile emissions have been found even in the Arctic!

Other areas of concern are the problems of **land and water pollution**. Getting rid of wastes safely is an increasingly difficult affair. Comedians commonly make jokes about the hazards of drinking the water in other countries, but believe it or not, a Public Health Service list in the late 1960's indicated more than sixty U.S. cities with unsatisfactory water! To make matters worse various insecticides (chemicals used in agriculture to kill insects), exotic chemicals from industry etc. continue to contribute to the problem.

Some of the more widely publicized pollutants have included DDT (an insecticide) and Lead.

I remember "going into shock" when I first saw a poster with a picture of a human breast and the accompanying statement "unsafe for human consumption." Yet most mothers' milk in the U.S. contains levels of DDT higher than the legal limits allowed for that chemical in cow milk to be shipped in interstate commerce. DDT has been found to increase cancer in rats, has various bad effects on animals' reproduction etc.

Lead poisoning is nothing new. Some scholars noted that the Romans, particularly the upper classes, used lead lined containers for their cooking and eating. It's curious to think that lead poisoning impairing the efficiency of Roman leaders, may have contributed to the downfall of that civilization.

Well, as I said, these are but a few of the better publicized pollutants. The scary thing is that **some** (though not necessarily all) chemicals build up in concentration along the food-chain (In other words as bigger animals eat smaller ones some of chemical x in the smaller ones gets absorbed into the bigger ones, and thus there gets to be a larger and larger concentration). What's even more frightening is that scientists still don't really know the total effects of all of the junk being poured out into the environment. Scientists don't know all of the effects of various chemicals in terms of individual physiological damage. They're even uncertain as to what extent these pollutants may affect our entire global environment.

For example, from time to time, there are debates pro and con as to whether all of the stuff spewed into the environment (not to mention the great amount of heat given off by humankind's various activities) are possibly contributing to a change in weather. This might sound harmless but it really isn't. Various outcomes suggested range from drought in major food producing areas, to flooding of coastal cities and even large glaciers. Yet as I said before, the experts aren't entirely certain as to what the results could be and often disagree even among themselves.

Another scary trend is that ten years after some product is out on the market, someone will discover that that item is harmful for some reason or another. (For example at presstime of this book both lead paint and certain food dyes were in the news!)

POPULATION AND RESOURCES

Ecological discussions frequently deal with the topic of the proper (or improper) disposal of wastes as mentioned above. Another subject that is commonly raised is the need for raw materials (energy, mineral or food) which are derived from our environment. Yet if you think carefully for a second these two areas — waste products and raw materials are really influenced by the size of the population:

It is common sense that more people generally require more raw materials. Larger numbers of people also result in greater outputs of waste (e.g. garbage, pollution etc.).

Yet when we look at the human demographic (numbers of people) situation, we note a large increase in population size over the past few thousand years. Another way of saying it is that **the time required for the world's human population to double has been steadily decreasing!**

It's estimated that there were five hundred million people on earth in the mid 1600's. It took until the mid 1800's, a period of **two hundred years** for the population to double and go to one billion. It took **eighty more years** until 1929 for the population to double again to two billion. The 1975 figures are around four billion, requiring only **forty-six years** to have doubled again!

Doubling time

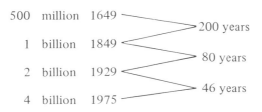

Thus I think you can see that the time required for the population to double has been steadily decreasing with the numbers of people simply soaring! Why has population gone up that way? Well, in general, health conditions have improved! A case of something such as appendicitis (very minor today) could have resulted in death but a few hundred years ago. Better sanitation, control of disease etc. have certainly helped people live longer lives in modern times.

Yet as was indicated earlier with more people comes the need for more food and resources. With regard to food, such factors as the development of higher yield crops, new farming machinery etc. have helped considerably yet the situation is still inadequate. The Food and Agricultural Organization of the U.N. estimated that there was barely enough food in the world to feed everyone in the mid 1960's. **But the catch is that distribution both between countries and even inside some countries results in inequalities in the amount of resources people get!** This is an interesting point. Even with the best production that scientists can develop, if politicians are inefficient etc. then people will starve. Thus we live in a world where somewhere between one and two billion people are hungry. It was found that even in the United States (as of 1969) that ten to fifteen million people were undernourished. Incidently the effects of malnutrition are pretty gross especially with small children (e.g. stunting of physical growth, mental growth — to name but a few results). But the problem is not likely to get better. With rapidly increasing population even the best efforts of scientists are not necessarily going to be able to produce enough food for everybody.

Then there is a need for other resources (minerals etc.) necessary for society to function. The projections are not encouraging. Even at the best estimates, at our current rates of usage, many of these various resources will be in short supply in the next few hundred years. There are of course all kinds of possibilities. Perhaps materials will be recycled, new sources of supply in space etc. found. The fate of various industries as these resources become scarce, not to mention what kind of relations may develop between consuming and producing countries is a matter of speculation. However the point is that Spaceship Earth has its limits; limits upon the amount of waste that can be thrown out into it, and limits upon the amount of resources that can be drawn from it.

PROPOSED METHODS TO INCREASE FOOD PRODUCTION

While many ideas have been proposed to increase the amount of food it is debatable whether food production will be able to keep up with population growth:

1. **IRRIGATION** — Problems — There is a limited supply of H_2O on earth. The costs are high. Even the most ambitious water projects may contribute little when compared to the increase in population. Desalting H_2O? — economic difficulties.

2. **HARVESTING THE SEAS** — A myth. The oceans' supply of food is actually rather restricted with the exception of nutrient rich areas. Currently we hunt the seas. Yet only about one fifth of the world's animal protein is from the oceans. At best, perhaps, a 2-2.5 times increase in catch could come about before 2000. Problems: Many of the world's fish species are already dangerously overfished. Also increasing pollution can spoil this source of supply. Farming the seas? Well there's a potential, but whether that will produce enough to feed the world's population is doubtful. In addition the same problems listed above apply to "sea farming." (not to mention additional technological ones).

3. **USE ALGAE** — A number of problems involved:
   - Educating people to eat it, taste etc. Even hungry people don't like eating something "strange."
   - Getting rid of water cheaply (1000 tons of Algae contain 836 tons of water).
   - Currently there is a lack of basic knowledge. Research is needed concerning algae growth, mortality, optimum conditions, diseases, etc.
   - There is even debate over algae's nutritional value — human enzymes are unable to digest much of their carbohydrates.
   - Pollution could also mess this idea up too!

4. **INCREASE ACREAGE** — Involves all the problems discussed under Irrigation. In addition there have been attempts in such places as the plains of Kazakhstan (U.S.S.R.), Brazil, and Tanzania that have been disasters due to climate, etc. (In other words it's not as easy as it sounds). Also the soils in large parts of South America, Africa, and Southeast Asia are lateritic (see p. 125) and/or unsuitable (also see #5).

5. **IMPROVE CROP YIELDS** — This does have possibilities, but also poses problems as well. For example there are the economic requirements of paying for fertilizers and mechanized equipment (not so easy in underdeveloped countries). There are only so many resources to go around. If India alone were to use proportionately the same amount of fertilizer that Holland uses, it would utilize half of the current world output. There are ecological problems involved with using large amounts of pesticides and fertilizer. Increased amounts of a particular crop may lower prices, and result in resistance from producers.

Possible climatic changes on earth could further complicate the mess. As you can see increasing food production may not be all that easy.

JEWISH PERSPECTIVES

In the chapter on charity, it was indicated that as God is the creator, everything we have is in a sense "on loan" from that Divine Source. As it is written:

> *The earth is the Lord's and the fulness thereof,*
> *The world and they that dwell therein.*
>
> *Psalm 24:1*

Where does humankind fit in? Well we are in a rather unique position. While our species is very small in the vastness of the universe, we nonetheless are the dominant life form on earth with the capability of destroying the entire world:

> *Oh Lord our God, how glorious is your name in all the earth . . .*
> *When I look up at your heavens, the work of your fingers,*
> *The moon and the stars which you set into place;*
> *What is man, that you should remember him?*
> *And the son of man, that you should think of him?*
> *Yet you have made him but little lower than the angels and have crowned him with glory and honor.*
>
> *From Psalm 8*

If you borrowed a Jaguar (the car) for a weekend you'd be careful to return it to its owner in good condition. Therefore humankind has a kind of special trust to take care of the earth and keep it in good condition also. In our traditions there's an interesting story:

> *When God finished creating everything he took Adam out to see all of the trees and paradise that was the Garden of Eden. God cautioned Adam, "Behold my works . . . all that I've created . . . Now don't you go and mess it up and do any damage to my world, because if you do there will be none to restore it!"*

EVEN IN A BUSH

In the Bible we read (Exodus 3) that God revealed himself to Moses from a bush . . . Centuries later the sages pondered the situation . . . Out of all of the ways that God could make himself known, why was a bush chosen? The answer: To show us that there is no place where God is not found . . .

Thought Question: What would this imply in terms of our discussion about ecology? Analyze in detail.

Our traditions therefore inform us of this special trust to take care of the world.

In the chapter on war some particular comments were made concerning ecological affairs. You will recall:

> When you are making war and besieging a city for a long time to take it, don't destroy the trees in the area by taking an ax against them. You may eat of them, but you can't cut them down. The trees of the field aren't men that you should besiege them!
>
> *Deuteronomy 20:19*

We therefore noted a strong concern with humankind's effect on the environment even during a wartime situation.

EVEN A SPIDER HAS ITS PLACE

As you'll recall from your Biblical history, there was a period of time before David became King of Israel, during which he was pursued by an unhappy and insecure King Saul.

Legend tells us that a rather interesting event occured during this period of David's life. Apparently, he had been wondering if God was all that clever. "After all," reasoned David "how could God be so smart if he created something as worthless as spiders?" Then one day David was forced to hide in a cave to escape Saul's troops. "Hey Moe, go over and check out that cave!" David, hearing the soldiers was understandably a little nervous. Then, the story tells us, God had a spider weave a web over the entrance to the cave. The soldiers seeing the web, assumed that no one was there and David was saved! Moral: Every living thing has its place in nature!

Our ancestors had a keen recognition of how any environmental change can affect an area's ecosystem. For example when the children of Israel are told that they will inhabit the land of Canaan, the comment is made:

> The Lord your God will put out those nations before you little by little. You may not consume them at once, lest the beasts of the field increase upon you.
>
> *Deuteronomy 7:22*

In other words, if the earlier population of Canaan were suddenly evicted the area could turn wild and desolate before it would again be inhabited. (See also II Kings 17:23-26).

Earlier we noted the following practice with regard to charity:

> For six years you may sow your land and gather it's fruits; but every seventh year you'll let it rest and lie still. Anything that grows there the poor can have, and what they leave wild animals may eat. Do the same with your vineyard and oliveyard.
>
> *Exodus 23:10-11*

There is an additional rationale behind this procedure beyond charity. The idea of leaving "reserves" for wild animals to eat from is an advanced concept. The practice of allowing the land a year "of rest" is sound agricultural practice. (particularly in those times). But we find even more in our traditions than that. There is a strong concern for the public good. We read in the Mishnah:

> A human being is always Muad (forewarned, liable) whether s/he causes damage on purpose or by accident, whether awake or asleep. If one blinded another's eye or broke his/her vessels s/he must pay full damages.

And this comment:

> If someone digs a pit in a private domain and opens it into the public domain, or in the public domain and opens it into a private domain, or in a private domain and opens it into another private domain, that person is liable, should anyone be injured.

Centuries ago our ancestors were even concerned with noise pollution!

> If a person wants to set up a shop in a courtyard another can complain and say to him "I can't sleep because of the noise of the people going in and out."

Believe it or not there is even legislation in the Mishnah regarding air pollution! A permanent threshing floor could be built no closer than fifty cubits from a town (a cubit is about 18 inches). Carcasses, graves and tanneries also had to be at least fifty cubits away. Tanneries could be established only on the east side of town. This was because in Israel the prevailing wind is from the north-west. The east wind wasn't strong enough to really carry the smell of a tannery (rather strong!) back to the town's inhabitants.

233

TU BI-SHEVAT – JEWISH ECOLOGY DAY

Question: How many new years are there in Judaism? Answer: One or two? Wrong! Believe it or not there are **four** new years within the Jewish calender. Three of them are Rosh Hashanah, The New Year for Kings, and the New Year for the Tithing of Cattle. The fourth — and most important for this chapter, is Tu Bi-Shevat the New Year for Trees. Plants and trees are essential for life on earth. They give off oxygen which we breath. They provide us with food. We make many useful things out of wood including furniture and homes. Plants and trees give shade and help drain swamps. Just as importantly they help give a higher quality of life. Can you imagine a world without any grass or trees? Beautiful flowers made into pretty floral designs help express emotion and provide beauty in our otherwise quite artificial environments.

Centuries before the word "ecology" was invented our ancestors recognized our dependance upon the environment. Tu Bi-Shevat acknowledges the importance of nature. Hundreds of years ago in Europe Jews made a special effort to eat different kinds of fruit on Tu Bi-Shevat. In fact a rather interesting observance grew up around that holiday. A seder, similar to the one held on Passover was developed about four hundred years ago. It would involve the eating of fruit and drinking of wine — a special Tu Bi-Shevat Seder!

234

ENDANGERED
SPECIES

COMMENTARY:

You will recall the problem of "divine punishment" raised in the unit "Why Laws?" We noted how whenever someone does something ignoring the laws of nature such as putting one's hand in a fire etc., that person is looking for trouble! In a sense the whole ecological mess brings that earlier issue up once again. It's highly unlikely that anybody one hundred years ago in charge of an industrial plant would have thought that the smokestack spewing out soot would harm a soul. It was thought at that time that the earth's resources were unlimited. Indeed barely a hundred years ago nations that had a lot of smokestacks viewed them as very progressive signs of manufacturing — a symbol of industries that would make them prosper! People in those days were ignorant of (or ignored) the fact that we are now quite aware of; that the earth's resources are quite limited and that abuse of the environment could bring disaster. In a sense then the same issue of ignoring scientific laws resulting in possible "punishment" is at play again here.

The entire ecological mess raises a complex variety of ethical problems. There is the ethical issue of abusing the earth — with the possible disastrous results. There is the ethical issue of individual freedoms vs. societal needs. The solutions proposed to the various issues that come up could very well conflict with individual freedoms. For example, how will the various realities of population, pollution and resources affect our way of life? Will people be able to travel in whatever vehicles they desire, whenever they want to? Will the form of homes we live in change, and will that change be voluntary or not? Will these factors affect our private lives even to the extent of determining the size of our families? How will some of these decisions be made — by voluntary means, or by government regulation? The various problems involved with the distribution of a limited amount of resources to a very large world population also raises ethical problems. The current situation consists of the developed nations using a huge amount of the world's resources. For example Americans make up about six percent of the earth's population, yet its been estimated that we use about forty percent of the earth's resources! Underdeveloped countries, many of which help supply those resources, would like to attain our standard of living. If this were to come about it's questionable how long anyone would maintain that level due to rapid resource depletion. Will resources become a tool to force political objectives? How will "Have" and "Have-not" nations reach an accomodation? I think you can see that this chapter can but merely pose the questions. I believe that you can also see just how complex the issues become. Yet these problems are not merely technological; they involve value judgements as well. Dealing with these issues may not only determine your and your children's lifestyles. It may indeed determine humankind's ultimate survival or decline.

235

SUMMARY

In this chapter we discussed some of the problems of ecology. Any discussion of ecology inevitably involves the subjects of **Population, Resources** and **Pollution.** An increasingly larger world **population** makes greater demands upon the environment for such **resources** as energy, food and minerals. We noted that the time required for the world population to double has been steadily decreasing. Yet the amount of natural resources available on Earth are quite limited, and are also decreasing. It is even a matter of debate if enough food can be produced to feed an increasingly large world population, (and if that is possible, whether dis-

Pretend these dots are people.   Pretend these dots are resources.
Six percent of the earth   **use**   forty percent of the earth's resources.

tribution could be such that no one would go hungry). As there are more and more people consuming more and more resources, so too can we expect more and more **waste products** (garbage). Yet current methods of handling these waste products has all too often been inadequate, resulting in pollution of various kinds. The effect of all of this junk being tossed into our environment isn't even fully known. Yet from available knowledge it is by no means a positive situation.

236

In this chapter we also looked at some Jewish perspectives on the ecological situation. Humankind occupies a unique position as the highest life form on earth. Our traditions point to a responsibility to protect the environment. We find a strong recognition of humankind's influence upon ecosystems and even specific Jewish legal legislation concerning pollution!

❖❖❖❖❖❖❖

FOCUS ON: A TRADITIONAL REGARD FOR ANIMAL LIFE

— Animals are allowed to rest on the Sabbath.

Exodus 23:12

— Ploughing with an ox and donkey harnessed together (they didn't have mechanized farm machinery then) is forbidden. Can you figure out why?

Deuteronomy 22:10

— Before one sits down to eat s/he must first feed his/her animals.

Talmud

— A traditional Jew may say a prayer, the She-Heheyanu, when s/he gets new clothes:

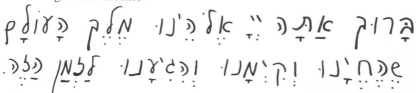

Blessed are you, O Lord our God, King of the universe who has kept us alive and preserved us and enabled us to reach this season.

This is not said when one gets a pair of shoes, because an animal had to die to provide the leather!

— If a person sees the ass (donkey) of someone s/he hates loaded with a burden, that person should help unload the animal. (After all the quarrel is with the person, not with the poor animal!)

Exodus 23:5

— Legend has it that both Moses and David were tested by God as shepherds. Moses, for example, cared for Jethro's flocks quite carefully. Each day he would lead the youngest animals out to pasture first, then the older ones and finally the fully grown ones. The idea was to make sure the younger animals would be able to get the food best suitable for them. When a kid wandered off to get a drink, Moses was sympathetic and even carried the animal back. God was so impressed with this behavior that Moses was deemed suitable to be a leader of Israel.

— One is not supposed to buy an animal unless s/he can feed it etc.

Talmud

The remarkable thing is that these Jewish concerns about tsa'ar ba'ale hayyim, the pain to living creatures, were expressed thousands of years ago. Has modern society caught up with them yet? Not really. Many species have become extinct through humankind's influence. In the news we occasionally hear of abandoned pets. (Something that occurs more often than people would care to admit). You'll appreciate the above comments even more should you ever go to a bullfight.

237

238

CONSIDER THIS:

1. What were some of the traditional views underlying the Jewish approach to charity? How could these be related to an approach to ecological concerns?

2. In the Bible we read (Genesis 1:28):

   > *And God blessed them and said "Be fruitful and multiply and replenish the earth and subdue it; and have dominion over the fish of the sea and over the fowl of the air and over every living thing that moves on the earth."*

Would this give license for ecological destruction? Why? Why not? Taken in the context of other traditional comments about ecology, how would it fit in? Why?

239

3. Earlier in the book, the author discussed the concepts of Divine punishment and reward. Analyze as they relate to this chapter.

4. Look up the following passages:
   Exodus 23:29-30
   Deut. 22:6-7
   Lev. 22:27-28
   Discuss how they relate to this chapter.

5. Write a report on one of the following:
   a. Population control — pros and cons.
   b. Pollution (air, water etc.)
   c. Judaism and birth control.
   d. Pollution is (bad) good for business.
   e. New ideas for dealing with food (resource) depletion.
   f. Will solutions to ecological problems hurt individual rights?

A REAL BORE

A story from our tradition:

> One day some people were sitting in a boat out in the ocean. Suddenly one of them pulled out a tool and began to drill a hole in the bottom of the vessel.
> "Hay, what are you doing, you Klutz?" the man's shipmates screamed in alarm.
> "What's it to you?" responded the man, as he continued to drill. "After all aren't I just drilling the hole underneath my own seat?"

240

— What is this story really trying to tell us?

— How could this be related to a discussion about ecology? Analyze in detail.

PIGS AND ECOLOGY!

You have, I am sure, heard of the term "Kosher." Generally when we talk about Kosher foods we refer to foods that are permitted in accordance with Jewish law. The dietary laws are interesting, detailed and beyond the scope of this book. One creature, however, worth our consideration here is the pig! Pigs are not kosher and Jews following the dietary laws aren't supposed to eat them. Why?

An answer is found in the Bible (Leviticus 11:7). But could there be any reason beyond the stated Biblical one? "Sure," you say. "Pigs sit around in excrement and can also transmit disease." (e.g. trichinosis). O.K., but pigs can be raised in cleanliness and many animals permitted by tradition carry other diseases. Surely this was known to our ancestors.

A fascinating theory suggested by anthropologist Marvin Harris, would be that pigs were not allowed because they are not suitable to the ecological conditions of the Middle East. Our ancestors originally were nomadic, but settled down became urbanized etc. Even in a more settled lifestyle herds of cattle, sheep etc. were important. Pigs were not the most advisable creatures to raise for a number of reasons:

1. Pigs are much more difficult to herd over long distances when compared to other animals.

2. Pigs are not very well adapted to the hot, dry weather of the Middle East. They don't have much hair to reflect sunlight and don't really sweat very much. Thus they have a hard time cooling themselves in a hot environment.

3. Pigs can eat many things, but gain the most weight from such foods as grains and fruits — foods that people eat. Goats, sheep etc. on the other hand eat such things as grass.

4. In a pastoral economy such animals as sheep, goats and cattle would be important for providing many necessities such as milk, clothes, cheese, pulling plows etc. Meat was only a small part of the yield. Pigs weren't a really good source of milk and certainly couldn't pull a plow.

It's no wonder then, that an animal that thrives on the same food as human beings, is badly adapted to hot weather (comparatively speaking), and doesn't provide a wide variety of uses would be looked down upon by the establishment at that time.

Now many people won't be happy with the above comments. Traditional Jews may argue that these laws are not a reflection of ecological knowledge but are the word of God. Others may say that the prohibition against eating pig, doesn't by any means, make up the entire body of Jewish dietary law. Still others would say that regardless of the origin of these laws, they are still valid for a number of reasons. They reflect our desire to affiliate as Jews, our attitudes towards the sanctity of life etc. You may want to discuss some of these issues with your teacher.

The major point in presenting this material about pigs is that, in my view, it represents but another example of our ancestors' awareness of ecological issues.

unit fourteen

The Ethics of Technology

THE INCREASE IN KNOWLEDGE

I think that one thing that should be clear from our discussion in the past few units is that modern day science gives humankind great power never before equalled in our history.

Moreover we are learning more about the world and universe around us today than ever before. To give you an idea of this fact, it's estimated that before 1500 perhaps one thousand different books at best were authored **each year** in Europe. By the 1960's, on a worldwide scale, about one thousand new books were produced **each day!** It is interesting to note that if we consider sheer numbers of scientists who have ever lived on this earth, ninety percent are still alive — which shows just how much activity is going on! Thus we are in the midst of a knowledge explosion, the likes of which has never been seen on this earth!

Coupled with this incredible increase in knowledge, there has been a decrease in the time necessary to apply and use new data. Companies work very hard to develop new techniques and equipment and to use them as quickly as possible. This wasn't always so. In addition communication today on a worldwide basis speeds things up. If there is a war or a discovery etc. on one side of our planet, the rest of the world hears about it in a matter of hours. Specialized journals give details within a matter of days. Thus things happen much more quickly today than ever before!

Changing technology and a rapidly moving world shape our approaches to various problems and have an impact upon each and every one of us. How do people react to this rapid change? Our reactions are varied. While technology is reshaping our world and life styles, human beings themselves haven't really changed that much in the past few thousand years. Naturally a rapidly changing situation doesn't always make everyone happy. So you may very well hear people on occasion reacting quite strongly against technology and scientists in general. On the other hand, while it is always risky to generalize, I would venture the opinion that North Americans as a group display a special fascination with mechanical gadgetry and the fruits of science and technology! Thus the reactions we see in our society towards science are often quite mixed!

SCIENCE — GOOD OR EVIL?

Are scientific discoveries good? Are they evil? That's a good question, one that you should consider quite carefully. My own view is that **science alone is neither good nor evil.** Science represents humankind's attempt to learn in a systematic way as much as possible about the cosmos and the various laws that govern it. However, a basic problem comes up. Knowledge is a wonderful thing. Yet there is nothing present in mere factual information that really tells us whether our application of that knowledge is necessarily "good" or "bad." These are value judgements that people have to make. Thus, as we indicated on p. 223, we may someday have the knowledge to make clones, "copies" of individuals. The fact that we may eventually possess the information and techniques enabling us to do this, doesn't tell us that we should; it doesn't really make the ethical choice.

Now let's consider the field of religion for a moment. Religion is a tough word to define. Generally when one talks about religion such things as "prayer," "God," "ethics," and "Sunday school" come to mind. Yet if you consider it for a moment, religion is really also concerned with finding as much as possible about the cosmos and how it operates. No, not the way that science does. Religion is concerned with the same realities, but in a different way. For example a scientist might ask the question "Why death?". S/he may be concerned with what actually causes an animal to die, what the physiological signs are etc.

A person whose field is religion may ask the same question but be concerned with such things as "Why was such a thing as death created?", "Is the existence of death good or bad?" etc. Now I think you can see considerable possibility for overlap! Sometimes religion has been severely criticized when it has speculated (and made errors) in the area of factual scientific data. As modern Jews we recognize that such errors simply reflect the less accurate scientific data that was available to our ancestors. Nonetheless, we still find a great deal of thinking about human problems, about ethical situations etc. within religion which is quite useful today. We may not, for example, literally believe that the first man and first woman were Adam and Eve and that two of their children were Cain and Abel. Yet some of the concerns that the story raises — "Why do people have to work for a living?", "Why isn't life always a paradise?" etc., are still quite relevant. And for those of you who occasionally "do battle" with a brother or a sister, the story of Cain and Abel is as noteworthy now as it was thousands of years ago. The ethical issue of "Am I my brother's keeper?" is raised in every generation!

Science, on the other hand, has often been severely criticized for its so-called "moral neutrality," (the idea that science is only concerned with the discovery of facts and not in the ethical or social problems that may result from those findings). An extremely encouraging phenomenon has been to find some scientists becoming actively involved not only in the search for knowledge, but indeed more concerned than ever before with the ethical problems raised by their research.

My bias should be obvious. Religion cannot ignore the factual data presented by science. Science, however, needs more than ever before, the ethical insights of religion! Both are necessary.

But what about various specific scientific discoveries? Are they "good" or "bad"? Well, I think that depends on how they are used. Let's say you buy a book. You can read it and learn something from it — a very positive use of the book. You could possibly use it as a projectile and throw it at someone. That's a bad use for the book. (Remember this **is** an Ethics text!) If you accumulate a lot of books your house may become quite cluttered. You may find yourself bumping into stacks of books. They may collect a lot of dust and make you sneeze! That is the "social cost" of having the books. Well, scientific discoveries can cause a similar situation. They can be used in a very positive fashion. They can also be used in a harmful manner as well. When new knowledge results in change in our lives we can say that there is a "social cost" as a result of the discovery. Is that social cost justified? Is it good? That depends on the particular situation at hand.

Obviously your own set of values and personal ethics will help you evaluate each situation. This evaluation will continue to be increasingly important.

At this point to underscore some of the general comments made about the "good and evil" of science, I would like to take various scientific and technological advances, and briefly analyze some of the pros, cons etc. of them.

1. The Automobile — One way of getting an idea of just how rapidly the world is changing is to compare notes with someone just a few years older than oneself. I find it fascinating, for example, to find that my grandmother remembers when there were no cars. My father at my age drove a Model A Ford; a machine that I find rather amusing and quaint when I consider the average car of today. Moreover, just consider how that one invention has influenced our entire life-style in a short period of only about a half a century. It has resulted in a remarkable system of national highways which make it possible to travel long distances in relatively short times. The superhighway system of America is an incredible engineering accomplishment that we often take for granted (until we visit a less developed country)! The automobile has thus "reduced" distances. It has helped make a suburban life-style possible. It has become, directly or indirectly, a substantial means of earning a living for many of our population. Automobile related industries are quite important in our national economy. Yet on the other hand, automobiles are blamed in a variety of ways for hurting the environment. Their emissions dirty the air. Superhighways etc., just don't make the prettiest landscape, and the automobile contributes to using up energy resources. Are the benefits equal to the social costs?

2. Hand Calculators — Hand calculators are a wonderful invention. Certainly they make computations quickly and accurately. Yet some people argue that they undermine one's own ability to do math. Others believe that due to their ease of operation and low cost, calculators enable and encourage us to try problems much more complex and involved than we might otherwise tackle (if we had to do the math by hand).

3. Lasers — Here is a fascinating invention with all kinds of possibilities. Lasers are beginning to be used as a tool for medical surgery. If three dimensional pictures etc. ever really become commonplace it will be due to laser technology. To give you an idea of just how versatile lasers are, they are being used in such varied fields as communications and surveying. Then of course one occasionally hears talk about the possible military uses of lasers as potential weapons as well ...

4. D.N.A. Research — This was discussed in greater detail earlier but the basic issue remains. This technology will perhaps eventually help cure hereditary diseases, stop the scourge of cancer, and could even make it possible to speed up bodily repairs or to slow the aging process. It also may contribute to such things as cloning and "test-tube" babies. The same knowledge could conceivably be used by a dictator with rather nasty results. In addition the ability to alter the genetic material of organisms could be used accidently or militarily to create new and exotic forms of disease!

5. Nuclear Energy — Nuclear energy is a very clear-cut example of a scientific achievement being used for possible "good" or "evil." It can be used with devastating results to kill people. It can also be used in a positive manner to generate power. Yet **even that** has been a matter of debate. Many people have questioned the continued use of nuclear power plants. There are some very strong arguments both in favor of and against their use. In favor:

1. We certainly need energy for our society to function. — That is crucial!

2. If nuclear power is discontinued and such things as coal are substituted, air pollution levels could go up greatly. These air pollutants have already been linked to a number of problems such as respiratory diseases, etc. not to mention a dirty environment.

3. The chances of a major accident in a nuclear power plant have been calculated at being incredibly small.

And against:

1. While chances of an accident are small, projections of the possible results of such an occurrence are grim (e.g. contamination of an area at least the size of Pennsylvania, many thousands of deaths etc.).

2. The effectiveness of safeguards in case of an accident are in doubt.

3. There is the possibility of sabotage, problems with terrorists etc.

4. Radioactive wastes that must be safely stored for hundreds of years are a by-product of these plants.

5. Nuclear plants emit low levels of radiation (e.g. radioactive gases) into the environment. Scientists really don't know the long-term effects of this.

The arguments raised by both sides are equally impressive. Inevitably it's a comparison of possible benefits vs. risks.

6. Plant Hormones — Remember the discussion of herbicides — chemicals that destroy plant life that was presented in the section on war? Well the research that enabled that application was, at first, quite innocent. All that scientists were originally interested in was chemical substances within plants that would help cause growth. That knowledge has had very positive results in growing bigger and better agricultural products for food. Yet from the same basic research came the tools used to create a great deal of ecological damage.

7. Public Health Advances — Here is a tricky one for you to consider. Public health advances in sanitation, drugs, etc. coupled with better food technology has contributed to a longer and healthier life for many people than ever before in human history. "So is there anything wrong with that?" you ask. "Good question," I would answer. Please keep in mind that more people living a longer life span contribute to an increasingly larger population, which uses increasingly larger amounts of resources. Can one say that the public health advances are therefore "evil"? Or are they "good"? Why?

8. Weizmann and Explosives — Here is another rather interesting situation. During World War I a scientist named Chaim Weizmann invented a synthetic substance that was needed for the production of explosives. Incidently one of the ingredients that he used was horsechestnuts (a seemingly innocent item!). Explosives can be used very nicely for building purposes but I'm sure you can guess how they can also be used in war as well! At any rate the British Government was quite pleased with Weizmann and wanted to reward him. Weizmann asked that the British Government help establish a Jewish homeland. It was in part due to Weizmann's efforts that the Balfour Declaration, which advocated the establishment of a Jewish homeland in Palestine, came into being. It's curious to think that a scientific discovery utilized to help in a war effort, may have contributed to the establishment of Israel!

TRADITIONAL VIEWS

Here's a neat story:

> *A Roman general named Turnus Rufus was chatting with Rabbi Akiba. "Hey Akiba, here's a tough problem for you . . . What's better, God's works or man's works?" Akiba thought for a second and then picked up a loaf of bread in one hand, and some grain in the other. "I frankly would prefer to eat the loaf of bread . . . he said . . . God might have created the world but some things were left to humankind to do . . . Incidentally Turnus, old boy, that's also why we have commandments to follow . . . to help us improve ourselves! As human beings we have an obligation to try to apply our creative talents to all of our existence!"*

It seems that in those days, as today, some individuals take delight in trying to ask smart people tough questions! But the issue is clear. Rufus was questioning whether we have the right to meddle in science and technology. Akiba felt that the products of technology (e.g. bread) can be far better suited to human existence than the mere natural substance (e.g. grain). (Then as a Rabbi he even managed to insert a little comment about following the commandments. Sneaky, huh?)

247

Here's another story about the issue of whether humans have a right to meddle in science and technology. This one refers to the health sciences:

> *One day a couple of Rabbis were wandering along the street when they came upon a sick person. "Oh am I sick!" groaned the poor fellow. "Yeah you do look a bit under the weather," responded the Rabbis. The Rabbis proceeded to give the man advice as to what he should do in order to relieve his symptoms. Rather than being grateful the man responded "God afflicted me, and you are interfering. Why don't you two mind your own business?" The two Rabbis asked him — "Buddy, what do you do for a living?" "I tend a vineyard," came the response. "Well God created the vineyard — you have no business interfering there," commented the Rabbis. "Yeah, but if I didn't fertilize, weed and take care of it, the vineyard would be in bad shape and wouldn't produce any fruit." "O.K. then, don't be a sap." The Rabbis smiled. "Your body is like that vineyard. If you don't seek medical aid when it's run down you'll be in bad shape too!"*

Again a position very much in favor of human involvement with science!

Let's take it one step further. In order to apply the possible benefits of science to human needs, one has to first gain the necessary knowledge. Our traditions have always been very much in favor of studying and learning. Now at this stage you might be ready to say, "Yuch! Homework is not that much fun!" You may very well be right! Yet the really fun part of learning can often come in the practical application of that knowledge later. For example can you think of how many hours of homework had to be done by a lot of different people before T.V. was invented? Anyhow, in order to simply survive in our world an education today is a must. Yet from an early period our ancestors had this "thing" about education. For example:

> — *A midrash tells us that everyday an angel comes by to destroy the world. But then, seeing people studying, the angel refrains from its destructive mission (So do your homework)!*

> — *Another neat story concerns the Hebrew letter Lamed. Why is the Lamed so tall when it is compared to other letters? Because the Lamed announces the Hebrew word for "learn!", and naturally an announcer of such an important message would stand high!*

Thus our tradition certainly supports learning in general!

"Well this is all good and fine," you might say. "But what if scientific data proves that traditional beliefs on a given subject are wrong? Then I bet the tradition isn't so open-minded!" Well, it is interesting to note that a question was once put to Maimonides that raised that very issue. Maimonides as you'll recall was one of our greatest Jewish philosophers. He was also considered one of the outstanding physicians of his day. I'm sure you've noticed references earlier in this book to him. At any rate when asked what he would do in a given situation involving a possible conflict between the Torah and scientific data, he indicated that he would just have to try to look for insight in the Torah more carefully. In effect he was aware of the fact that scientific knowledge is but a product of its age. He also recognized that while we may not be able to accept everything in the tradition as scientifically valid, we nonetheless can find much meaning and moral guidance from those sources.

As I indicated earlier in unit five, the Talmud is virtually an encyclopedia of traditional thought. Mixed in with legal thinking, ritual, etc. is even medical advice! Now as I'm sure you can guess some of the remedies that are suggested, while rather quaint, may be a little dated! Thus we find Jewish authorities as far back as 1000 years ago cautioning people against trying any of these remedies unless first consulting with a physician! Does this diminish the authority of the Talmud? Well, it certainly would say that science has advanced since those days (and that this was recognized a long time ago by Jewish authorities)! But the variety of subjects dealt with in the Talmud cover a wide range of moral, ritual and philosophical issues. Much of this thinking is just as relevant, if not more so, today than ever before, and can offer us much guidance and insight.

"Well so what? Let's say the Jewish tradition has shown some flexibility towards advances in scientific knowledge. What's the big noise?" you ask. Well, while you may at this stage take it for granted that science and religion can coexist, there have been situations in world history where there has been some antagonism between the two. When Copernicus suggested that the earth rotated around the sun, it was considered a rather interesting theory. After all everybody believed it was the opposite . . . Indeed in the Bible (Joshua 10:12, 13) Joshua (with God's help) made the sun stand still (which could be interpreted to mean that it was the sun which traveled around the earth, and not the earth around the sun). At any rate as long as this was mere theory it was one thing, but you'd be amazed at the controversy that erupted when Galileo went around proclaiming that the Copernican theory was **fact**! Why the noise? Because it challenged accepted beliefs and was interpreted by some as a threat to religious faith. Even in the mid-1800's many people were quite disturbed when Darwin's work on evolution implied that humankind had evolved from earlier life forms (as opposed to the account given in Genesis). **As I hope has been made quite clear above, such conflict is quite alien to Judaism.**

Interestingly enough there have been a number of Jews who have made outstanding contributions in many scientific fields. Some very obvious modern examples are Freud, Einstein and Salk. There are numerous suggestions as to why many Jews have been involved in the sciences. One suggestion has been that the whole stress that Judaism has put on learning in general (discussed above) certainly would encourage academic pursuits. Other comments would focus on Jewish history. I am sure you have been told time and time again how our ancestors were often the victims of much discrimination. Could it be that Jews were unafraid of public rejection for holding new or different ideas simply because they had already encountered much hostility for merely being Jews? Another possiblity is that because Judaism has displayed flexibility in accepting new scientific facts, Jews would be adventurous in treading in new and untraveled areas. Of course it is always dangerous to generalize. It could very well be that all, some, or none of these factors, concerning Jewish activities in the sciences are significant.

SUMMARY

The rapid increase in scientific knowledge has been playing a major role in shaping the world around us. Yet, as these discoveries have an impact upon our society and way of life, our reactions are often mixed. Are scientific discoveries "good" or "evil"? Neither, in my opinion. It really depends on how they are used. The same basic knowledge can be used in a very positive way as well as in a negative manner. What about the relationship between science and religion? In a sense both are concerned with finding out about the cosmos and how it operates. Yet they are not the same. Science has been strong in dealing with factual data. Religion has been invaluable in providing insights into human problems and giving ethical guidance. While religion has often been criticized for mistaken speculation about factual data (e.g. Creation) science has also been criticized for its so-called "moral neutrality." Both need each other. Scientific evidence cannot be ignored by religion. Scientists cannot ignore the ethical problems that are arising, now more than ever before, from their work.

To dramatize the fact that scientific knowledge can be utilized for good or for evil a number of examples were given. Each one of these discoveries has had a "social cost" in its application. Whether the "cost" is equal to the benefits is a matter of speculation. The following were mentioned:

1. The automobile.
2. Hand calculators.
3. Lasers.
4. D.N.A. research.
5. Nuclear energy.
6. Plant hormones.
7. Public health advances.
8. Weizmann and explosives.

It is quite obvious that these are but a few examples. Many, many more could be enumerated!

An examination of traditional sources indicates the following:

1. Judaism has maintained that humans have a right to apply technology to the world around us.

2. Judaism has always put a high value upon learning and study.

3. While there have been situations in world history where science and religion have been at odds with each other, such confrontation is, in general, alien to Judaism.

CONSIDER THIS:

1. Find six examples of scientific or technological products (not discussed in the text). Discuss the good, and bad points, social costs etc. of each.

2. Here is a neat midrash:

   Rabbi Meir was asked how he could possibly learn anything from an individual like Aher. Meir took a piece of fruit, ate the insides and threw away the peel.

   What was Meir trying to say? How does that relate to our comments in this unit?

3. In what ways are science and religion similar? In what ways are they different?

4. In this unit you have seen how various scientific advances have an impact upon our lifestyles. Take the following topics. Discuss in detail the various changes that these things could bring about in our **values**:
   a. The population explosion and increased crowding.
   b. Modern medical technology (the specifics are up to you).
   c. The increase of automation.
   d. The rise of the welfare state.
   e. Human-machine symbiosis.

FOCUS ON: PRIVACY

In modern times the problem of privacy has been quite prominent in the news:

1. Small, elaborate and extremely effective mechanical devices have been developed that can quite easily invade an individual's or company's privacy. While this kind of equipment can very easily be used to abuse citizens' rights to privacy, it can also be used as an important tool to fight crime.

2. Some people have argued that advertising in appealing to our inner weaknesses, desires, etc. forms a very subtle invasion of our privacy.

3. As our society has become very complex there has been a tendency to keep more records about people. The records come in many forms. There are school records, recording not only grades, but teachers' reactions and opinions, test scores etc. for one's entire academic career. There are police records, mental hospital records, medical records, insurance records, and credit records. As of 1974 there were at least fifty-four U.S. federal agencies with well over a million records about individuals. Now, let's complicate the matter a little. Because of the huge amount of knowledge in our society in general, there has been a necessity to develop faster methods of storing and retrieving information. The computer serves that purpose. Thus it should come as no surprise that many of the records about individuals have been stored in computers. The potential for abuse has been enormous. Often a record (sometimes inaccurate or outdated) can emerge twenty years after it was made to hurt an individual's ability to get credit, a job etc. Moreover there is a great deal of exchange of information between various institutions that collect information about people.

Some Traditional Comments:

Item One: When you lend your brother anything, you shall not go into his house to fetch his pledge. You will stand outside and the man to whom you did lend will bring the pledge outside to you.

Deut 24:10, 11

Item Two: A man shouldn't let his windows open into a courtyard which he shares with others . . . In a courtyard which one shares with others a person shouldn't open a window facing another person's window, or a door across from another person's door . . .

Mishnah

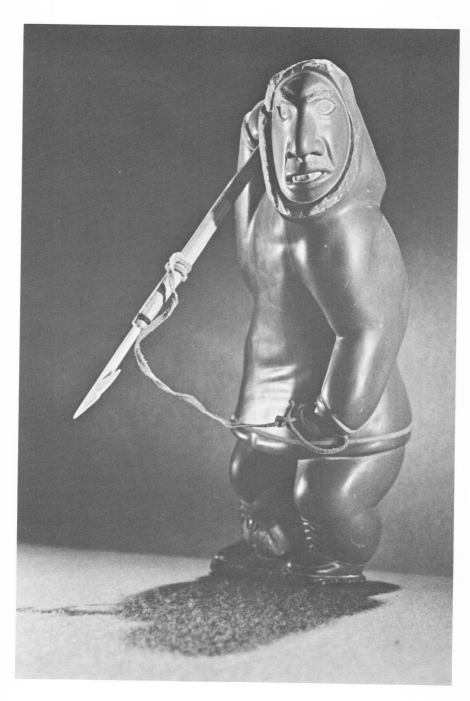

We are all hunting for meaning and purpose in life.

Epilogue

So, this is it! **Jewish Ethics For The 21st Century!** I hope that you've found both this book and your course in Jewish Ethics stimulating and enjoyable. Certainly it is my desire that it got you thinking!

In closing this book, there a few thoughts which I would like to leave with you:

First and foremost, I believe that by now you have a far better conception of the meaning and implication of the subject of "ethics" than you did when you started to read this book. Virtually every interaction that you have with any other human being can be seen as an ethical situation. Our dealings not only with people, but indeed with animal life, with the environment and even with the physical objects of our technology can also be viewed in moral terms. It is my hope that you have learned to approach things with this new perspective in mind. Regardless of what moral choices you decide to make, recognition of this underlying ethical perspective can help as you make your own decisions.

A second thing that I hope you have gained from this course is a better understanding of Judaism. Judaism is more than a religion. It is a culture, an approach to the human condition. As a civilization which has existed for many thousands of years, Jewish perspectives can give us much insight and guidance. You will note that I said perspectives with an "s". Judaism has been broad enough to encompass many different thinkers over many different ages. The comments made from a Jewish perspective in this book, whether you agree with all of them or not, are meant only as a starting point. It is my hope that you are stimulated to investigate Jewish thinking further. It's almost like having a conversation with great minds who lived many thousands of years ago about common problems.

Still another point that I hope you keep in mind as you encounter ethical problems is the importance of keeping your sense of humor and being able to laugh. It is interesting to note that in the Talmud we are told that one of the ancient sages commonly used humor as an instructional tool. He would first tell a humorous story, and then use it as a basis for his religious lesson or message. Keeping a sense of humor is an important part of staying cool when dealing with ethical problems. It also makes life much more pleasant.

I'd like to close with a story that an Israeli friend once told me:

> *There was once a man who had a terrible dilemma. Every night he would undress to go to bed . . . But he never could remember where his clothes were the next morning. That can be a bit of a problem, as you can imagine. Well, finally he decided to be very methodical. When he went to bed, he wrote down on a piece of paper just what he was wearing and where he put it. That worked out very nicely, as his system speeded things up considerably the next morning. However, he still had a problem! He couldn't remember where he was!*

In a sense we all share that man's dilemma. We are all trying to find out "where we are." We are all, in a sense, hunters. No, to be sure, we aren't armed with spears trying to bring home food. Yet we are all looking for meaning and purpose in life. We seek what is important in existence. Every person, shares much in common with all other human beings. We are similar in even more ways, with other human beings of our own nationality, or group. Yet each person is also unique. It is the values you hold and the ethical decisions that you make that contribute much to what kind of person you are.

254

ABOUT THE AUTHOR

Steve Rittner has been involved in Religious Education for a number of years, and is currently a member of the faculty at Temple Israel, Boston. He holds degrees in biology, religion and education. His first book **All That You Want To Know About The Bar-Bat Mitzvah** *has been well received throughout the United States and Canada.*

 **Temple Israel**
Minneapolis, Minnesota

IN APPRECIATION OF THE LOVE,
KINDNESS AND CARING OF
GERT GLASS
FROM
LIZ FREIDMAN DOUGLIS &
CINDY FREIDMAN SUTTON